Railroad Maps of North America

THE FIRST
HUNDRED YEARS

Railroad Maps of North America

THE FIRST HUNDRED YEARS

By Andrew M. Modelski
Geography and Map Division

LIBRARY OF CONGRESS
Washington 1984

Library of Congress Cataloging in Publication Data

Modelski, Andrew M., 1929-
    Railroad maps of North America.

    Includes index.
    1. Railroads—North America—Maps.
2. Cartography—North America. 3. North America—
Maps. I. United States. Library of Congress.
II. Title.
G1106.P3M6   1984   912'.1385'097   82-675134
ISBN 0-8444-0396-2

Passenger train on Markham
Trestle, Bingham, Utah, ca. 1914.

For sale by the Superintendent of Documents,
U.S. Government Printing Office,
Washington, D.C. 20402

Contents

Preface

Railroads could not have developed in North America without maps. The builders of the railroads depended on surveys to help determine the best routes, and when the subsequent lines were in operation railroad companies used maps to promote them. (Some lines on the survey and promotional maps, of course, were never built.)

Today these maps represent an important historical record, illustrating the growth of travel and settlement and the development of industry and agriculture. This atlas is published in response to the needs of scholars and railroad enthusiasts who seek graphic portrayal of the railroad network that spread across the North American continent, reaching as far north as Alaska and as far south as the Isthmus of Techuantepec, Mexico.

The ninety-two maps included in *Railroad Maps of North America* are a representative sample of the five thousand railroad maps preserved in the collections of the Library of Congress. They illustrate the development of cartographic style and technique and highlight the achievement of early railroaders. The maps selected vary in size from small foldout sketches to large-scale surveys and wall maps for display in ticket offices (dimensions follow the map descriptions, with height preceding width). There are progress report surveys for individual lines, official government surveys, promotional maps, maps showing land grants and rights-of-way, and route guides published by commercial firms. Many of the original maps are in color, as the descriptions indicate, and some of these are shown in color here. Only original separately printed and manuscript maps preserved in the Library's Geography and Map Division are included. Photocopies, facsimiles, and maps from volumes housed elsewhere in the Library are not. All the illustrations that accompany the maps or that will be found elsewhere in this book were selected from the collections in the Library's Prints and Photographs Division and Geography and Map Division.

Railroad Maps of North America begins with an introductory essay that traces the history of this continent's first hundred years of railroad mapping. The maps themselves are arranged according to the three North American countries, and then by types of maps beginning with early surveys and maps of entire regions and leading to maps that show particular locations or serve particular purposes. The arrangement reflects in general the geographical filing system of the Geography and Map Division and is intended to demonstrate the variety, richness, and numerous special types of railroad maps in the collection. Concluding the atlas is an analytical index that should be of great use to researcher or railroad buff. It was compiled with skill and imagination by Brian J. Svikhart.

The publication of these maps was suggested by the Library's Director of Publishing, Dana J. Pratt, and the book was edited by James Hardin, who also selected the illustrations. The design was planned by Diane Wolverton, John Sapp, and Charles McKeown and executed by William Rawley, all of the Division of Typography and Design, Government Printing Office.

For locating old railroad properties, stations, yards, and individual structures, fire insurance plans from the late nineteenth and early twentieth centuries are extremely useful. The Library of Congress has also published a detailed guide to its holdings of some fourteen thousand maps of particular cities and towns, *Fire Insurance Maps in the Library of Congress*. This publication is available from the Superintendent of Documents, U.S. Government Printing Office, Washington, D.C. 20402. When requesting information on how to order, cite stock number (S/N 030-004-00018-3).

How to Order Reproductions

Uncolored photoreproductions and color transparencies of the maps reproduced in this atlas (many of which use color to identify railroad lines) may be ordered from the Library of Congress, Photoduplication Service, Washington, D.C. 20540. Prices may be requested from the Photoduplication Service. In requesting prices or ordering reproductions, refer to this publication by title, *Railroad Maps of North America,* and cite the entry numbers of the maps wanted.

Maps are most economically reproduced by the positive photodirect print process. This process provides black-and-white prints on resin coated paper of archival quality. Material exceeding 34 × 46 inches (86 × 117 cm) is subject to a surcharge. Sizes are included with the map descriptions.

If reproductions are needed for use in publications, 8 × 10-inch glossy photographic prints should be requested. The only color reproductions available from the Photoduplication Service are transparencies in sizes 2 × 2 inches (35 mm), 4 × 5 inches, and 8 × 10 inches.

Photographic prints of the illustrations used throughout this book are also available from the Photoduplication Service. Again, prices should be requested from the Photoduplication Service. When ordering, identify the illustration from the information provided in the caption and cite negative number or G & M location, as listed on page 178.

Introduction

by Andrew M. Modelski

Surveying and mapping activities flourished in North America as people began moving inland over the inadequately mapped continent. The settlement of the frontier, the development of agriculture, and the exploitation of natural resources generated a demand for new ways to move people and goods from one place to another. Privately owned toll or turnpike roads were followed first by steamships on the navigable rivers and by the construction of canals and then in the 1830s by the introduction of railroads for steam-powered trains.[1]

The United States

Railways were introduced in England in the seventeenth century as a way to reduce friction in moving heavily loaded wheeled vehicles. The first North American "gravity road," as it was called, was erected in 1764 for military purposes at the Niagara portage in Lewiston, New York. The builder was Capt. John Montressor, a British engineer known to students of historical cartography as a mapmaker.

The earliest survey map in the United States that shows a commericial "tramroad" was drawn in Pennsylvania in October 1809 by John Thomson and was entitled "Draft Exhibiting . . . the Railroad as Contemplated by Thomas Leiper Esq. From His Stone Saw-Mill and Quarries on Crum Creek to His Landing on Ridley Creek." Thomas Leiper was a wealthy Philadelphia tobacconist and friend of Thomas Jefferson, who owned stone quarries near Chester. Using his survey map, Thomson helped Reading Howell, the project engineer and a well-known mapmaker, construct the first practical wooden tracks for a tramroad. Thomson was a notable land surveyor who earlier had worked with the Holland Land Company. He was the father of the famous civil engineer and longtime president of the Pennsylvania Railroad, John Edgar Thomson, who was himself a mapmaker. In 1873 the younger Thomson donated his father's 1809 map to the Delaware County Institute of Science to substantiate the claim that the map and Leiper's railroad were the first such works in North America.[2]

In 1826 a commercial tramroad was surveyed and constructed at Quincy, Massachusetts, by Gridley Bryant, with the machinery for it developed by Solomon Willard. It used horsepower to haul granite needed for building the Bunker Hill Monument from the quarries at Quincy, four miles to the wharf on the Neponset River.[3]

These early uses of railways gave little hint that a revolution in methods of transportation was underway. James Watt's improvements in the steam engine were adapted by John Fitch in 1787 to propel a ship on the Delaware River, and by James Rumsey in the same year on the Potomac River. Fitch, an American inventor and surveyor, had published his "Map of the Northwest" two years earlier to finance the building of a commercial steamboat. With Rober Fulton's *Clermont* and a boat built by John Stevens, the use of steam power for vessels became firmly established. Railroads and steam propulsion developed separately, and it was not until the one system adopted the technology of the other that railroads began to flourish.

John Stevens is considered to be the father of American railroads. In 1826 Stevens demonstrated the feasibility of steam locomotion on a circular experimental track constructed on his estate in Hoboken, New Jersey, three years before George Stephenson perfected a practical steam locomotive in England. The first railroad charter in North America was granted to Stevens in 1815.[4] Grants to others followed, and work soon began on the first operational railroads.

Surveying, mapping, and construction started on the Baltimore and Ohio in 1830, and fourteen miles of track were opened before the year ended (see entry 2). This roadbed was extended in 1831 to Frederick, Maryland, and, in 1832, to Point of Rocks. Until 1831, when a locomotive of American manufacture was placed in service, the B & O relied upon horsepower.

John Stevens's experimental railway at Hoboken, New Jersey, 1825. Courtesy of the Library of the Stevens Institute of Technology.

George Stephenson's locomotive engine *The Rocket,* 1830.

"Types of American Locomotives." No. 1, from 1804 up to 1876. No. 2, from 1876 to 1882. Pen and ink drawings by Theodore West, 1885. Printed by Harrison Penny.

Soon joining the B & O as operating lines were the Mohawk and Hudson, opened in September 1830, the Saratoga, opened in July 1832, and the South Carolina Canal and Rail Road Company, whose 136 miles of track, completed to Hamburg, constituted, in 1833, the longest steam railroad in the world. The Columbia Railroad of Pennsylvania, completed in 1834, and the Boston and Providence, completed in June 1835, were other early lines (see entries 1 and 18). Surveys for, and construction of, tracks for these and other pioneer railroads not only created demands for special mapping but also induced mapmakers to show the progress of surveys and completed lines on general maps and on maps in "travellers guides" (see entry 18).

Planning and construction of railroads in the United States progressed rapidly and haphazardly, without direction or supervision from the states that granted charters to construct them. Before 1840 most surveys were made for short passenger lines which proved to be financially unprofitable. Because steampowered railroads had stiff competition from canal companies, many partially completed lines were abandoned. It was not until the Boston and Lowell Railroad diverted traffic from the Middlesex Canal that the success of the new mode of transportation was assured. The industrial and commercial depression and the panic of 1837 slowed railroad construction. Interest was revived, however, with completion of the Western Railroad of Massachusetts in 1843. This line conclusively demonstrated the feasibility of transporting agricultural products and other commodities by rail for long distances at low cost.

Early railroad surveys and construction were financed by private investors. Before the 1850 land grant to the Illinois Central Railroad, indirect federal subsidies were provided by the federal government in the form of route surveys made by army engineers. In the 1824 General Survey Bill to establish works of internal improvements, railroads were not specifically mentioned. Part of the

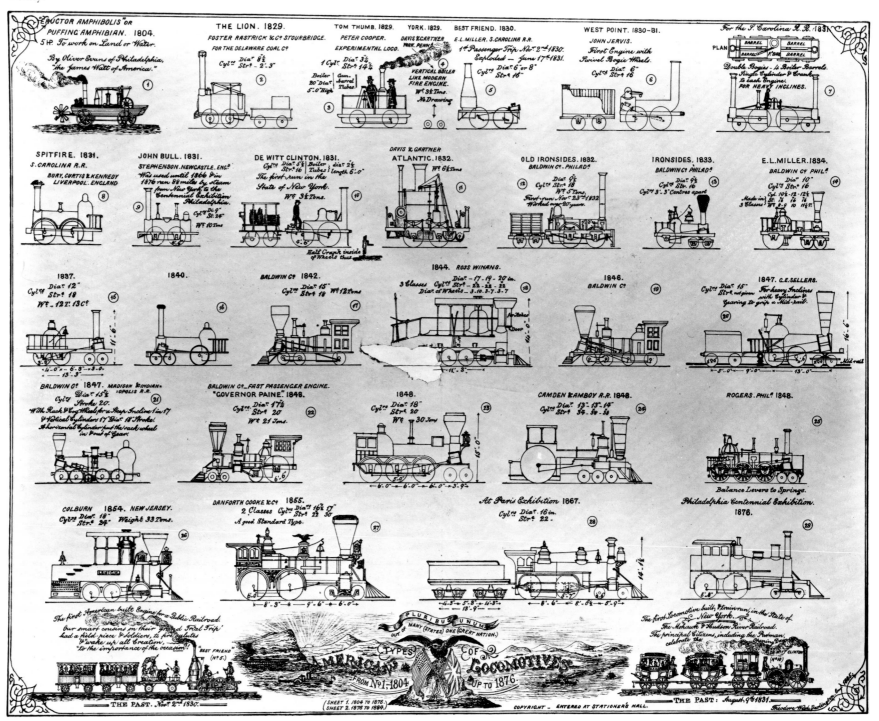

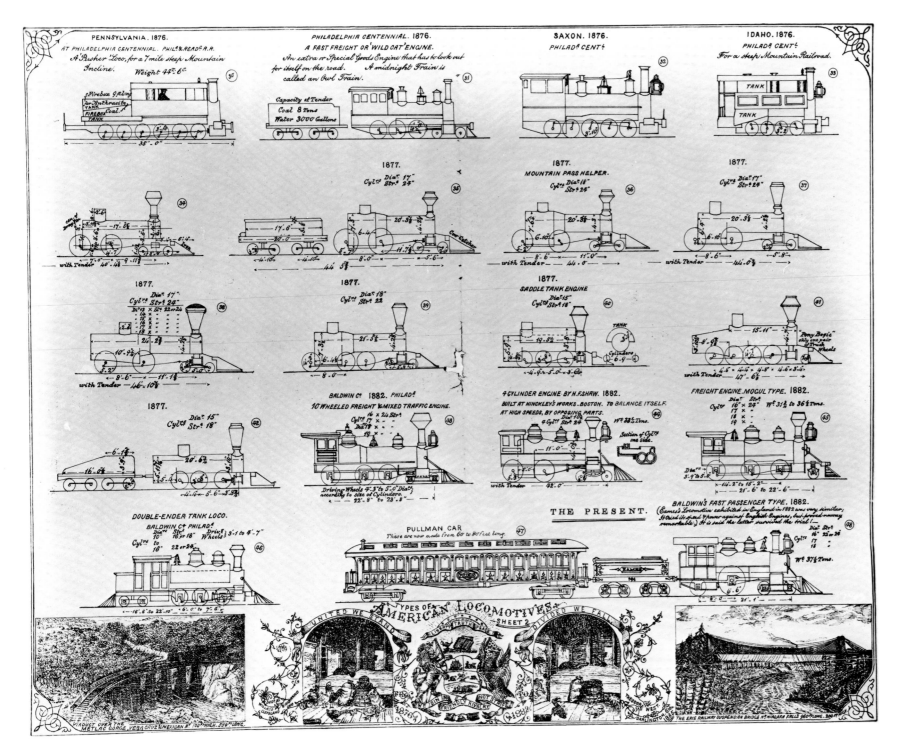

appropriation under this act for the succeeding year, however, was used for "Examinations and surveys to ascertain the practicability of uniting the head-waters of the Kanawha with the James river and the Roanoke river, by Canals or Rail-Roads."[5] In his *Congressional History of Railways,* Louis H. Haney credits these surveys as being the first to receive federal aid. He notes that such grants to states and corporations for railway surveys became routine before the act was repealed in 1838.

The earliest printed map in the collections of the Library of Congress based on government surveys conducted for a state-owned railroad is "Map of the Country Embracing the Various Routes Surveyed for the Western & Atlantic Rail Road of Georgia, 1837" (see entry 6). The surveys were made under the direction of Lt. Col. Stephen H. Long, chief engineer, who ten years earlier had surveyed the routes for the Baltimore and Ohio[6] (see entry 2). Work on the 138-mile Georgia route from Atlanta to Chattanooga started in 1841, and by 1850 the line was open to traffic. Its strategic location made it a key supply route for the Confederacy. It was on this line that the famous "Andrews Raid" of April 1862 occurred when Union soldiers disguised as railroad employees captured the locomotive known as the *General.*[7]

Canada

In Canada, to a much greater degree than in England, Mexico, or in the United States, the railroad was designed to serve long-distance traffic, but it was regarded at first as only a very minor form of transportation. Rivers and canals were considered to be the great highways of commerce. Only where there were distances to be bridged between the more important waterways were railroads thought profitable.

In 1832, two years after the completion of the Liverpool and Manchester Railroad, a charter was granted by the legislature of Lower Canada to the Company of the Proprietors of the Champlain and St. Lawrence Railroad for a line from Laprairie on the St. Lawrence to St. Johns, sixteen miles away on

"The New Railroad Bridge Across the Susquehanna, From Havre de Grace to Perryville, Md." Wood engraving after a photograph by Schrieber & Son, Philadelphia. *Frank Leslie's Illustrated Newspaper,* December 22, 1866.

the Richelieu River, just above the rapids. From St. Johns it was possible to travel on the Richelieu River to Lake Champlain and then down the Hudson. The portage road promised to shorten substantially the journey from Montreal to New York.

A manuscript survey map for this first Canadian railroad was made by William Casey, civil engineer, and Hiram Corey, land surveyor. The map, entitled "Map and Section of the Intended Champlain and Saint Lawrence Rail Road," is preserved in the Public Archives of Canada. Construction for the line was begun in 1835, and the railroad opened for traffic in July 1836.

By 1852 the rails had been extended to St. Lambert, opposite Montreal, and southward to Rouse's Point, on Lake Champlain. Twenty years later this pioneer road, after a period of leasing, was absorbed by the Grand Trunk Railway (see entry 84).

For ten years the sixteen-mile Champlain and St. Lawrence was the sole steam railroad in British North America, while by 1846 England had built over twenty-eight hundred miles, and the United States nearly five thousand. Political unrest, commercial depression, and the diversion of public funds to canals hindered development in Canada. Many projects were formed and charters secured for roads in the western peninsula of Upper Canada, between Cobourg and Rice Lake, on the Upper Ottawa, in the Eastern Townships, and elsewhere. But they all came to nothing.

The railroad picture changed by the mid-1840s. In that time of frenzied speculation in both England and the United States, money for investment in Canadian railroads was easier to obtain. The Montreal and Lachine Line extended for eight miles around the Lachine Rapids on the north shore of the St. Lawrence. On November 19, 1847, Montreal had its first train.

Five years later, another railroad was built that extended from the south bank of the river across the border to connect with the American railroad system. The Grand Trunk Railway was completed from Lake Huron to the Atlantic Ocean in 1860.

The early railroad policy of Canada was embodied in the Guarantee Act, which undertook to guarantee a part of the debt of any company which built a railroad of at least seventy-five miles. The result of this act was speculation in many small, unnecessary railroads that helped bring about the financial panic of 1857, halting almost all construction.

In 1879 the Canadian government completed building the Intercolonial Railway (see entry 75). The Canadian Pacific was completed in 1885 with public support, to connect British Columbia with the east. At the turn of the century, many small Canadian lines were absorbed by the Canadian Pacific and the Grand Trunk (see entries 78 and 84).

The early twentieth century brought another railroad building boom (see entries 78 and 85). All the lines, except the financially stable Canadian Pacific, were consolidated by the government into the Canadian National Railways in 1923[8] (see entry 85).

Mexico

Mexican railroad development was the result of foreign capital and enterprise, attracted by national franchises or "concessions" and encouraged later by subsidies. This policy was adopted by President Porfirio Diaz in 1880 after the failure of an attempt to promote railroad building by Mexicans under state concessions. A concession is not a corporate charter, as it is under English law, nor is it a grant of funds or other aid. It is in effect a lease for a definite term of years to build a line largely or wholly out of private funds. The public authority in the end assumes proprietorship over all fixed properties and an option upon the movable ones.

In considering the introduction of railroads into Mexico, one should remember that the first important railroad company in the United States—the Baltimore and Ohio—was chartered in 1827 and that the experiments which demonstrated the practicality of Stephenson's locomotive were conducted in England in 1829. It is remarkable

The Mexican Central Railroad, ca. 1885. Detroit Photographic Company.

that the possibility of a line from Veracruz to the City of Mexico was being considered as early as 1833. We know this from the narrative of Hall Jackson Kelly, the eccentric Boston schoolmaster and engineer, who in that year crossed Mexico en route to Oregon.

Four years later, in August 1837, under the administration of Anastasio Bustamante, a concession was granted to Francisco Arillage, a merchant of Veracruz, for a railroad from Veracruz to the City of Mexico, with a branch in Puebla. Under this concession a preliminary survey was made, but nothing further was done and the concession was forfeited. The earliest railroad survey map of Mexico in the Library of Congress resulted from the Mexican concession granted on March 1, 1842, to Jose Garay for a line to cross the Isthmus of Techuantepec. Surveys for this line were made by U.S. Army engineers under the direction of Gen. John G. Barnard (see entry 86). Other railroad surveys in Mexico conducted by U.S. Army engineers were made in 1858 under the direction of Capt. Andrew Talcott, a graduate of West Point. Talcott was assisted by a party recruited in New York, his chief assistants being Robert B. Gorsuch and M. E. Lyons of Reading, Pennsylvania.

In the middle years of the nineteenth century, and through the Diaz regime (1877-1911), rail lines were surveyed and developed to facilitate the export of raw materials to the borders of the United States and to port facilities on both coasts. Routes were also built to speed import goods to Mexico City. Most of the extensive Mexican railroad network, therefore, was surveyed, mapped, and constructed between 1880 and 1910. This activity is reflected in the many maps produced during this period. The consolidation of many lines, which began in 1908, resulted in the creation of the National Railways of Mexico (Ferrocarriles Nacionales de Mexico), which composed 70 percent of all Mexican lines[9] (see entry 90).

The Transcontinental Railroad

The possibility of railroads connecting the Atlantic and Pacific coasts was discussed in Congress even before the treaty with England which settled the question of the Oregon boundary in 1846.[10] Chief promoter of a transcontinental railroad was Asa Whitney, a New York merchant active in the China trade who was obsessed with the idea of a railroad to the Pacific. In January 1845 he petitioned Congress for a charter and grant of a sixty-mile strip through the public domain to help finance construction.[11] Whitney suggested the use of Irish and German immigrant labor, which was in great abundance at the time. Wages were to be paid in land, thus ensuring that there would be settlers along the route to supply produce to and become patrons of the completed line. The failure of Congress to act on Whitney's proposal was mainly due to the vigorous opposition of Sen. Thomas Hart Benton of Missouri, who favored a western route originating at St. Louis.

In 1849 Whitney published a booklet to promote his scheme entitled *Project for a Railroad to the Pacific.* It was accompanied by an outline map of North America which shows the route of his railroad from Prairie du Chien, Wisconsin, across the Rocky Mountains north of South Pass. An alternate route to the south of the pass joined the main line at the Salmon River and continued to Puget Sound. Proposed lines also extended from St. Louis to San Francisco and from Independence, Missouri, to New Mexico and the Arkansas River. This is one of the earliest promotional maps submitted to Congress and was, according to its author, conceived as early as 1830[12] (see entry 19).

Although Congress failed to sanction his plan, Whitney made the Pacific railroad one of the great public issues of the day. The acquisition of California following the Mexican War opened the way for other routes to the coast. The discovery of gold, the settlement of the frontier, and the success of the eastern railroads increased interest in building a railroad to the Pacific.[13] Railroads were also needed in the West to provide better postal service, as had been developed in the East, by designating railroad lines "post roads" in 1838. Strengthened by other proposals such as those of Hartwell Carver in 1849 and of Edwin F. Johnson in 1853 (see entry 20), such leading statesmen as John C. Calhoun, Stephen A. Douglas, and Jefferson Davis declared their support for linking the country by rails. The lawmakers, however, could not agree on an eastern terminus, and they did not see the merits of the several routes west. To resolve the debate, money was appropriated in 1853 for the Army Topographic Corps "to ascertain the most practicable and economical route for a railroad from the Mississippi River to the Pacific Ocean."

Under the provisions of the Army Appropriation Act of March 1853, Secretary of War Jefferson Davis was directed to survey possible routes to the Pacific. Five selected routes, roughly following specific parallels, were to be surveyed by parties under the supervision of the Topographical Corps. The most northerly survey, between the 47th and 49th parallels, was under the direction of Isaac Ingalls Stevens, governor of Washington Territory. This route closely approximated that proposed by Asa Whitney.

The ill-fated party under Capt. John W. Gunnison was to explore the route along the 38th and 39th parallels, or the Cochetopa Pass route, which was advocated by Missouri Senator Thomas Hart Benton. Because he failed to get John Charles Fremont appointed to head this particular expedition, Benton promoted two other well-publicized, privately financed ventures in the same year, one headed by Edward F. Beale and the other by Fremont. After Gunnison's death at the hands of hostile Indians, Lt. Edward G. Beckwith continued the survey along the 41st parallel. Capt. Amiel W. Whipple, assistant astronomer of the Mexican Boundary Survey, and Lt. Joseph Christmas Ives surveyed the routes of the 35th parallel westward to southern California. This line was favored by Jefferson Davis and was essentially the route traversed

Mining for gold, El Dorado, California.

Northern Pacific Railroad car on the way to the Klondike. Keystone View Photo.

Central Pacific Railroad Company, Kern County, California.

170. Cement Ridge—Old Man Mountain in dist.

by Josiah Gregg in 1839 and later surveyed by Col. John J. Abert (see entry 14). When the results of the surveys were analyzed, it was apparent that additional data on the roadbeds, grades, and passes were needed for the 32d parallel route to California. Lt. John G. Parke resurveyed along the Gila River between the Pima villages and the Rio Grande. Capt. John Pope mapped the eastern portion of the route from Dona Ana, New Mexico, to the Red River. Topographical surveys to locate passes through the Sierra Nevadas and the Coast Range in California and to determine the route that would connect California, Oregon, and Washington were made under the direction of Lt. Robert S. Williamson[14] (see entry 17).

These surveys showed that a railroad could follow any one of the routes, and that the 32nd parallel route was the least expensive. The Southern Pacific Railroad was subsequently built along this parallel (see entries 17 and 22). The southern routes were objectionable to northern politicians and the northern routes were objectionable to the southern politicians, but the surveys could not, of course, resolve these sectional issues.

While sectional issues and disagreements were debated in the late 1850s, no decision was forthcoming from Congress on the Pacific railroad question. Theodore D. Judah, the engineer of the Sacramento Valley Railroad (see entries 15 and 16), became obsessed with the desire to build a transcontinental railroad. In 1860 he approached Leland Stanford, Collis P. Huntington, Mark Hopkins, and Charles Crocker, leading Sacramento merchants, and soon convinced them that building a transcontinental line would make them rich and famous. The prospect of tapping the wealth of the Nevada mining towns and forthcoming legislation for federal aid to railroads stimulated them to incorporate the Central Pacific Railroad Company of California. This line later merged with the Southern Pacific (see entries 25 and 59). It was through Judah's efforts and the support of Abraham Lincoln, who saw military benefits in the lines as well as the bonding of the Pacific Coast to the Union,

"Camp Victory," Utah Territory, April 28, 1869, the day the Central Pacific Railroad laid ten miles of track in twenty-four hours.

that the Pacific Railroad finally became a reality. The Railroad Act of 1862 put government support behind the transcontinental railroad and helped create the Union Pacific Railroad (see entries 64 and 65), which subsequently joined with the Central Pacific at Promontory, Utah, on May 10, 1869, and signaled the linking of the continent.

Mapmaking and Printing

Technological advances in papermaking and printing which permitted quick and inexpensive reproduction of maps greatly benefited railroad cartography. Before the introduction of these new techniques early in the nineteenth century, maps were laboriously engraved, in reverse, usually on copper plates, and printed on hand presses. Although the results were excellent, this slow and costly process could not keep pace with the demand for railroad maps. The process of lithography was invented in 1798 by Alois Senefelder of Bavaria and came to America at an opportune time, just as the first railroad charter was being granted in 1815. This invention revolutionized map printing and provided the means for inexpensive map reproduction. Within two years after William and John Pendleton established the first important lithographic printing house in Boston, in 1825, their firm was printing railroad surveys and reports for the earliest New England railroad companies.[15]

Even after lithographic printing in map production became common, engraving was used for many years for finer and more limited works. As late as 1848 Peter S. Duval of Philadelphia engraved map plates of Virginia for Claudius Crozet, principal engineer to the Commonwealth.

Technical advances were quickly adapted to map printing. The transfer process eliminated most of the laborious procedure of drawing on stone in reverse. It allowed an illustration or a newly drawn map, using specially prepared paper and ink, to be transferred directly to a stone or a zinc plate. The early use of "zincography" in America,

in 1849, is credited to P.S. Duval's Swiss shop foreman, Frederick Bourquin. Zinc plates were adaptable to the rotary steam power press, which was first installed by Duval in his Philadelphia lithographic establishment.

Another important printing process, cerography, or wax engraving, was introduced in America by Sidney Edwards Morse, whose father, Jedidiah Morse, published the first geography book in the United States, *Geography Made Easy*, in 1784. The process was first used in 1839 for Morse's "Cerographic Map of Connecticut" and in 1842 for the *Cerographic Atlas of the United States.* This was an ingenious method of making a mold from which a printing plate was cast. On a thin layer of wax applied to a copper plate, lines and symbols, and later type, were inscribed or impressed. Through the means of an electroplating process, a relief mold was produced from which single sheet maps were printed. The process was kept secret by Morse. It became more widely used after Rand McNally introduced its "wax engraving process" in 1872.

From the 1870s through the first four decades of the twentieth century, this method of printing, sometimes called "relief line engraving," became very popular with large map printing houses in the United States. The firm of George F. Cram and Company, well known for its railroad maps and other geographic publications, adopted the process in the 1880s with the introduction of its *Universal Family Atlas of the World.* Matthews-Northrup and Company and Poole Brothers also used this method for printing their numerous railroad maps. Multicolor printing, the development of photolithography, and the offset press further accelerated railroad map production and greatly reduced prices.[16]

Color lithography to distinguish regions and administrative divisions on maps was introduced as early as the 1850s. Color to accentuate the many lines of intricate railroad networks, however, continued to be manually applied to many maps at the end of the century.

"Deadwood Central Railroad Engineer Corps." Deadwood, South Dakota, 1888. Photograph by Grabill.

The Growth of Mapping

The wealth of data derived from the Pacific surveys stimulated cartographic activities. The data used in compiling twenty-two large individual maps published with the thirteen handsomely illustrated volumes of the *Pacific Railroad Surveys,*[17] for example, was the basic source material for Lt. Gouverneur Kemble Warren's "Map of the Territory of the United States from the Mississippi River to the Pacific Ocean." With Warren's map the work of the topographical engineers on the preliminary Pacific surveys came to an end.[18]

The accelerating flow of new information, Warren recognized in his *Memoir to Accompany the Map,* made it difficult to keep such a map up to date. He said that "the work of compilation . . . must necessarily be frequently repeated; and to aid the future compiler, I have prepared the accompanying memoir upon the different maps and books used, and upon the manner in which their discrepancies have been resolved." He gratefully acknowledged the work of Edward Freyhold in "the beautiful execution of the topography upon the map." The first revision, drawn by Freyhold, was engraved on stone by Julius Bien of New York. A copy of this map is preserved in the Library's President Millard Fillmore Collection and bears his signature and the date December 19, 1863. This map, like the first edition, lists forty-five major surveys and mapping reports from the time of Lewis and Clark to the General Land Office Surveys of the late 1850s.

The Civil War provided another stimulus for railroad mapping because of the strategic importance of rail transportation to the armies (see entries 29 and 30). After the war, railroad builders became aware of the traffic-generating potentials of the scenic wonders of the West. Jay Cooke and Company, financiers of the Northern Pacific Extension Project, and other promoters lobbied for the establishment of Yellowstone National Park. To make

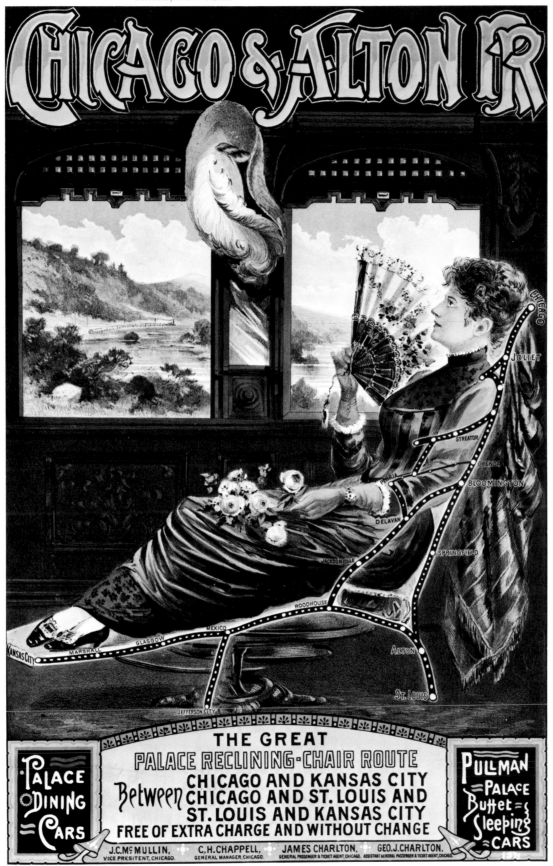

"The Great Palace Reclining-Chair Route." Chicago & Alton Railroad. Lithograph by Ballin & Liebler, New York.

it accessible to tourists, they persuaded park promoters to support completion of the railroad to coincide with the opening of the park in 1872. Not until 1883, however, did a rail spur extend to within three miles of the park (see entry 45). Other railroads followed the lead in promoting the establishment of resorts and national parks.[19] This created additional demand for maps to illustrate reports, promotional literature, displays, and timetables from the thousands of railroad and promotional firms which sprang up in the nineteenth century.

Land Grants

The second half of the nineteenth century was the era of railroad land grants. Between 1850 and 1872 extensive cessions of public lands were made to states and to railroad companies to promote railroad construction.[20] Usually the companies received from the federal government, in twenty- or fifty-mile strips, twenty alternate sections of public land for each mile of track that was built. Responsibility for surveying and mapping the grants fell to the U.S. General Land Office, now the Bureau of Land Management. Numerous maps of the United States and individual states and counties were made which clearly indicated the sections of the granted land and the railroad rights-of-way.

Land grant maps were frequently used by land speculators to advertise railroad lands for sale to the public. As early as 1868 most western railroads established profitable land departments and bureaus of immigration, with offices in Europe, to sell land and promote foreign settlement in the western United States. Consequently, the Library's collections also include some foreign-language maps aimed at both the immigrant already on the East Coast and the prospective one in Europe.

Competition between speculators may have led to the idea of the distortion of railroad maps to emphasize one state, area, or line to the advantage of the advertiser. This idea, derived from the government land grant maps, may have been perpetuated by the mapping of the Illinois Central Railroad after it was granted land along its path in 1850. In

"Departure of a Colony of
Emigrants for Colorado."
Chicago & St. Louis Railroad
Station. *Harper's Weekly*, 1870.

John W. Amerman's book entitled *The Illinois Central Rail-Road Company Offers for
Sale Over 2,000,000 Acres Selected Farming
and Wood Land* (New York, 1856) appears an
"Outline Map of Illinois" which emphasizes
the Illinois Central Railroad by a heavy black
line, with stations placed evenly along the
line to give the illusion of proximity of towns
along the lines. This practice of manipulating
scale, area, and paths of railroads became
common practice in advertising maps of the
1870s and early 1880s and in railroad
timetable maps.

Map Publishing Firms

Perhaps 30 percent of the commercially
produced railroad maps were published by
the New York City publishing house
established by Joseph Hutchins Colton in
1831. This firm was known the world over
for the quality, quantity, and variety of its
publications, including maps, atlases, and
school geographies.[21] Henry Varnum Poor, in
the introduction to his *History of the
Railroads and Canals of the United States of
America,* commends the series of Colton's
railroad maps which illustrate his work. "All
the maps," Poor wrote, "are drawn and
engraved under the supervision of G.
Woolworth Colton, Esq., whose diligence, accuracy and extensive information are sufficient guarantee for their correctness."[22]

Indeed, Colton's maps from the early
1850s to the last decade of the century, most
of which were subtitled "Colton's Railroad
and Township Map," surpassed in quality and
quantity other maps published in the nineteenth century. Other reputable map
publishing firms of the period include Asher
& Adams of New York, James T. Lloyd and
Company of New York and London,
Matthews-Northrup and Company and J. Sage
and Sons of Buffalo, Gaylord Watson of New
York and Chicago, and later in the century,
the Chicago firms of Rand McNally, Poole
Brothers, and George F. Cram. The Poole and
Cram firms originally stemmed from the Rand
McNally Company, and all three are still in
business today.

From a booklet distributed by Rand McNally & Company about 1879.

Map Drawing and Designing Room.

"Map 'Designing,' to other than a railroad official, might seem a peculiar phrase, but the majority of railroad maps have some 'peculiar designs' hidden under the careful pencil of the draughtsman. It requires a faculty only acquired by experience and a perfect knowledge of the railroad system of the country, to 'design' a good railroad advertising map. The various friendly interests must be shown to best advantage, and the rival interests disposed of in a manner that 'no fellow can find out.' The drawing of a good map is a matter of considerable difficulty, but the 'designing' of a good map involves the exercise of tact and ingenuity.

"Probably more *original* map projections have been made by our map drawing room than have ever been produced in the United States. It is not generally known that our large railroad and county map, which is 58 × 100 inches, is the second *original* projection of a United States map ever made. Our United States and Canada Atlas is made from the same projection."

Map Engraving Department.

"Our illustration gives a view of the Engraving Room of this department. It is situated in the building which we occupy fronting on State Street, and is composed of three rooms, only one of which is illustrated.

"It is generally admitted that our map engraving is not excelled in the world for clearness of outline and beauty of execution. We have frequent orders from Europe for map work, and the liberal patronage received from all sections of the United States, attests in a gratifying manner the superiority of our work in this line. Our new wall map of the United States and our Business Atlas, is the largest work ever attempted by our process of engraving. It required the services of ten compilers and engravers nearly two years, and cost about $20,000."

Cylinder Press Room.

"It is with considerable pride that we invite your attention to this department. It is without doubt by far the most extensive and best equipped cylinder press room in the United States. After the Great Fire we purchased such presses as could be had quickest, and started them running, and at once ordered built the best presses that could be manufactured, and as the new presses were received, the old machines were taken out and sold. Nearly all our cylinder presses have from four to eight rollers, and to this may be attributed the great superiority of our press work, especially on colored printing. The printing of colored maps has frequently been attempted by other concerns on the ordinary two-roller presses, but never successfully.

"The press seen above in our engraving prints a sheet larger than any fine printing press in the country, 42 × 58 inches, and was built expressly for colored map printing. The presses on this floor cost over $70,000."

Following the consolidation and rapid growth of North American railroads after the financial panic of 1873, many commercial maps were produced to show the spreading network. One company signaled its emergence into this field by announcing in January 1873 that "the house of Rand, McNally & Co., beg leave to inform their railroad friends, and the patrons of the [Railway] Guide generally, that they have lately made extensive additions to their engraving department, and are now prepared to execute Map and all kinds of Relief Plate Engraving [i.e., wax engraving] in the very highest style of the art."[23] Rand McNally's output in the late nineteenth century rivaled the volume of maps, guides, illustrated timetables, and atlases produced by Colton.

In 1858 William H. Rand, a native of Boston, established a printing office in Chicago and employed as a printer Andrew McNally. By 1868 Rand and McNally formed a partnership which soon acquired a reputation for printing railroad publications. In 1871 they introduced the *Rand McNally Railway Guide*. Less than a year after their business was destroyed in the 1871 Chicago Fire, the company's first two maps appeared in the December 1872 issue of the *Guide*. In response to the need by the railroads for maps, in timetables and other publications, Rand and McNally opened a map department in late 1872. With the adoption of the wax engraving process, followed in May 1873 by the employment of a color printing process, the company's reputation as one of the world's leading commercial mapmakers was established.[24]

A major accomplishment of Rand McNally was the publication in 1876 of the "New Railroad and County Map of the United States and Canada. Compiled from Latest Government Surveys, and Drawn to an Accurate Scale," which is not reproduced in this atlas because of its size. That same year, the company used the plates from this map to produce its famous *Commerical Atlas and Marketing Guide,* which is now in its 114th edition. The map and the *Business Atlas,* as it was then known, required the services of ten

"In the Waiting Room." Advertisement for the St. Louis and San Francisco Railroad. The Strobridge Lithograph Company, Cincinnati, Ohio, 1899.

compilers and engravers for nearly two years and cost about $20,000.[25] Today the atlas continues to be an indispensable reference tool for the business world and the librarian, for it contains the most complete index to place names in the United States, as well as useful railroad information. There is a complete list of railroads in the United States, mileage and distance tables, freight and passenger service information, and a summary of the current status of major mergers. A map of the principal railroad network is also included, along with state maps that show and list the railroads serving each state.

Between 1882 and 1891 Rand McNally produced "elephant-size" maps at the scale of 1:506,880 or 1 inch to 8 miles, in twelve panels which formed a map more than 10 × 15 feet in size. The several editions of the map, which depicts the country from the East Coast to the 105th meridian of longitude, are entitled "Rand McNally & Co's New Railroad Junction Point and County Map of the Eastern & Middle States Prepared from Latest Government Surveys, and Verified by the Working Time Tables of the Various Railroads. Drawn, Engraved, Printed, Colored by Hand and Published by Rand, McNally & Co. Chicago." It shows county boundaries, all railroad junctions, and all railroads. This is probably the map which George H. Heafford stated was "freqently posted on the out-houses, dead-walls and fences of our large cities."[26]

Early Twentieth Century

Not all the commercial mapping ventures of the late nineteenth and early twentieth centuries represented large and diversified operations. Several interesting manuscript maps of the mid-western states portray routes of the "Railway Mail Service" and locate working post offices. These maps were designed by an enterprising Chicago railway mail clerk, Frank H. Galbraith.

The maps were devised to serve as memory aids for employees of the Railway Mail Service and the U.S. Post Office Department in quickly locating counties, routes, and post offices in the several states. The maps were not published but were rented, on a fee basis, to practicing or prospective postal workers (see entry 32).

Railroad map production continued at a strong pace into the early twentieth century, until expansion of the network was completed. It declined, slowly, after the peak of railroad building. The largest decline was in individual promotional maps and surveys as lines became abandoned or consolidated. General railroad maps, depicting continental and national areas and using the basic style developed in the previous century, continued to be popular until the beginning of World War II.

Today, separately published maps of individual consolidated systems and small-scale maps printed in timetables and atlases, such as *Rand McNally's Handy Railroad Atlas of the United States* (Chicago, 1982), continue to reflect the influence of mapping and printing styles set in the nineteenth and early twentieth centuries.[27]

Andrew M. Modelski
Head, Acquisitions Unit
Geography and Map Division

Notes

1. Henry Varnum Poor, *Manual of the Railroads of the United States for 1870-71* (New York: H.V. & H.W. Poor, 1870), p. xxviii.

2. James A. Ward, *J. Edgar Thomson: Master of the Pennsylvania* (Westport: Greenwood Press, 1980), p. 11.

3. Daniel J. Boorstin, *The Americans: The Democratic Experience* (New York: Random House, 1965), p. 18.

4. Thurman W. Van Metre, *Transportation in the United States* (Brooklyn: Foundation Press, 1950), p. 31.

5. The reports to these surveys have not been found. See Louis H. Haney, *A Congressional History of Railways* (1908), 1:111. See also Joseph Carrington Cabell, *Notes Relative to the Route, Cost and Bearing of a Railway from Covington to the Head of Steamboat Navigation on the Kanawha River . . .* (Addressed to Walter Gwynn, Chief Engineer, February 10, 1851.)

6. *Report of the Engineers, on the Reconnoissance and surveys, made in reference to the Baltimore and Ohio Rail Road* (Baltimore: Printed by W. Wooddy, 1828). William Howard, C.E., Stephen Harrison Long, Jonathan Knight, William Gibbs McNeill, Joshua Barney, and Isaac R. Trimble were the surveyors. Joshua Barney's "Map of the Country Embracing the Various Routes Surveyed for the Balt. & Ohio Rail Road by Order of the Board of Engineers" (Baltimore, 1828?, scale ca. 1:193,000, 27 × 61 cm) was prepared to accompany the report.

7. Slason Thompson, *A Short History of American Railways* (Chicago: Bureau of Railway News and Statistics, 1925), p. 154.

8. R. A. J. Phillips, *Canada's Railways* (Toronto: McGraw-Hill, 1968), pp. 81-94.

9. Fred W. Powell, *The Railroads of Mexico* (Boston: Stratford Co., 1921), pp. 1-42.

10. Louis H. Haney, *A Congressional History of Railways,* 2 vols. (Madison: University of Wisconsin, 1908-10; reprint ed., New York: Augustus M. Kelley, 1968), 1:234.

11. Memorial of Asa Whitney . . . Praying a Grant of Land, to Enable Him to Construct a Railroad from Lake Michigan to the Pacific Ocean (28th Congress, 2nd sess., Senate Doc. 69, Serial 451, Jan. 28, 1845).

12. Carl I. Wheat, *Mapping the Transmississippi West,* 5 v. (San Francisco: Institute of Historical Cartography, 1957-63), 2:187.

13. John F. Stover, *American Railroads* (Chicago: University of Chicago Press, 1961), p. 53.

14. Gouverneur K. Warren, *Memoir to Accompany the Map of the Territory of the United States from the Mississippi River to the Pacific Ocean, Giving a Brief Account of Each of the Exploring Expeditions Since A.D. 1800, with a Detailed Description of the Method Adopted in Compiling the General Map* (Washington: U.S. Congress, Senate, 1859), p. 78.

15. "Single Rail Railway," [With lithograph plate by Pendleton. Boston, April 30, 1827] No. t.p.; date from end of article.

16. David Woodward, *The All-American Map* (Chicago: University of Chicago Press, 1977), pp. 26-36.

17. *Reports of Explorations and Surveys, to Ascertain the Most Practicable and Economical Route for a Railroad from the Mississippi River to the Pacific Ocean 1853-1856* (Washington, 1855-59). Published in a quarto set of thirteen volumes and commonly known as the "Pacific Railroad Surveys," it contains narratives of the explorations and accompanying maps of the surveyed routes.

18. Warren, *Memoir,* pp. 66-82.

19. Alfred Runte, "Pragmatic Alliance, Western Railroads and the National Parks," *National Parks* 48 (April 1974):14.

20. Haney, *History of Railways,* 2:13.

21. George Woolworth Colton, *A Genealogical Record of the Descendants of Quartermaster George Colton* (Philadelphia: Printed for private circulation, by John Milton Colton, 1912), p. 273.

22. Henry Varnum Poor, *History of the Railroads and Canals of the United States of America* (New York: John H. Schulz & Co., 1860), p. [vi].

23. Rand McNally and Co., [Untitled booklet distributed to customers by the company, circa 1879].

24. Rand McNally and Company, *Railway Guide The Travelers' Hand Book,* (Chicago, 1873), p. xvii, and "A Tradition is Born . . . Rand McNally's First Maps," *Ranally World* (December 1962), p. 8.

25. *Ranally World* (February to June 1956) and Andrew McNally III, *The world of Rand McNally* (New York: Newcomen Society of North America, 1956).

26. Rand McNally and Co., [Untitled booklet distributed to customers by the company, circa 1879].

27. Andrew M. Modelski, *Railroad Maps of the United States: A Selective Annotated Bibliography of Original 19th-century Maps in the Geography and Map Division of the Library of Congress* (Washington: Library of Congress, 1975), p. 13.

Ensenore Glenn House. Plate from F. Mayer's *Atlas of County of Cayuga, New York* (1875).

Railroad Maps of North America

T H E   F I R S T
H U N D R E D   Y E A R S

United States

California & Oregon Coast
Railroad surveying crew, Grants
Pass, Oregon, to Crescent City,
California, ca 1900.

Boston and Providence

1828

1.   Hayward, James. Plan of a survey for the proposed Boston and Providence Rail-Way. Jan. 1828. Boston, Annin & Smith, 1828. 19 × 109 cm (7½ × 41½ in).

From Massachusetts Board of Commissioners of Internal Improvements, *Report in Relation to the Examination of Sundry Routes for a Railway from Boston to Providence; with a Memoir of the Survey* (Boston, 1828).

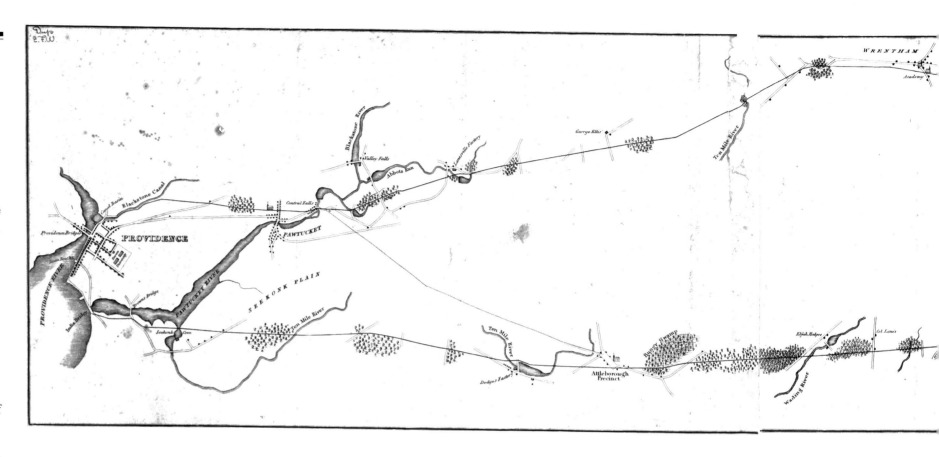

Uncolored topographic strip map showing proposed lines of survey. This is the earliest railroad map represented in the Library's map collections. It is listed as one of the "Rail Roads Never Before Delineated" by Henry S. Tanner in his *Memoir on the Recent Surveys . . .* (Philadelphia, 1829). It was incorporated in June 1831.

The report mentioned above reveals that the commissioners believed "horse power will be most expedient for application to the uses of this road."

Two major routes were surveyed. The first began at South Boston, continued through Milton, Sharon, and Attleborough, and terminated at the India Bridge in Providence. The second survey began at "Madam Swan's" residence in Roxbury, continued west of the first survey, through Purgatory Meadows, Walpole, and Pawtucket, and terminated at the Blackstone Canal in Providence. Small alternate by-pass routes were also surveyed. The railroad company eventually selected and followed the more easterly survey route. This line became the New Haven Railroad.

The map is one of the very first products of George G. Smith and William B. Annin, who established, in 1828, a printing firm bearing the name of the inventor of lithography, the Senefelder Lithography Company of Boston. The firm was taken over by William Pendleton in 1830.

Early surveying and mapping activities for railroads are described by Thomas Curtis Clarke in *The American Railway* (New York, 1888):

. . . the first thing is to make the surveys and locate the position of the intended road upon the ground, and to make maps and sections of it, so that the land may be bought and the estimates of cost be ascertained. The engineer's first duty is to make a survey by eye without the aid of instruments. This is called the "reconnoissance." By this he lays down the general position of the line, and where he wants it to go if possible. Great skill, the result of long experience, or equally great ignorance may be shown here. After the general position of the line, or some part of it, has been laid down upon the pocket map, the engineer sends his party into the field to make the preliminary survey with instruments. . . . The chief of the party exercises a general supervision over all, and is . . . assisted by a topographer, who sketches in his book the contours of the hills and direction and size of the watercourses. . . . In a properly regulated party the map and profile of the day's work should be plotted before going to bed, so as to see if all is right. If it turns out that the line can be improved and easier grades got, or other changes made, now is the time to do it.

After the preliminary lines have been run, the engineer-in-chief takes up the different maps and lays down a new line, sometimes coinciding with that surveyed, and sometimes quite different. The parties then go back into the field and stake out this new line, called the "approximate location," upon which the curves are all run in. In difficult country the line may be run over even a third or fourth time; or in an easy country, the "preliminary" surveys may be all that is wanted.

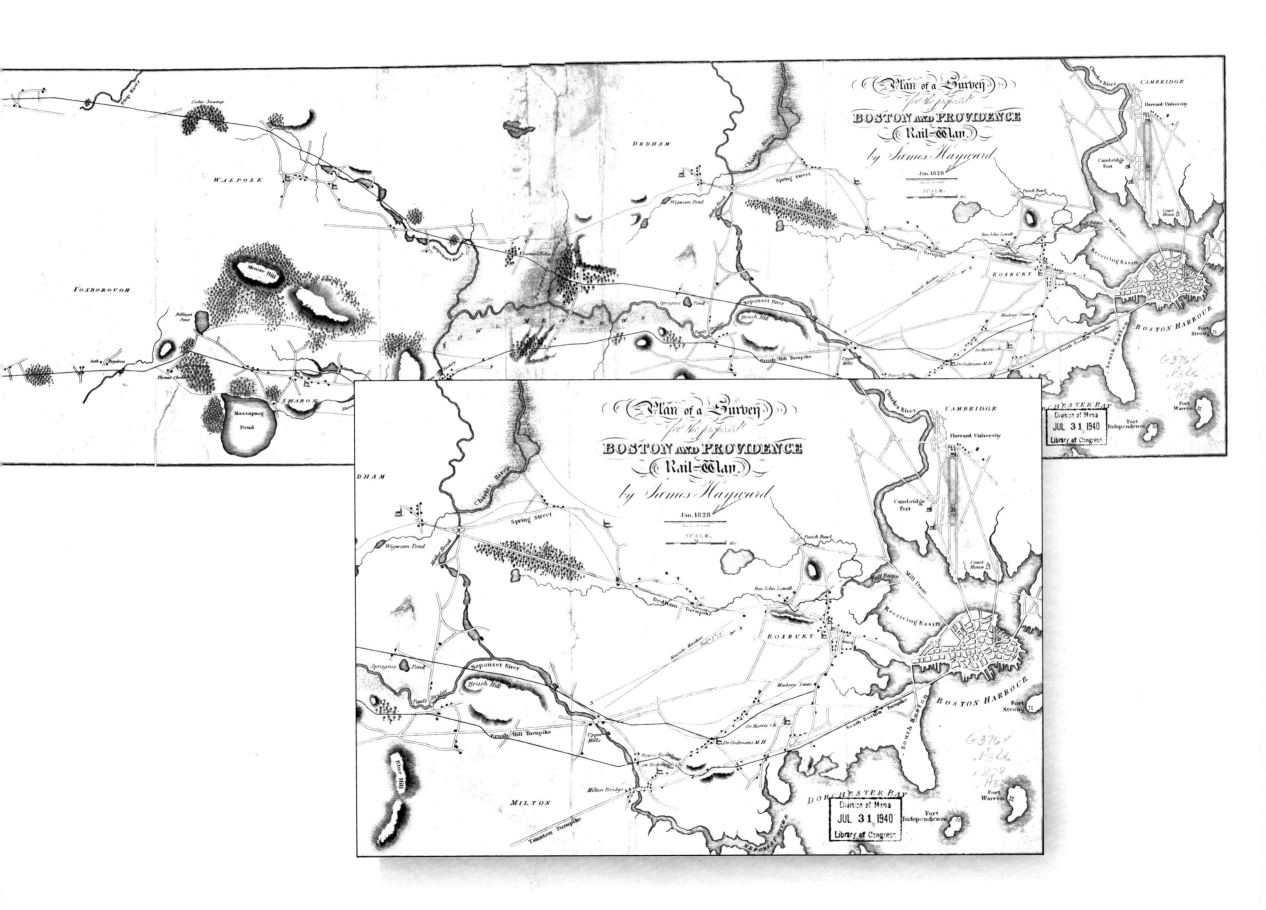

Baltimore and Ohio

1829

2. Barney, Joshua. Map of the country embracing the various routes surveyed for the Balt. & Ohio Rail Road by order of the Board of Engineers. Drawn by Lt. J. Barney U.S. Army. [1829]. (Peter Force map coll. no. 438) 27 × 61 cm (10½ × 24 in).
LC copy imperfect: Has crease lines.
A paste-on label states that this copy is presented to the subscribers of the "American," from Dobbin, Murphy & Bose. The label covers the statement "Engraved by John and Wm. W. Warr Philada." The map without this label, and Barney's published profiles of "Two Principle Routes Surveyed . . ." accompany the 1829 *Third Annual Report of the President and Directors, to the Stockholders of the Baltimore and Ohio Rail Road Company.*

Map of Baltimore, Ann Arundel, Montgomery, Frederick, and Washington counties, Maryland, showing drainage, roads, and important place names. Indicates "routes surveyed" and "location of rail road." Incorporated in 1827. First survey published in 1828.

This second published survey map of the Baltimore and Ohio Railroad shows the surveyed routes by dashed lines and the actual track location by solid black lines. The completed tracks begin at the Mount Clare Depot in Baltimore (not shown on this map) and continue over the Carrolton Viaduct (point A) through Ellicot's Mills to Gillies Falls, near Ridgeville, following the Patapsco River and its Western Branch. Construction is also shown progressing from Upper Point of Rocks (point G) to near Buckeystown.

Just a year after this map was published, the line was opened to horse-drawn cars for freight and passenger traffic to Point of Rocks, with an extension to Frederick.

The Frenchman Charles Varlé, a notable cartographer and canal engineer who spent some thirty years in America, has left us the first narrative description of a journey on the Baltimore and Ohio Railroad. In 1833 he published an interesting pocket guide to the city of Baltimore and its environs. *A Complete View of Baltimore with a Statistical Sketch* was accompanied by a folded "Plan of the City of Baltimore including the South Baltimore Cos. Grounds." In the third section of the guide, an interesting nineteen-page "Narrative of an Excursion on the Baltimore & Ohio Railroad — By the Author," Varlé describes a journey from Baltimore to Frederick, Maryland, taken by rail on March 13, 1832, "in one of the four cars running together, the number of the passengers amounting to 80, and each car drawn by a single horse." Varlé's trip on the B&O was taken shortly before steam-powered locomotives were introduced. He comments that "Arrangements are [in the] making to place on the road, a sufficient number of locomotive steam engines, which will supercede the horse power now in use, being more economical, and admitting greater speed."

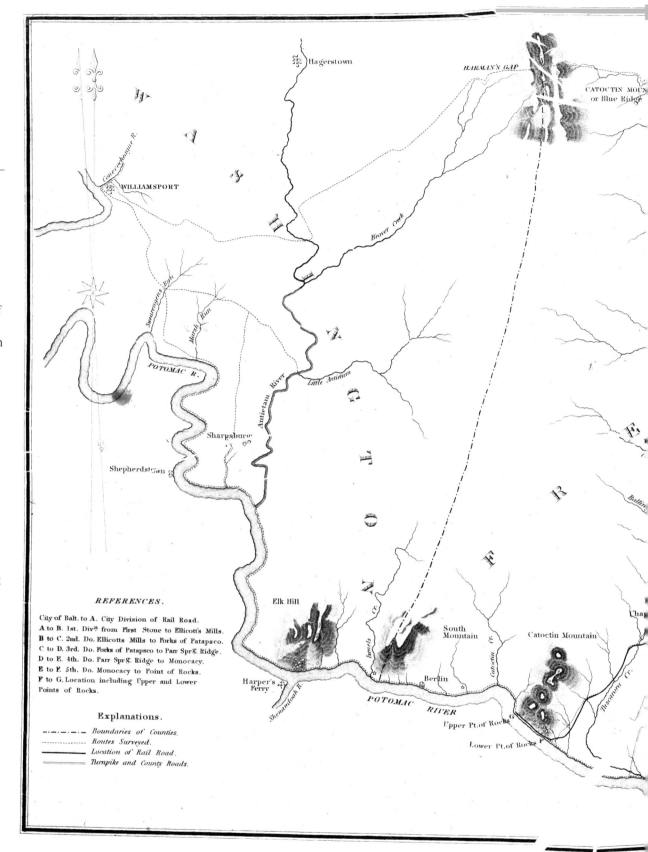

REFERENCES.

City of Balt. to A. City Division of Rail Road.
A to B. 1st. Divⁿ from First Stone to Ellicott's Mills.
B to C. 2nd. Do. Ellicotts Mills to Forks of Patapsco.
C to D. 3rd. Do. Forks of Patapsco to Parr Sprg. Ridge.
D to E. 4th. Do. Parr Sprg. Ridge to Monocacy.
E to F. 5th. Do. Monocacy to Point of Rocks.
F to G. Location including Upper and Lower Points of Rocks.

Explanations.

—·—·—· Boundaries of Counties.
············ Routes Surveyed.
———— Location of Rail Road.
════════ Turnpike and County Roads.

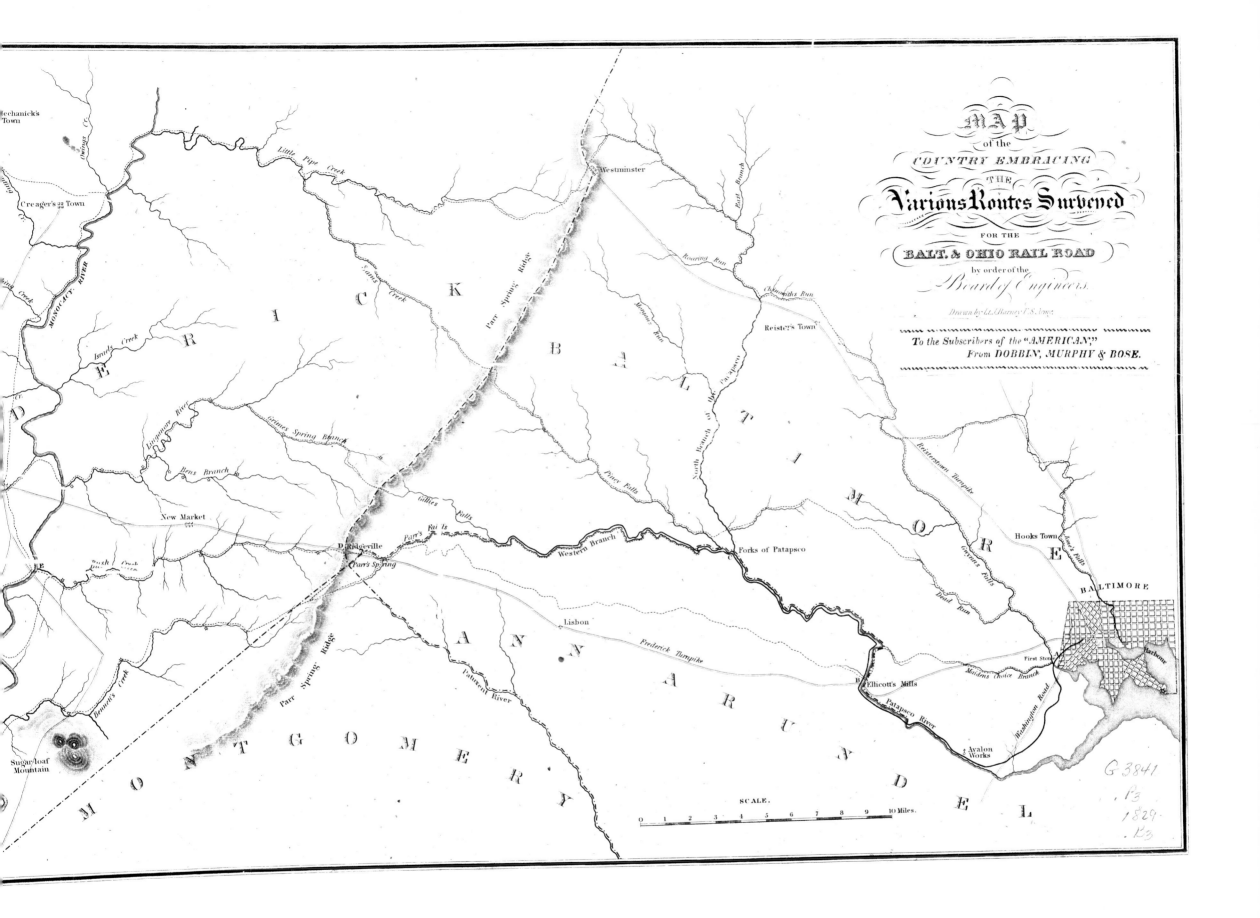

MAP
of the
COUNTRY EMBRACING
THE
Various Routes Surveyed
FOR THE
BALT. & OHIO RAIL ROAD
by order of the
Board of Engineers.

Drawn by Lt. J. Barney U.S. Engr.

To the Subscribers of the "AMERICAN,"
From DOBBIN, MURPHY & BOSE.

SCALE.
0 1 2 3 4 5 6 7 8 9 10 Miles.

G 3841
.P3
1829
.B3

Danville and Pottsville

1831

3. **Kennedy, David K.** *and* **Lucas, William B.** Plan
and profile of the Danville and Pottsville Rail Road. 1831.
Kennedy & Lucas's Lithography, Philadelphia. 47 × 63
cm (18½ × 25 in).
 Across bottom of map: "Profiles of grades."

   Detailed map of part of Pennsylvania between Sharp Mountain and the Susquehanna
River showing roads, drainage, and relief by
hachures along the survey route.

   Shows the east and west branches of the
Mount Carbon Railroad and the Mill Creek
Railroad, which began operation in 1829.
Chartered on April 8, 1826. Name changed in
1851 to the Philadelphia and Sunbury Rail
Road.

   Intense speculation in coal lands in the
Schuylkill region resulted in rapid construction of a local railroad net of wide ramifica-
tions there, and the success of the Delaware
and Hudson and Lehigh canals resulted in a
small amount of feeder construction by them
in the northern fields. The general agitation
for public improvements in Pennsylvania and
the commercial rivalry between trade centers
gave rise to several projects, in the decade
from 1825 to 1835, to build rail lines into and
through the coal region. None of these but
the Philadelphia & Reading succeeded,
although large amounts of money were spent
in projecting several of them.

   The Pottsville & Danville Railroad was to
give the Lehigh coal region an additional
outlet via the Schuylkill Navigation, while
providing a new route to the West. It was
also to connect Pottsville on the Schuylkill
Navigation with Sunbury on the Susquehanna. The company was chartered in 1826 and
was backed by a group of Philadelphia
capitalists of note, including Stephen Girard,
the wealthiest man of his day. He had bought
large tracts of coal land in the vicinity of the
proposed route and believed the new railroad
would prevent the Susquehanna trade from
going out of the state to Baltimore. In 1834,
at a meeting of stockholders in Philadelphia, a
special drive was launched to complete the
line, already built from Pottsville on the
Schuylkill to Girardville, a new settlement in
the Lehigh basin.

Winchester and Potomac

1832

4. Humphreys, Andrew A. Map of the routes examined and surveyed for the Winchester and Potomac Rail Road, State of Virginia, under the direction of Capt. J. D. Graham, U.S. Top Eng., 1831 and 1832. Surveyed by Lts. A. D. Mackay and E. French, 1st Arty., assistants in 1831, and Lts. E. French and J. F. Izard, assistants in 1832. Drawn from the original plot by Lt. Humphreys, 2d Artillery. 53 × 58 cm (21 × 27 in).

From *Documents Concerning Winchester and Potomac Railroad,* 24th Congress, 2d session., House doc. 465, serial 331.

Uncolored topographic map surveyed in strips along the railroad routes. Shows property owners and covers an area between the Shenandoah and Potomac Rivers to Winchester. Includes table showing ''a summary of the routes surveyed for the Winchester and Potomac Rail Road, State of Virginia.''

This is one of the earliest printed government surveys drawn from the original plot by Lt. Andrew Atkinson Humphreys, who as chief of the Office of Western Explorations and Surveys some years later supervised the making of the maps for the *Pacific Railroad Surveys,* including G. K. Warren's monumental map of the transmississippi West.

Humphrey's map was based on surveys by Lts. A. D. Mackay and E. French in 1831 and Lts. French and J. F. Izard in 1832.

This line, constructed to connect with the Baltimore & Ohio at Harpers Ferry, was designed to divert Shenandoah Valley wheat from the city of Alexandria, Virginia, and stimulate the growth of Baltimore. Completion of the line in 1836 greatly contributed to the decline of Alexandria.

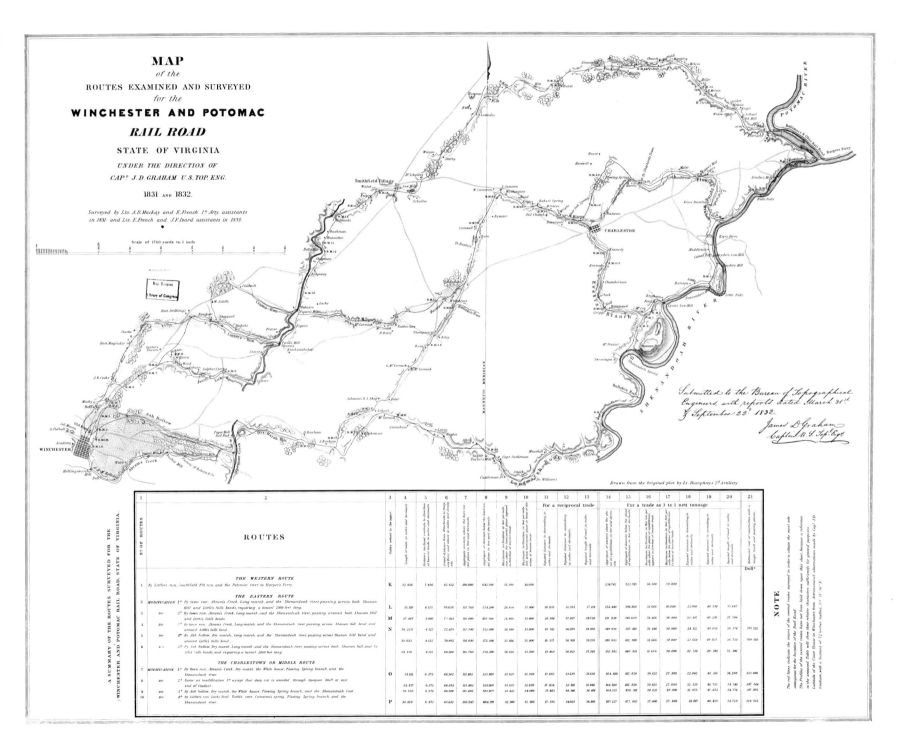

New York and Erie

1834

5.   Wright, Benjamin. Map of the route of the proposed New York & Erie Railroad, as surveyed in 1834, reduced from the plans as returned by Benjn. Wright, Civil Engineer. Printed by Cammeyer & Clark, N.Y. D. R. Harrison, sc. 59 × 113 cm (22½ × 44½ in).

Uncolored general survey map which shows New York's southern tier, from Westchester County to Lake Erie, and part of northern Pennsylvania and New Jersey.

This line, chartered on April 24, 1832, was formed as the result of demands of the southern counties to offset the economic advantages that the Erie Canal had brought to the northern part of the State. The 446 miles of line were built entirely within the State of New York, their eastern terminus on the west bank of the Hudson River at Piermont, some twenty-six miles from New York City. The western terminus was located on Lake Erie at Dunkirk instead of at Buffalo.

After financing was arranged and the difficulties of rough terrain overcome, the line forged ahead. By 1851 trains carried President Millard Fillmore and his cabinet to Dunkirk, on Lake Erie, over the longest continuous railroad line in the world. It was extended to Cleveland and Chicago and, in 1861, became the Erie Railroad.

The best account of this famous excursion is that given by Edward Harold Mott in his book, *Between the Ocean and the Lakes. The Story of Erie* (New York, 1899):

> A large number of Government and State officials, and other prominent men, were the guests of the railroad company and made the trip either in whole or part, between New York and Dunkirk, the western terminus. Mr. Fillmore was the guest of chief distinction, but popular enthusiasm along the route was equally shown towards him and Daniel Webster. The latter set out on the jaunt "on a flat car, at his own request, a big easy rocking-chair being provided for him to sit on. He chose this manner of riding so that he could better view and enjoy the fine country through which the railroad passed."

Benjamin Wright, the mapmaker, was born in 1770 in Connecticut and died in 1842 in New York. A well-known surveyor, engineer, and New York legislator, he was senior engineer in charge of construction of the Erie Canal's middle and eastern sections, chief engineer for the Erie Canal, the Chesapeake & Ohio Canal, and the St. Lawrence Canal, and consulting engineer for the New York & Erie Railroad and several other railroad lines.

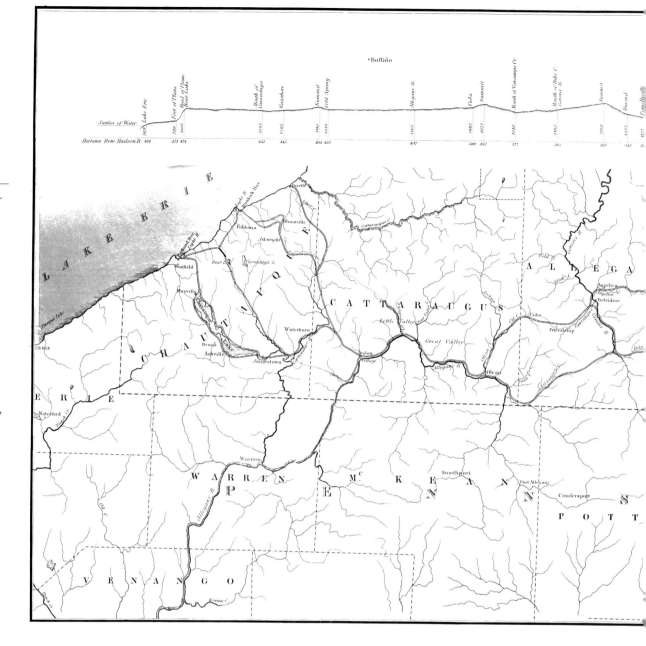

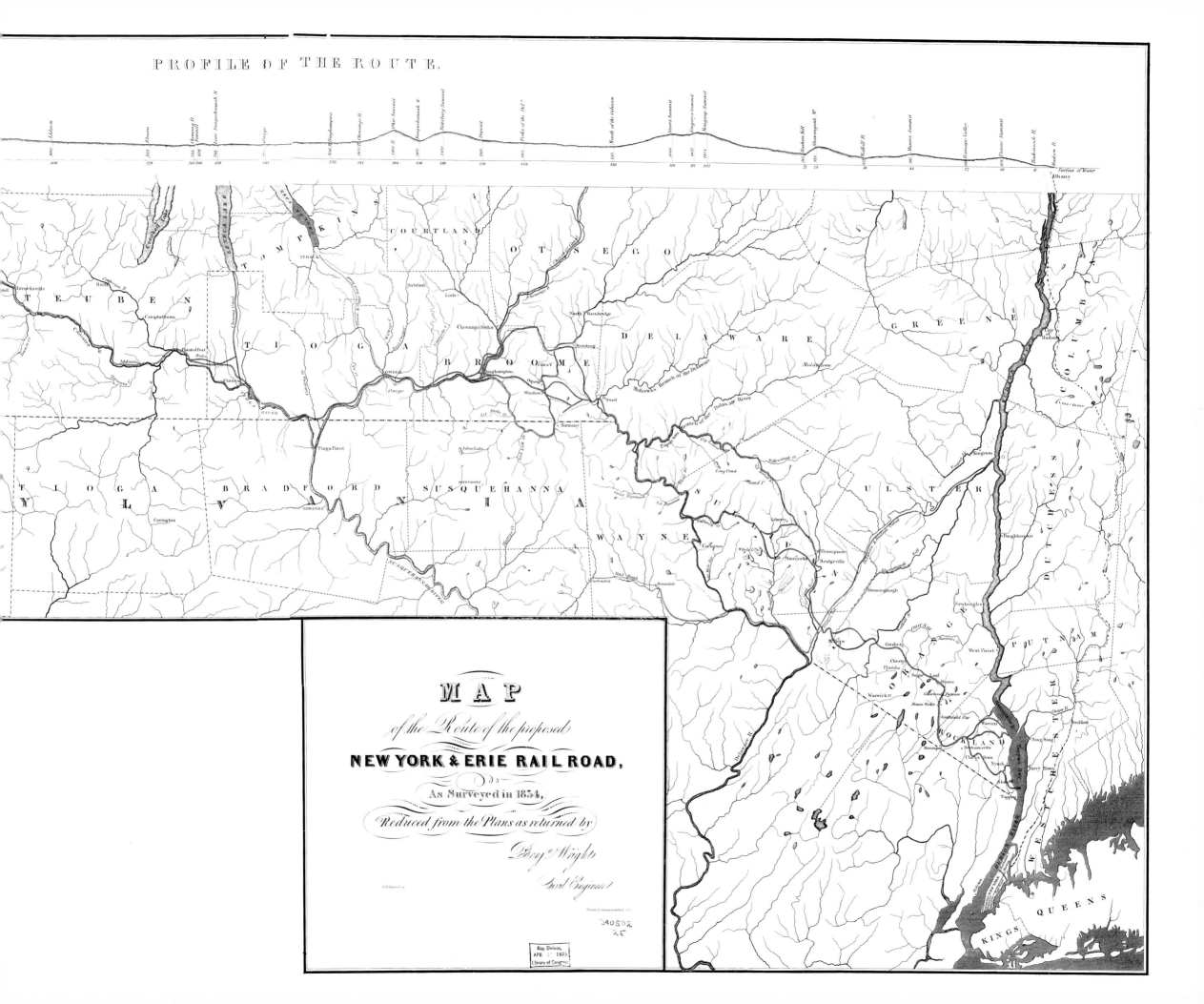

PROFILE OF THE ROUTE.

MAP

of the Route of the proposed

NEW YORK & ERIE RAIL ROAD,

As Surveyed in 1834,

Reduced from the Plans as returned by

Benj.ⁿ Wright

Civil Engineer

Western and Atlantic

1837

6. Cooper, J. F. Map of the country embracing the various routes surveyed for the Western & Atlantic Rail Road of Georgia. Under the direction of Lieut. Col. S. H. Long, Chief Engineer. 1837. U.S. Topographical Bureau M. H. Stansbury, Del. 20 × 55 cm (7½ × 21½ in).

From [*Report of Thomas Stockton, Asst. Engineer concerning Survey of said railroad, Oct. 25, 1837*] Senate doc. 57, 24th Congress, 2nd sess., 1836-37. p. 38. serial 314.

Accompanied by "profiles of the principal routes surveyed for the W.&A. Rail Road of Georgia."

Uncolored topographical map of northern Georgia, embracing the area between the Tennessee boundary and the Chickamauga River in the northwest, and the Chattahoochee River in the southeast.

When built, the line extended from Chattanooga, Tennessee, to a selected junction point in Georgia which became known as Terminus in 1836. This junction eventually became the city of Atlanta. Secondary surveys traversed from point A in Murray County to Taylor's Gap near Sliger's at point C and the Tennessee line, and from point R at "Atoona," near Allatoona Creek, east to the Chattahoochee River at point M.

This is the earliest printed map in the collections based on government surveys conducted for a state-owned railroad. It was similar to other internal improvements of the state. The surveys were made under the direction of Lt. Col. Stephen H. Long, chief engineer, who ten years earlier had surveyed the routes for the Baltimore and Ohio. Work on the 138-mile Georgia route from Atlanta to Chattanooga started in 1841, and by 1850 the line was open to traffic. Its strategic location made it a key supply route for the Confederacy. It was on this line that the famous "Andrews Raid" of April 1862 occurred when Union soldiers disguised as railroad employees captured the locomotive known as the *General.*

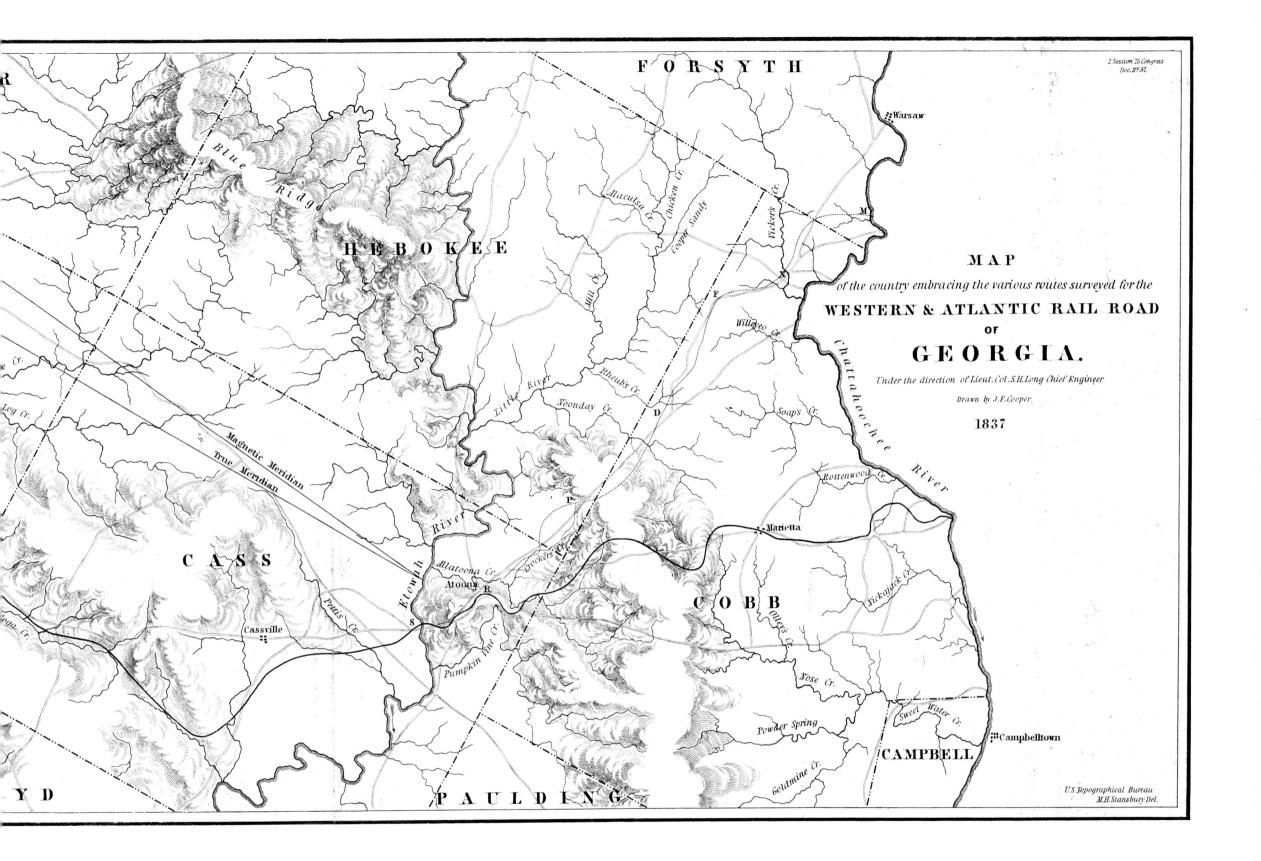

FORSYTH

Warsaw

MAP
of the country embracing the various routes surveyed for the
WESTERN & ATLANTIC RAIL ROAD
OF
GEORGIA.

Under the direction of Lieut.Col.S.H.Long Chief Engineer

Drawn by J.F.Cooper.

1837

2 Session 25 Congress
Doc. Nº 57.

HEBOKEE

Macutsa Cr.
Chicken Cr.
Cooper Sandy
Vicker's Cr.

M

Blue Ridge

Mill Cr.

Willkeo Cr.

F

Little River

Rheub's Cr.

Soap's Cr.

Chattahoochee River

Noonday Cr.

D

Magnetic Meridian
True Meridian

Log Cr.

Rottenwood Cr.

P

Marietta

River

Crocker's Cr.

CASS

Pettis Cr.

Allatoona Cr.

Atoona
B

Elowah River

S

Cassville

CAMPBELL

Olley's Cr.

Vickajack Cr.

Nose Cr.

Powder Spring

Goldmine Cr.

Sweet Water Cr.

Campbelltown

CAMPBELL

Pumpkin Vine Cr.

YD

PAULDING

U.S.Topographical Bureau
M.H.Stansbury Del.

13

Philadelphia and Reading

1838

7. **Osborne, R. B.** Topographical plan & profile of the Philadelphia and Reading Rail Road. [1838] J. Knight. Sc. Printed by G. F. Lewis. [Philadelphia, 1838?] 25 × 81 cm (10 × 32 in).

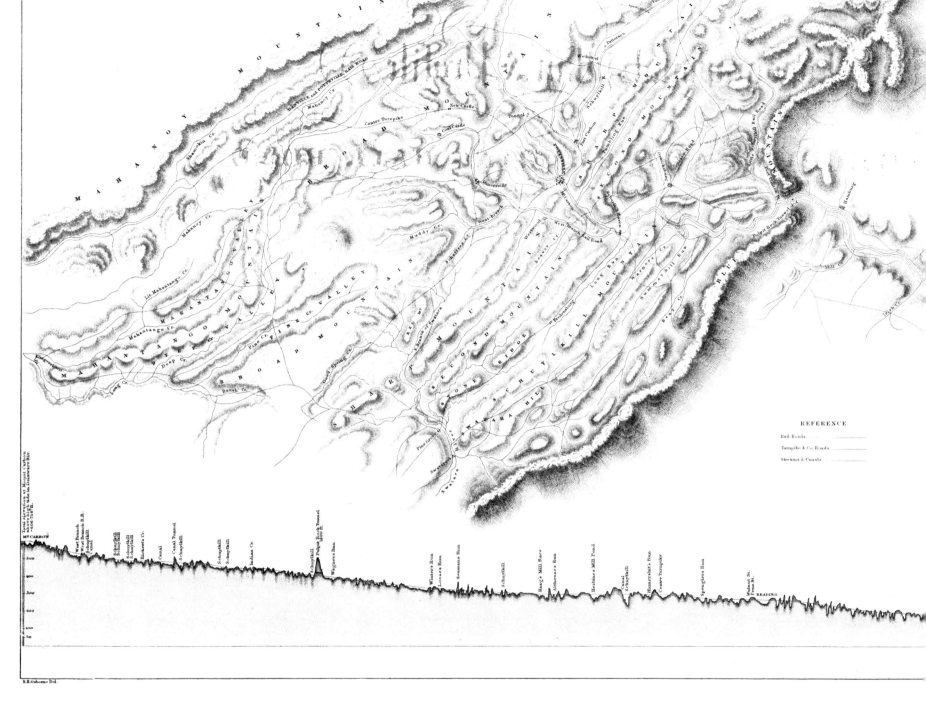

Uncolored topographic strip map of part of Pennsylvania from Mahanoy Mountain along Schuylkill River to Philadelphia.

The Philadelphia and Reading Company was chartered by the Legislature of Pennsylvania on April 4, 1833, to build a road from Philadelphia to Reading, a distance of fifty-eight miles. In 1835 work began and portions of the road were open for travel in 1838. At that time it was expected that the line would be continued to the coal fields by other companies, but as they were unable to do so, the right to construct the road to Pottsville was granted to the Philadelphia and Reading Company, and the time for its completion was extended to March 20, 1842. Construction began in 1836, and that part of the line between Reading and Norristown opened on July 16, 1838. On December 5, 1839, the section between Philadelphia and Norristown was completed, and on January 13, 1842, the entire line to Mount Carbon opened for the transportation of passengers and freight. On May 20, 1842, the Richmond line opened for coal trade. In 1851 the company purchased the railroad extending from the corner of Pine and Broad streets to a junction with the road on the west side of the Schuylkill, and in 1858 also purchased the Lebanon Valley Railroad.

Five great railroad companies have been built up on the anthracite trade, and three others secure a large part of their traffic from hard coal mines which they reach by branch lines. At the time, the Philadelphia and Reading was the only railroad to succeed in building lines into and through the coal region, and it remains the largest of the anthracite railroads. It played a leading role in the early history of American railroading. In density of traffic it has consistently stood first among American carriers, and first faced and solved many transportation problems of both engineering and financing. The development of anthracite transportation shows no orderly and symmetrical growth from canals to railroad lines. During the early years of railroad building, the canals formed the through routes, the railroad lines acting as feeders and covering the short, but to the canals inaccessible, distances from the mines where the traffic originated to the canals along the rivers.

Osborn is credited with building America's first iron bridge. The forty-two foot bridge spanned a creek tributary to the Delaware River near Manayunk, now part of Philadelphia.

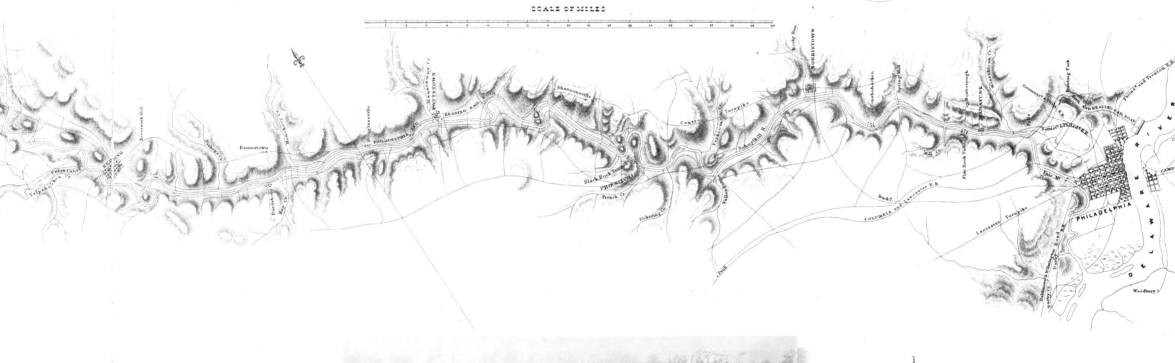

Topographical Plan & Profile

OF THE

PHILADELPHIA AND READING RAIL ROAD

SCALE OF MILES

Base line, level of high tide at Delaware

First iron bridge in the United States, Brownsville, Pennsylvania. Photograph by John Kennedy Lacock, 1910.

15

Baltimore and St. Louis

1843

8. Latrobe, Benjamin H. Map, exhibiting the railway route between Baltimore & St. Louis, together with the other principal lines in the eastern, middle & western states. Prepared under the direction of B. H. Latrobe, Ch. Engr. B. & O. R.R. Baltimore: A. Hoen [1843]. 38 × 76 cm (15 × 30 in).

An uncolored outline map of the eastern United States, covering the area from Portland, Maine, to Norfolk, Virginia, and west to the Mississippi River. The map was made by the son and namesake of the famous architect who was Thomas Jefferson's surveyor of public buildings. The younger Latrobe, a lawyer and civil engineer, was born in Philadelphia in 1806 and died in Baltimore in 1878. He became assistant to Jonathan Knight, chief engineer for the Baltimore and Ohio Railroad, and later succeeded him. He is noted for designing the Thomas Viaduct at Raley, Maryland, the world's oldest such stone structure still in operation, and had charge of building many miles of track, including the extensions to the Ohio River and to Pittsburgh. He was the first to employ the present type of railroad ferry (1835), originated the "ton mile" work unit, served as consultant in the planning of the first transcontinental railroads, and was a member of the committee for planning the Brooklyn Bridge.

16

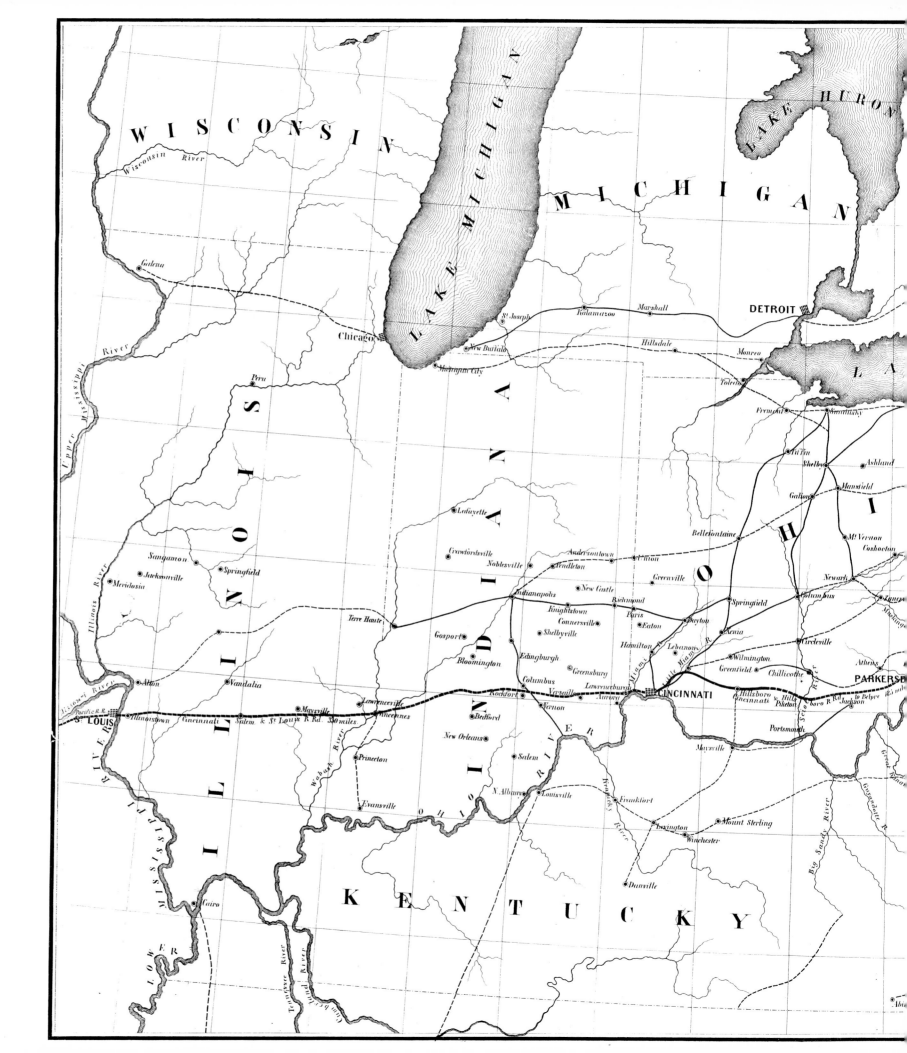

MAP,

Exhibiting the Railway Route between

BALTIMORE & St. LOUIS

TOGETHER WITH THE

OTHER PRINCIPAL LINES

in the

Eastern, Middle & Western States.

Explanations:

Rail Roads finished or under Contract _____
d°   projected   - - - - - - - -

Prepared under direction of B. H. Latrobe Ch. Engr. B. & O. R. R.

Scale 39 miles to the inch.   ⊏ 1843 ⊐

17

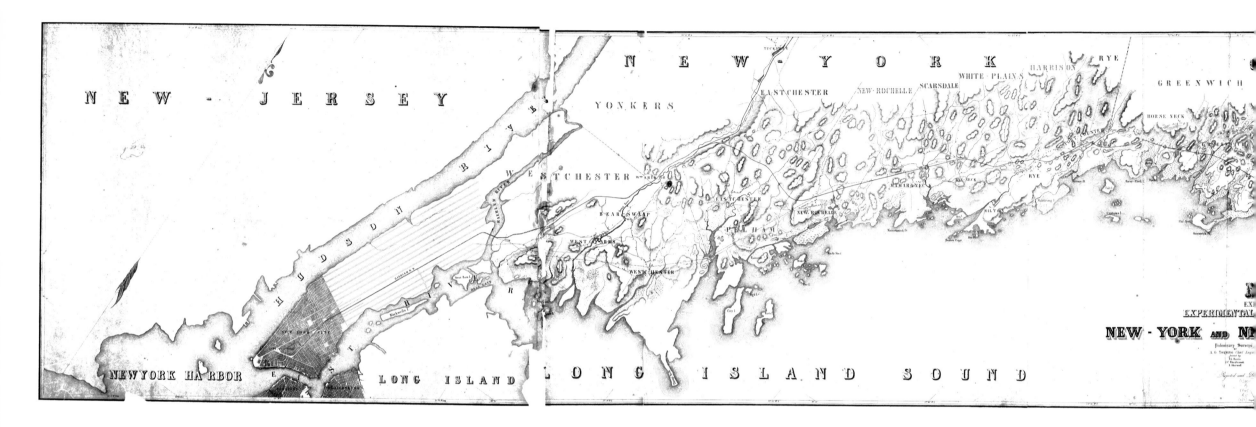

New York and
New Haven

1845

9.   Anderson, P. Map exhibiting the experimental and located lines for the New-York and New-Haven Rail-Road preliminary surveys by A. G. Twining, Chief Engineer. Assisted by D. L. Harris. J. C. Ehesbroush. E. Shotwell. Final location & construction by R. B. Mason, Chief Engineer. Asisted [sic] by B. B. Provost. P. Sours. Projected and drawn by P. Anderson, Civil Ingr. [sic] Febr. 1845. Snyder & Black Lithogrs. New-York. 47 × 315 cm (18½ × 124 in).

A greatly detailed uncolored topographic strip map measuring over ten feet in length. Indicates drainage, relief by hachures, cities and towns, individual houses, harbors, lighthouses, turnpikes, local roads, and trails. Shows connections at Bridgeport with the Housatonic Railroad, and the Naugatuck Railroad at Milford.

The main survey is indicated by a solid black line. The line was built along this survey and was opened to both passenger and freight traffic in January 1849. The company was chartered on June 20, 1844, construction began in 1847, and a double track was laid in 1854.

Beginning in the eastern part of the New Haven at Mill Run and connecting with the Hartford and New Hampshire and the New Hampshire and Northampton Railroad, the line extended through the Connecticut counties bordering Long Island Sound. It threaded its way through the towns of Milford, Bridgeport, Stamford, and Greenwich and entered the state of New York at Portchester, continued through New Rochelle, and joined the tracks of the Harlem Railroad near Williams Bridge. Secondary survey lines are indicated by dashed lines leading south from mile marker fifty-six at Mamaroneck, and west through Westchester to connect with the Harlem Railroad at the Harlem River Bridge (mile sixty-nine). Suggested bypass routes appear at several towns along the main route.

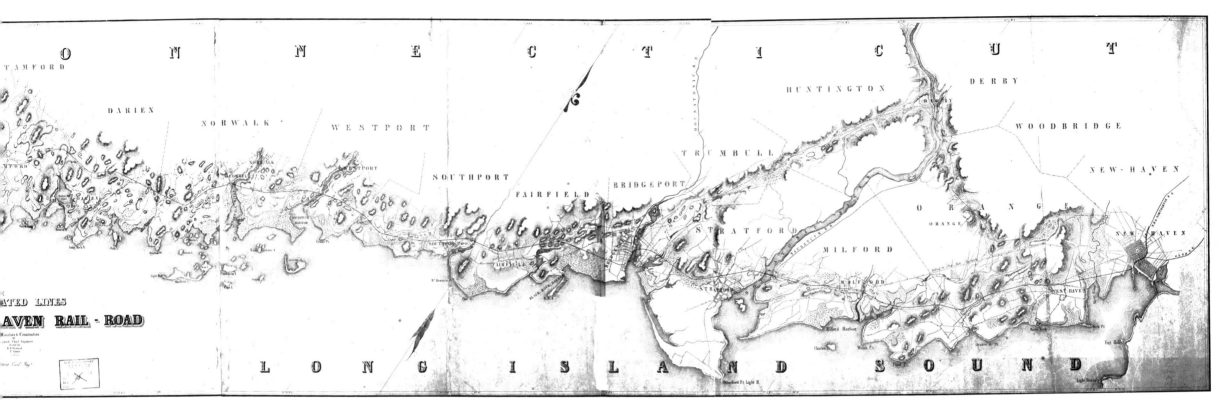

New Haven from Perry Hill.
Engraving by Wellstood & Peters
from a drawing by B. F. Smith,
Jr. Undated: mid-nineteenth
century.

Orange and Alexandria

1854

10.   Faul, August. Map and profile of the Orange and Alexandria Rail Road with its Warrenton Branch and a portion of the Manasses [sic] Gap Rail Road, to show its point of connection. Ackerman Lith. 379 Broadway, New York. [1854?] Colored. 40 × 119 cm (15½ × 47 in).

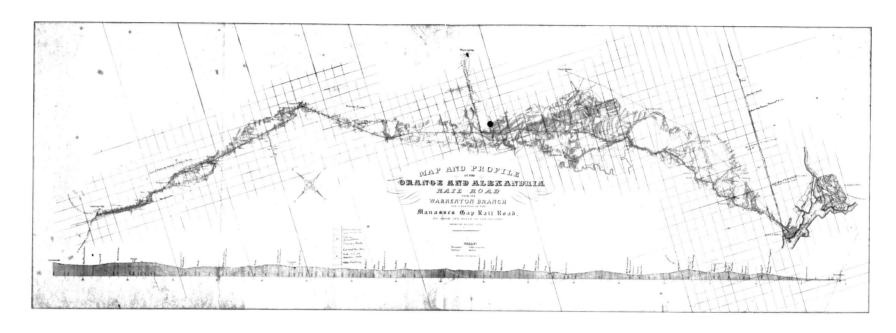

Printed topographic strip map with manuscript annotations to show the geologic structure along the route of the railroad. The Alexandria and the Chesapeake and Ohio canals and stage stable for horses used on the Piedmont stage route to North Carolina are also indicated.

The Orange and Alexandria Railroad Company was chartered in 1832. It was not until 1848, however, that this company was organized to recover for the city of Alexandria some of the trade previously lost to Baltimore and Richmond. Construction on the line began in 1850 and was completed to Culpeper by 1852 and to Gordonsville by 1854. The map shows a junction with the Virginia Central Railroad at Gordonsville. Warrenton was linked by a branch line in 1853. The Manassas Gap Railroad, the first to cross the Blue Ridge Mountains, was completed to Strasburg in 1854 to join Alexandria with the upper Piedmont Valley. Detailed descriptions of three original surveys were published in the *Proceeding of the Called Meeting of the Stockholders of the Orange and Alexandria Railroad Company, December, 1849.* The routes on the maps generally follow the survey lines as reported by Chief Engineer Thomas C. Atkinson at the fifth annual meeting of the stockholders, held in Alexandria, October 24, 1854. No original survey maps were appended to the report. This map was drawn by August Faul and printed about 1854 by Ackerman Lithography of New York. This copy, annotated in colors to show geological structures along the route of the railroad, is an example of the general survey maps prepared to illustrate progress reports of individual railroads.

Federal troops clearing up the damage to the military railroad controlled by General Pope. Orange and Alexandria Railroad, Union Mills, Virginia.

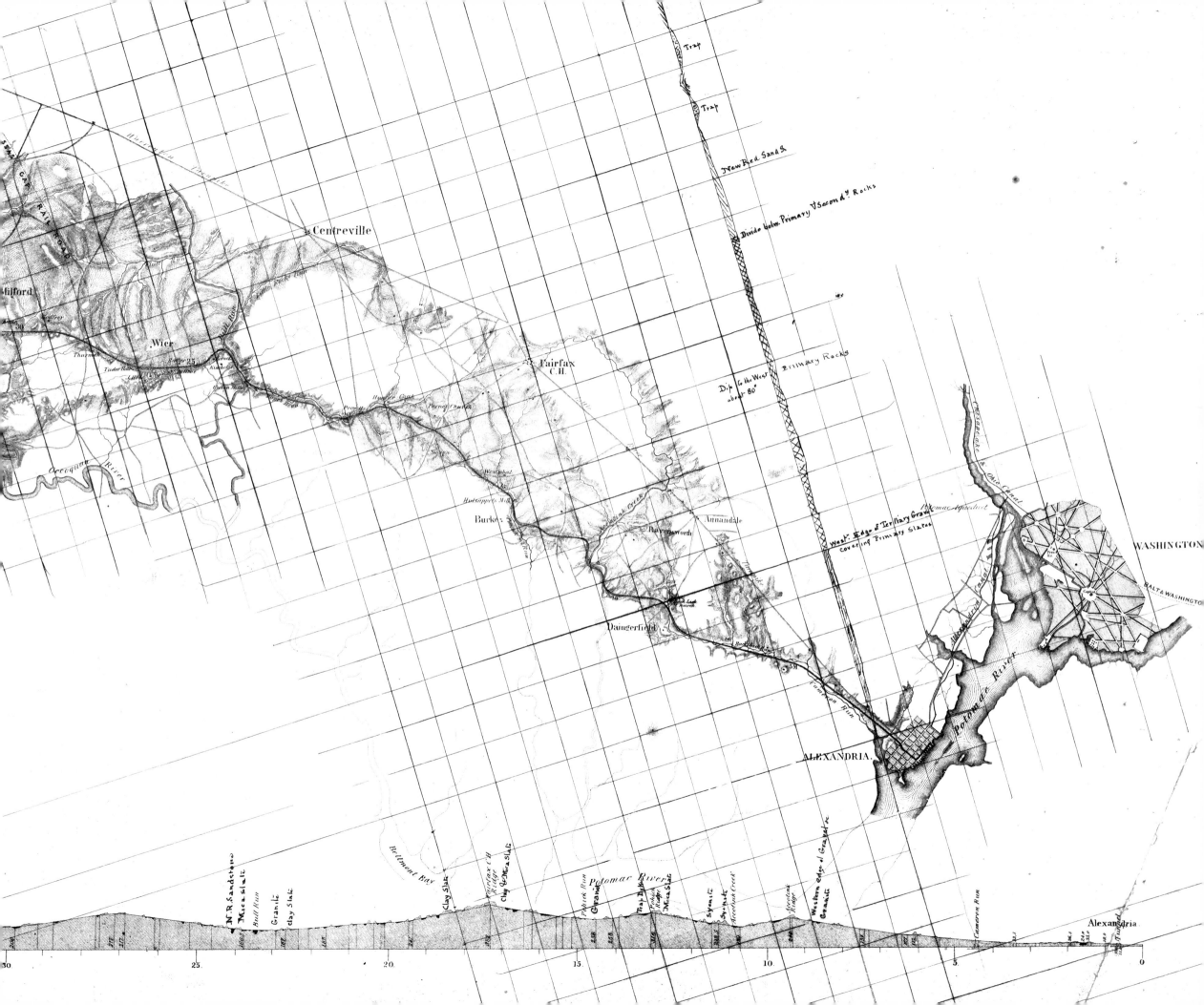

Trap

Trap

New Red Sand St.

Divide below Primary & Secondary Rocks

Primary Rocks

Dip to the West about 80°

West. Edge of Tertiary Gravel covering Primary Slates

Potomac Aqueduct

Chesapeake & Ohio Canal

WASHINGTON

BALT & WASHINGTON

Centreville

Milford

Wier

Fairfax C.H.

Warrenton Turnpike

Occoquan River

Parney Church

Westphal

Huntsapple's Mill

Burke

Annandale

Daingerfield

ALEXANDRIA

Potomac River

Alexandria

Belmont Bay

N. R. Sandstone
Mica slate
Bull Run
Granite
clay Slate

Clay Slate

Fairfax C.H. Ridge
Clay & Mica Slate

Pohick Run
Potomac River
Granite
Trap Dyke
Fisher
Ridge
Mica Slate
Syenite
Trap
Accotink Creek

Western edge of Granite
Granite

Hunting Run

Cameron Run

30   25   20   15   10   5   0

Manassas Gap

1855

11. Dwyer, Thomas. Map of the Manassas Gap Railroad and its extensions. September, 1855. Baltimore: A. Hoen & Co., 1855. 60 × 94 cm (24 × 37 in).

Topographical survey map of northern Virginia and part of West Virginia extending west from Washington, D.C., to the Allegheny Mountains, showing relief by hachures, drainage, cities and towns, counties, roads, and railroads with distances. Includes profiles. Chartered March 11, 1850, and opened in 1854 from Manassas Junction to Strasburg, Virginia, this railroad was consolidated June 1, 1867, with the Orange and Alexandria, forming the Orange, Alexandria, and Manassas Railroad.

The main line and the extensions and connections and the boundary of Loudoun County, Virginia, are hand-colored in brown. Profiles of the main line and its Loudoun Branch appear at the bottom and left margins of the map. This line was the first to cross the Blue Ridge Mountains in Virginia and was completed to Strasburg, Virginia, in 1854. A train on this line took Confederate soldiers to their victory at Bull Run in 1861.

At the first annual meeting of the stockholders, September 2, 1851, it was reported that construction had begun at a junction with the Orange & Alexandria Railroad. "The work was pushed diligently," so that trains were running to The Plains in May 1852, to Rectortown in August, and to Markham in December. The "top of the Ridge" was reached a year later (November 1853), and finally, after "distressing delays by reason of the heavy earth work" west of the Blue Ridge and the necessity of building bridges over both branches of the Shenandoah, Strasburg was attained on October 19, 1854. It was reported to the stockholders that "the iron horse of Manassa this day takes his first draught of limestone water." In four years a group of farmers had built sixty miles of railroad and could claim to be the first Virginians who had transcended the barrier of the Blue Ridge with a railroad.

Manassas Junction, Virginia, after its evacuation by Confederate troops, March 1862.

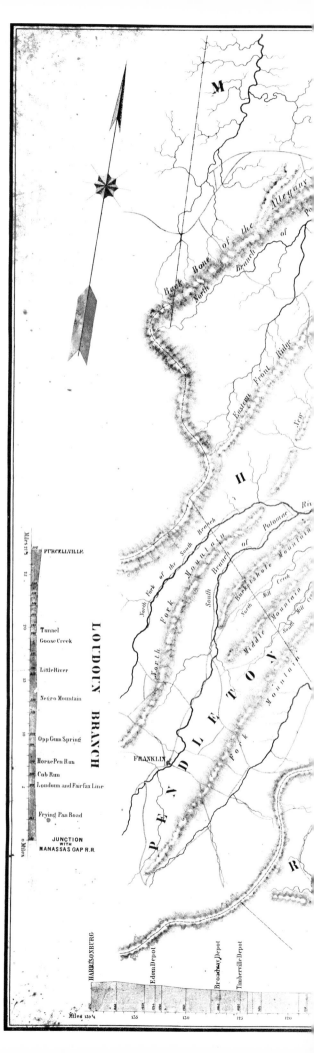

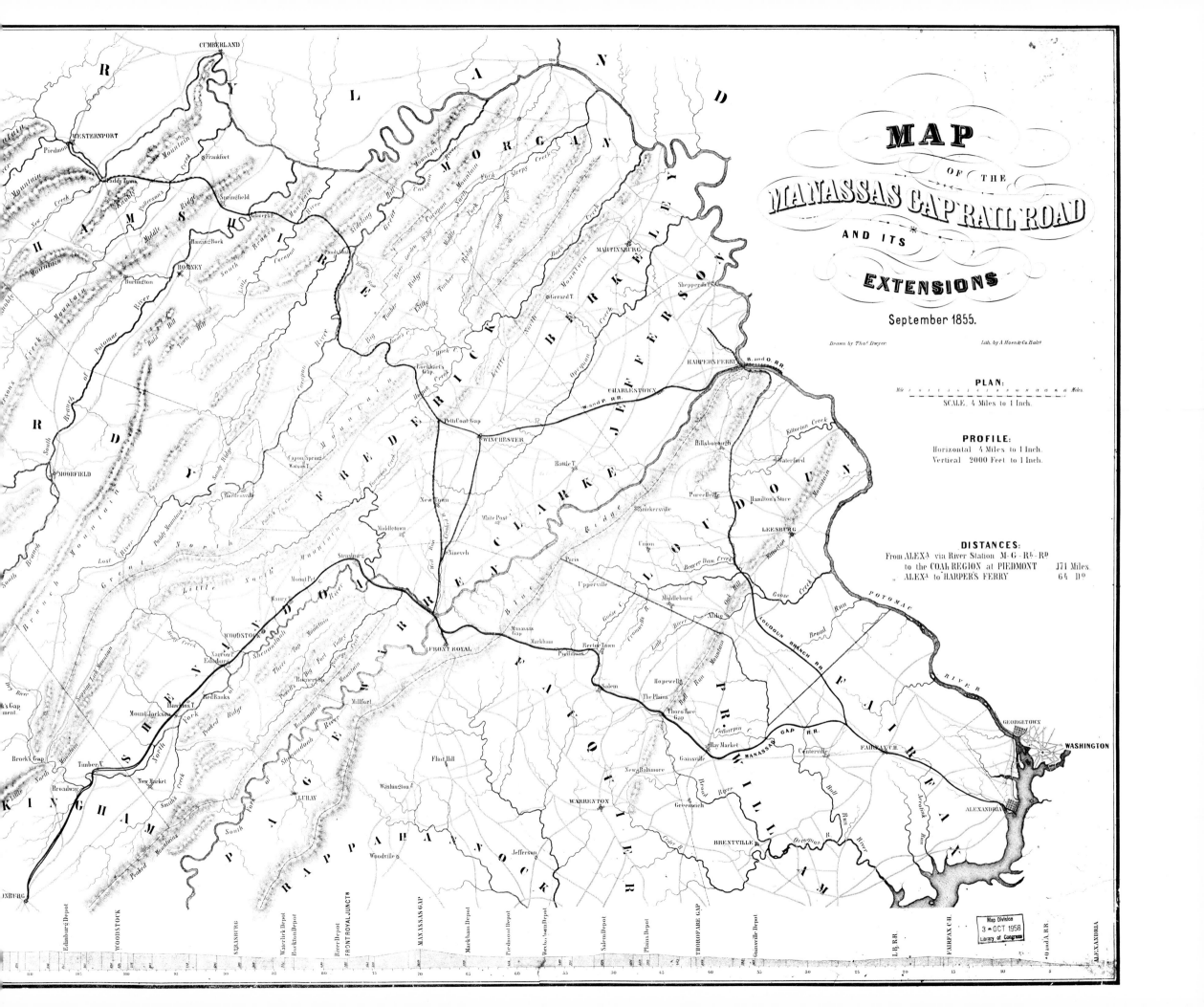

MAP
OF THE
MANASSAS GAP RAIL ROAD
AND ITS
EXTENSIONS

September 1855.

Drawn by Thos Dwyer

Lith. by A Hoen & Co Balto

PLAN:

SCALE, 4 Miles to 1 Inch.

PROFILE:

Horizontal 4 Miles to 1 Inch.
Vertical 2000 Feet to 1 Inch.

DISTANCES:

From ALEXᴬ via River Station M·G·Rᴸ·Rᴰ
to the COAL REGION at PIEDMONT 171 Miles.
ALEXᴬ to HARPER'S FERRY 64 Dᵒ

Baltimore and Ohio

1858

12. **Jacobi, L.** Map and profiles shewing the Baltimore and Ohio Rail Road with — its branches and immediately tributary lines. 1858. Compiled and drawn by L. Jacobi C.E. Baltimore. Published by Hunckel & Son and L. Jacobi Baltimore. Lithographed by Hunckel & Son Baltimore. c1857. Baltimore: Hunckel & Con, 1858. Colored. 61 × 127 cm (24 × 50 in).

"Baltimore and Ohio Rail Road being the main artery in the great national route between the east and west."

Detailed map of part of the middle Atlantic region showing drainage, cities and towns, counties, canals, roads, and the railroad network, with proposed extensions of lines. Includes profiles and distances and length of finished track.

The main line has connections with the Northern Central and the Philadelphia, Wilmington & Baltimore Railroad in the city of Baltimore, and with the Winchester and Potomac Railroad at Harpers Ferry. It connects with the coal and iron mine railroads in Western Maryland and the Central Ohio and the Cleveland & Ohio River Railroads by Wheeling, West Virginia. The map indicates the progress of work on the Pittsburgh and Connellsville Railroad, northwest of Cumberland, Maryland, and southeast of Pittsburgh. The main lines of the Baltimore and Ohio Railroad are printed in solid red lines. A list of branch lines and distances between cities appear at the left side of map. The location for the proposed Alexandria-Loudoun and Hampshire Railroad is shown as a dashed line connecting Alexandria with the B & O at Paddy Town, which today is Keyser, West Virginia.

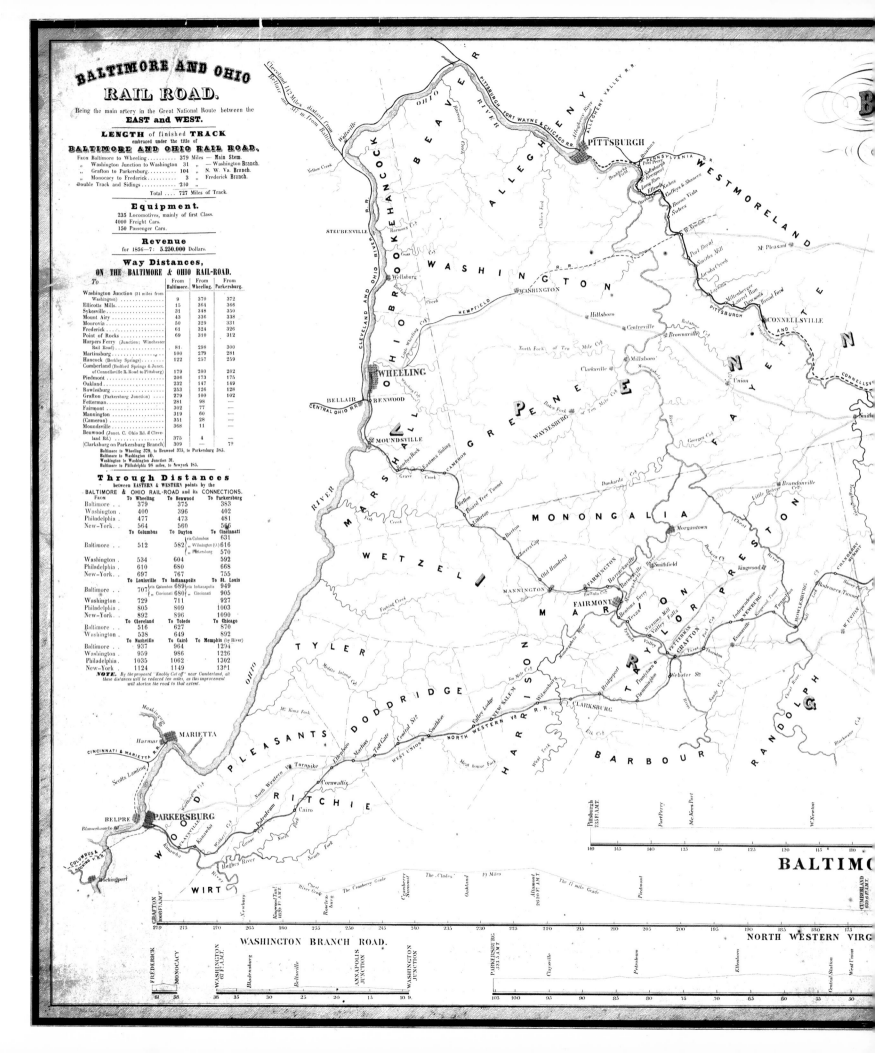

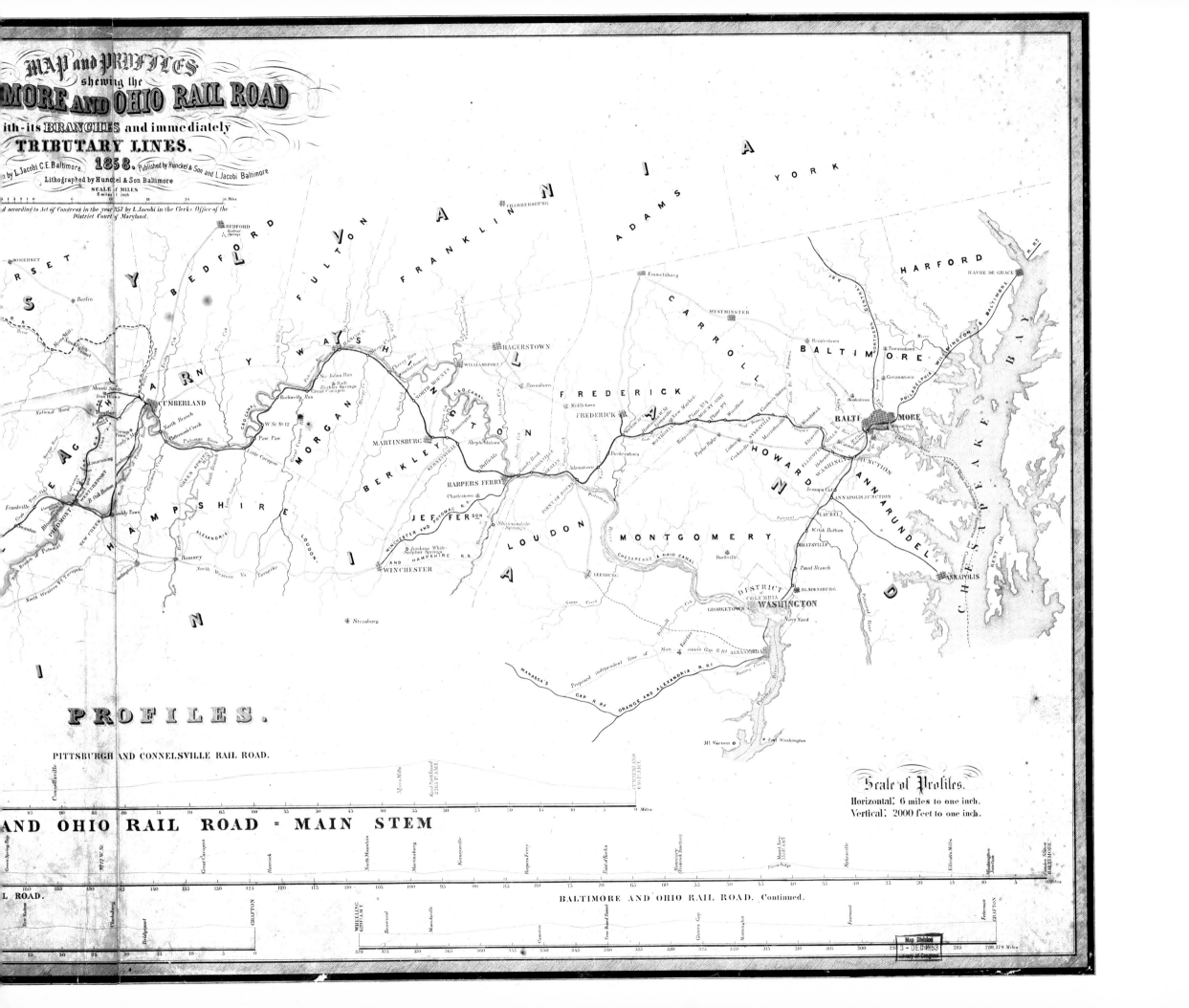

Pacific and Atlantic

1851

13. Lewis, William J. Route of the Pacific and Atlantic Rail Road between San Francisco, & San Jose. As located by Wm. J. Lewis, Chief Engineer, in Sept. Oct. & Nov. 1851. San Francisco: Britton & Rey, 1851. 20 × 69 cm (7½ × 27 in).

Uncolored survey map made to accompany the *Articles of Association and By-Laws of the Pacific and Atlantic Railroad Company. With Reports of the Chief Engineer and Secretary.* (San Francisco, 1854). Map of the southwest shore of San Francisco Bay, between San Francisco and San Jose, showing roads, cities and towns, the proposed railroad, property owners, streams, and relief by hachures.

This map was prepared three years earlier than the survey map for California's first railroad, the Sacramento Valley Railroad.

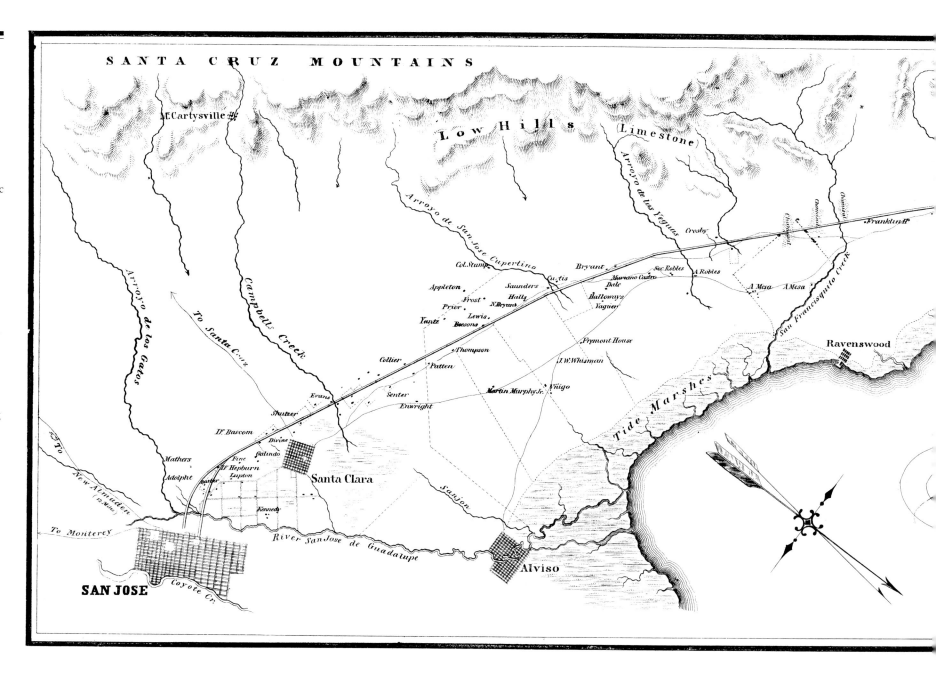

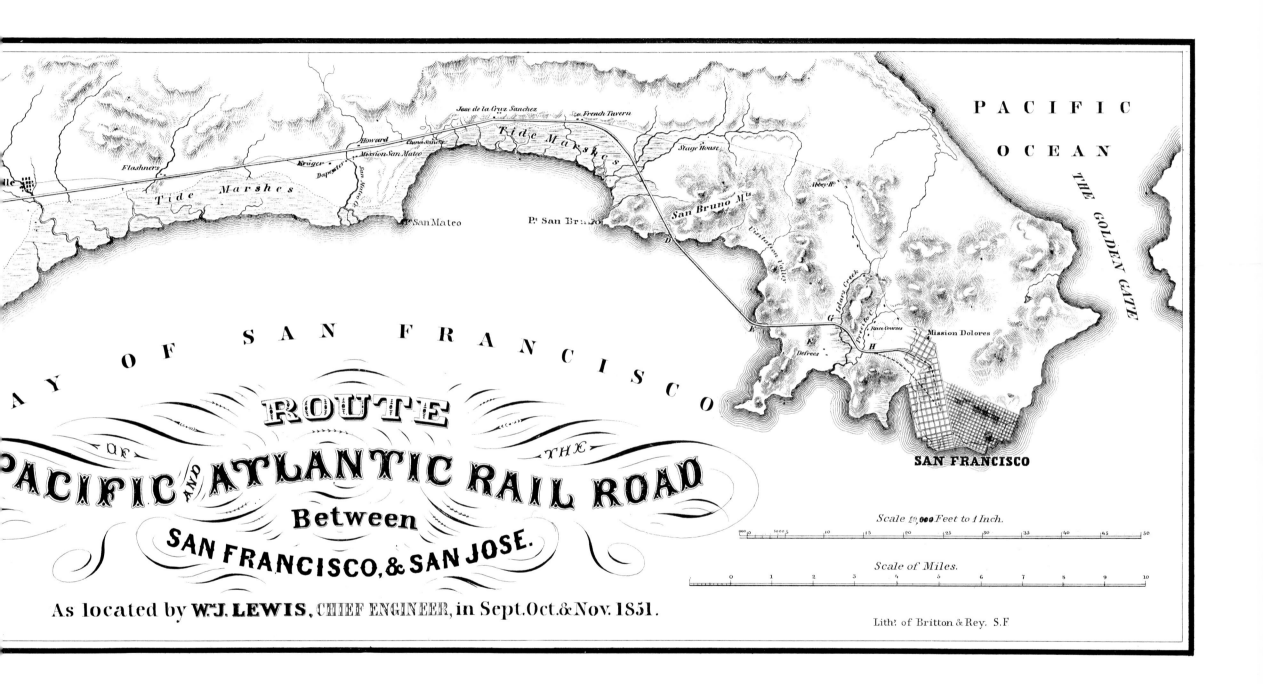

PACIFIC OCEAN

THE GOLDEN GATE

BAY OF SAN FRANCISCO

Tide Marshes

Flashners

Kruger

Dapester

Mission San Mateo

Howard

Chaves Sanchez

Jose de la Cruz Sanchez

French Tavern

Tide Marshes

Stage House

Abbey H.

San Bruno Mtn

Visitation Valley

Islais Creek

Precita

Race Courses

Mission Dolores

Defrees

P. San Mateo

P. San Bruno

SAN FRANCISCO

ROUTE

OF THE

PACIFIC AND ATLANTIC RAIL ROAD

Between

SAN FRANCISCO, & SAN JOSE.

As located by W. J. LEWIS, CHIEF ENGINEER, in Sept. Oct. & Nov. 1851.

Scale 12,000 Feet to 1 Inch.

Scale of Miles.

Lith. of Britton & Rey. S.F

27

Rio Grande to the Pacific Ocean

1854

14. Hoffmann, John D. From the Rio Grande to the Pacific Ocean from explorations and surveys made under the direction of the Hon. Jefferson Davis, Secretary of War by Lieut. A. W. Whipple, Topogl. Engrs. and Lieut. J. C. Ives, Topogl. Engrs. A. H. Campbell, Civil Engr. and Surveyor. Wm. White Jr., N. H. Hutton, J. P. Sherburne, Asst. Surveyors. 1853-4. Engraved by Selmar Siebert. 58 × 135 cm (22 × 53 in).

At head of title: "Route near the 35th Parallel. Map no. 2."

From U.S. War Department, Explorations and Surveys for a Railroad Route from the Mississippi River to the Pacific Ocean. Topographical Maps . . . to Illustrate the Various Reports . . . (Washington, 1859) 33d Congress 2d session. Senate. Ex. doc. no. 78.

Insets: Sketch of Aztec Pass. Drawn by C. Mahon. From a sketch by A. H. Campbell, Civil Engineer. Sketch of Campbell's Pass from Agua Azul to Salt Spring. Drawn by C. Mahon.

Under the provisions of the Army Appropriation Act of March 1853, Secretary of War Jefferson Davis was directed to survey possible routes to the Pacific. Five selected routes, roughly following specific parallels, were to be surveyed by parties under the supervision of the Topographical Corps. Illustrated here is an example of one of the twenty-two detailed topographic survey maps submitted to Congress at the completion of the work of the Pacific railroad surveys.

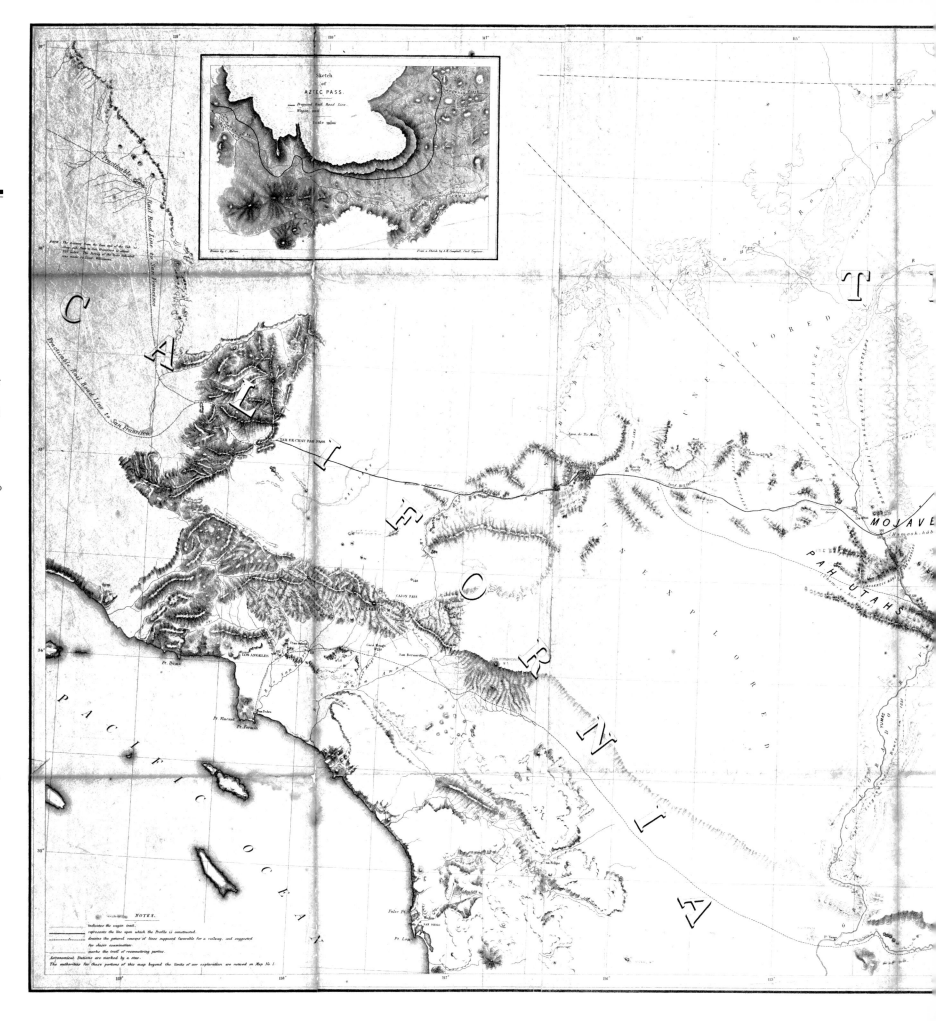

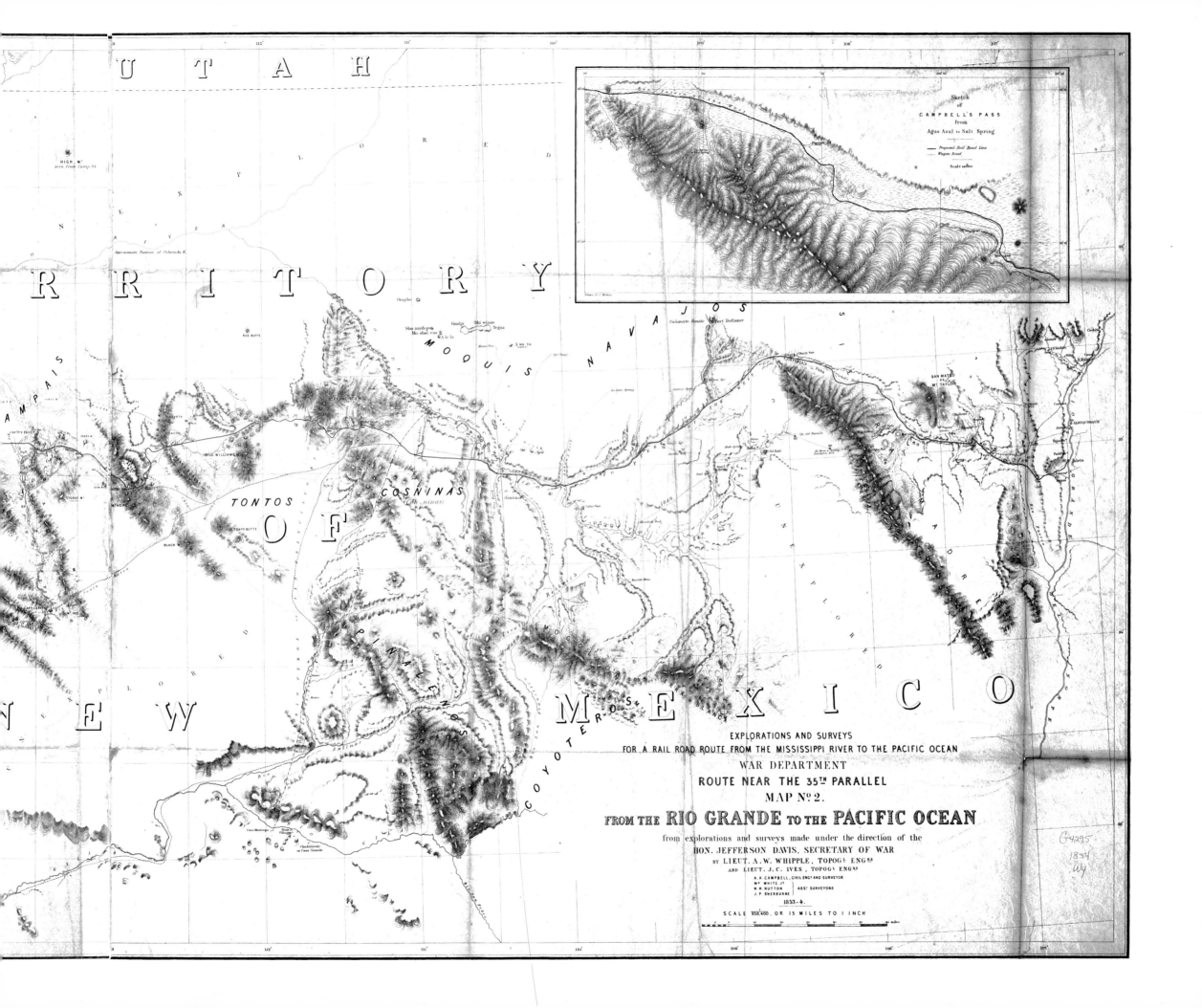

Sketch
of
CAMPBELL'S PASS
from
Agua Azul to Salt Spring

Proposed Rail Road Line
Wagon Road

Scale 12000

EXPLORATIONS AND SURVEYS
FOR A RAIL ROAD ROUTE FROM THE MISSISSIPPI RIVER TO THE PACIFIC OCEAN
WAR DEPARTMENT
ROUTE NEAR THE 35TH PARALLEL
MAP Nº 2.
FROM THE RIO GRANDE TO THE PACIFIC OCEAN
from explorations and surveys made under the direction of the
HON. JEFFERSON DAVIS, SECRETARY OF WAR
BY LIEUT. A.W. WHIPPLE, TOPOG.L ENG.RS
AND LIEUT. J.C. IVES, TOPOG.L ENG.RS
A. H. CAMPBELL, CIVIL ENG.R AND SURVEYOR
W.M WHITE J.R
N.H. HUTTON   ASS.T SURVEYORS
J.P. SHERBURNE
1853-4.

SCALE 950,400, OR 15 MILES TO 1 INCH

Sacramento Valley

1854

15. Judah, Theodore Dehone. Map of the Sacramento Valley Railroad from the City of Sacramento to the crossing of American River at Negro Bar, Sac. Co. San Francisco: B. F. Butler's Lith., 1854. 68 × 44 cm (10½ × 21½ in).

Uncolored survey map of part of Sacramento County showing rivers and streams, relief by hachures, vegetation, mile markers, settlements, and landowners' names, including the William A. Leidesdorf Rancho, Nueva Helvetia, and the Mining District.

The railroad depicted in this map was organized on August 16, 1852, and incorporated in October 1853. Leidesdorf, of Danish-Negro parentage, was vice consul to Mexico.

This is the official survey for the first California railroad and was made by the famous engineer Theodore D. Judah (1826-1863), who was later the guiding spirit in building the Central Pacific Railroad across the Sierra Nevada Mountains. He was persuaded to come to California from the East by Col. Charles Lincoln Wilson, a successful transportation executive, to build the railroad that transported men and freight from Sacramento to the goldfields.

The map identifies many landowners along the line of survey but does not name the property of the colorful "widow Harper," who it is said faced the grading teams at her property line with a shotgun. The widow's property is adjacent to the Collins property, on which two hills are shown. The survey paralleled the plank road, which ran east out of Sacramento, and then followed the rutted and dusty roads along the American River. At

Lost Camp Spur Cut, eighty miles from Sacramento, California, Central Pacific Railroad.

the nine-mile marker a secondary survey line extended to the Cosumnes River.

In 1855 Judah laid out the town of Folsom at Negro Bar, which was named after the first black gold miners who settled there in 1849. A copy of his *Map of the Town of Folsom, California* (San Francisco: F. Kuhl, 1855) survives in the collections of the Bancroft Library in California.

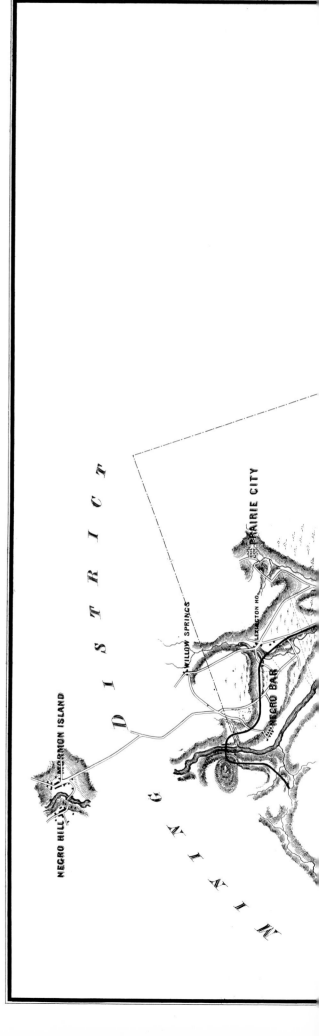

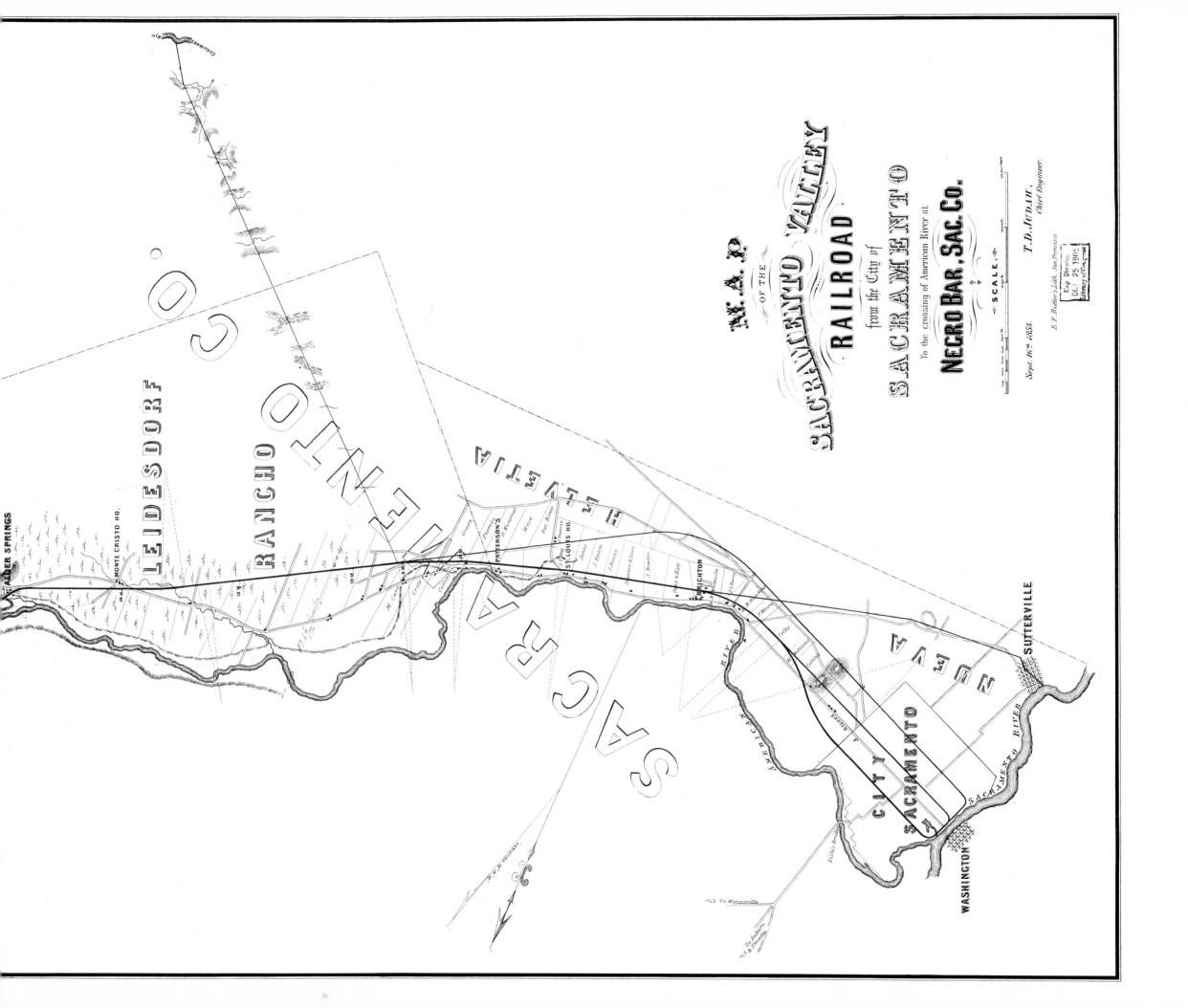

MAP
— OF THE —
SACRAMENTO VALLEY
RAILROAD
from the City of
SACRAMENTO
To the crossing of American River at
NEGRO BAR, SAC. CO.
→ SCALE. ←

Sept. 16th 1854.

T. D. JUDAH,
Chief Engineer.

B. F. Butler's Lith. San Francisco.

Sacramento Valley

1854

16. Judah, Theodore Dehone. Map showing the location of Sacramento Valley Railroad, Cal. Sacramento, Septr., 1854. T. D. Judah, Chief Engineer. B. F. Butler's Lith. San Francisco. Scale 27 × 55 cm (11 × 17 in).

From *Report of the Chief Engineer of the Preliminary Surveys and Future Business of the Sacramento Valley Railroad* (Sacramento: Democratic State Journal, 1854).

Uncolored sketch map of the first railroad in California, showing drainage, marshes, relief by hachures, mining areas, and the projected extensions of the Sacramento Valley Railroad in the state. The map is oriented to the west and covers central California and its mining district. From San Francisco to San Jose it uses the survey lines of the Pacific and Atlantic Railroad (see entry 13), then extends to Sonora, California, which was founded by Mexican gold miners. An extension on the main line crosses the "Emigrant's Trail" at Bear Creek and ends at Tehama.

View of Sacramento. Inset on S. G. Elliott's 1860 Map of Central California (see entry 35).

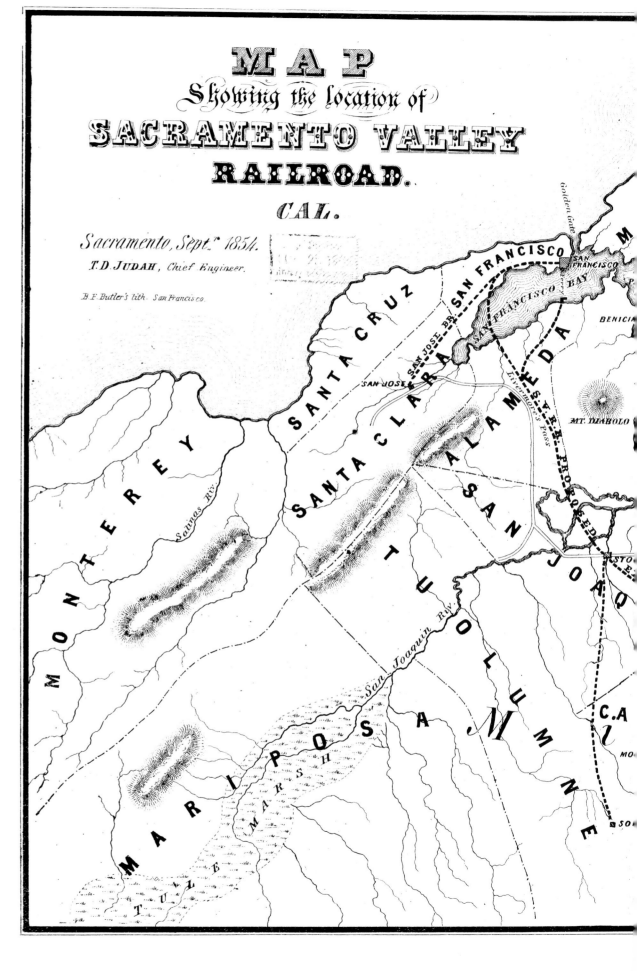

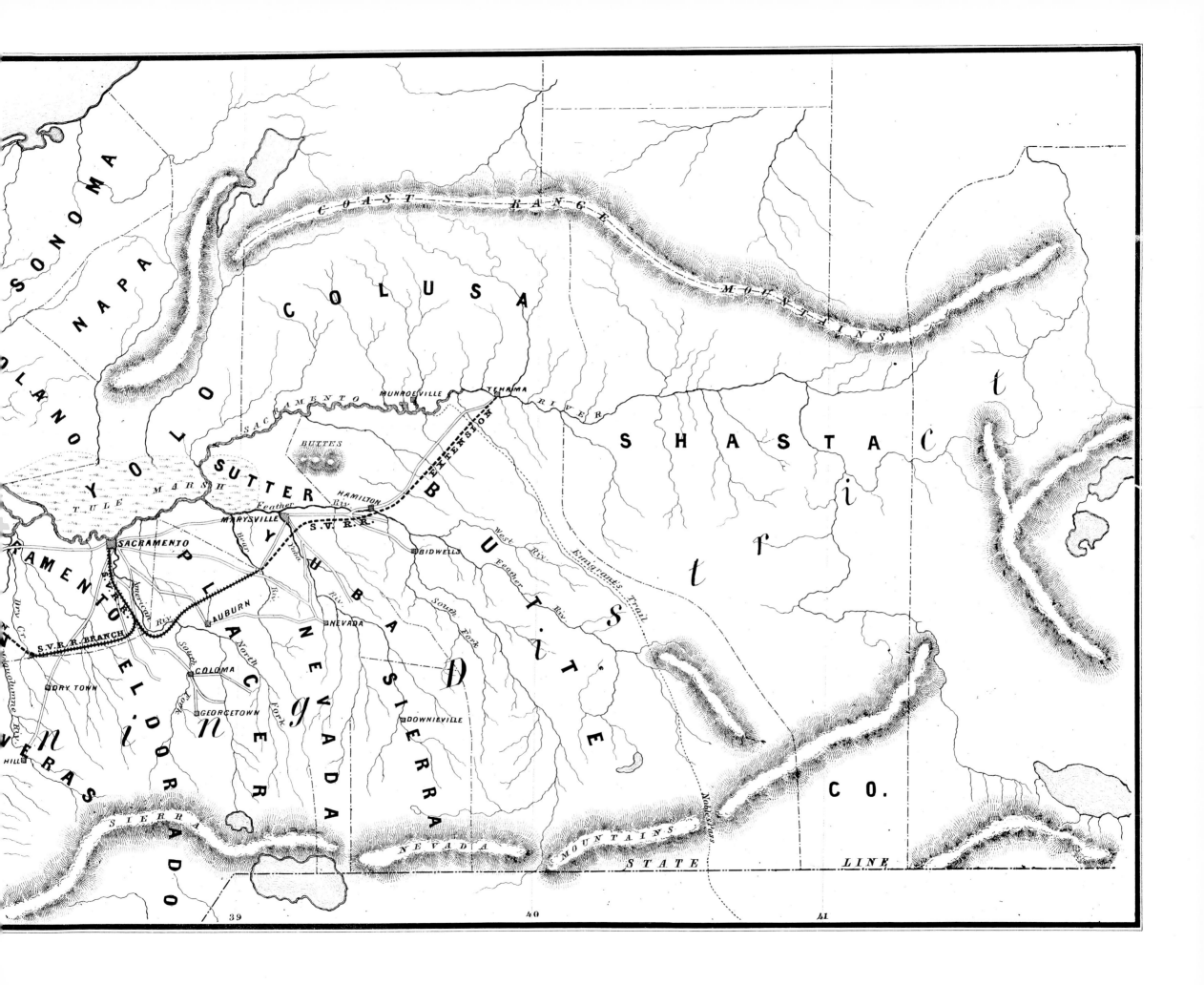

Pacific Railroad

1855

17. Warren, Gouverneur Kemble. Map of routes for a Pacific railroad, compiled to accompany the report of the Hon. Jefferson Davis, Sec. of War. G. K. Warren. 1t. top engrs. 1855. Rev. Jany. 1857. N[ew] Y[ork] Lith. of J. Bien [1857]. Colored 52 × 59 cm (21 × 23 in). (Millard Fillmore map Coll.)

Outline sketch map of the United States west of the Mississippi River designed to show the relationship of the proposed railroad routes.

First edition of the map appears in U.S. War Department, *Report of the Secretary . . . Communicating the Several Pacific Railroad Explorations* (Washington, 1855). 33d Congress, 1st session, House. Ex. doc. no. 129.

Note: "This is a hurried compilation of all the authentic surveys and is designed to exhibit the relations of the different routes to each other: the topography represents only those great divides which form summits on the profiles of the routes. An elaborate map on a scale of 1:3,000,000 is being compiled and is in an advanced state. Revised Jany. 1857. G. K. Warren, Lt. Top. Engrs."

Annotated in pink to show boundaries and names of states and territories. Signed in ms., on the verso: "Millard Fillmore."

Warren's large and elaborate map incorporating the Pacific railroad surveys was heavily used by commercial publishers such as Joseph H. Colton, J. T. Lloyd, Rand McNally, and Gaylord Watson to revise their maps.

This map is from President Millard Fillmore's extensive map collection, which is now in the Library of Congress Geography and Map Division.

"Through to the Pacific."
Currier & Ives, 1870.

MAP OF ROUTES
FOR A
PACIFIC RAILROAD

Compiled to accompany the Report of the

HON. JEFFERSON DAVIS, SEC. OF WAR

In Office of P. R. R. Surveys

1855.

Statute Miles   4533

1: 4000000

Note — This map is a hurried compilation of all the authentic surveys
and is designed to exhibit the relations of the different routes to each
other. the topography represents only those great divides which form
summits on the profiles of the routes. An elaborate map on a scale of
1: 3000000 is being compiled and is in an advanced state.
Revised Jan.ʸ 1857.

G. K. Warren.
Lt Top. Engrs.

Lith. of J. Bien 60 Fulton St. N.Y.

General Maps

United States

1834

18. Norris, William. Map of the railroads and canals finished, unfinished and in contemplation in the United States. Drawn and engraved for D. K. Minor editor of the Railroad Journal. New York [1834] 62 × 94 cm (24½ × 37 in).

One of the earliest general maps of the United States, made exclusively for D. K. Minor, editor of the *Railroad Journal.* The map names the larger rivers and steams, shows ridges of the Appalachian Mountains by hachures, and includes major cities and towns. Watercolor has been neatly added to emphasize state boundaries. Canals and railroads are distinguished by line symbols. Around the sides of the map there are route profiles for the Baltimore and Ohio, the Columbia, and the "Massachusetts Railroad." Eleven canal profiles are also included. Below the title cartouche there is an engraved view showing the Erie Canal at the Little Falls of the Mohawk River near Herkimer, New York.

This map was made by the locomotive designer and builder William Norris. It includes detailed graphic information about the planning and construction of U.S. railroads and shows the desire of the eastern seaports for western markets. It indicates railroads under construction and lines completed in the Northeastern, Middle Atlantic, and Southern states. For example, in New York it shows the surveyed lines for the New York and Erie Railroad projected by Benjamin Wright in 1834 (see entry 5). In Pennsylvania it shows the Philadelphia and Columbia Railroad, the first state-owned railroad, completed as far as Columbia, Pennsylvania. It

also shows the inclined plane Allegheny Portage Railroad, the first line to cross the Allegheny Mountains, completed between Johnstown and Hollydaysburg, providing a link to the Pennsylvania Canal. This stretch of railroad line is credited with having the first railroad tunnel built near Johnstown. The tunnel, dug through slate, measured 901 feet in length and 25 feet in diameter.

In Virginia, the map shows the Winchester and Potomac Railroad, completed to Harpers Ferry just before its connection with the B & O. This transportation link, completed in 1836, was designed to divert Shenandoah Valley wheat from the city of Alexandria and to stimulate the growth of Baltimore. It greatly contributed to the decline of Alexandria.

In South Carolina the map shows the "Charleston & Augusta Rail Road," constructed in 1833 to Hamburg by the South Carolina Canal and Railroad Company. At the time its 136 miles of track constituted the longest railroad in the world. First regular passenger service was established on this line using the steam engine *Best Friend of Charleston.*

William Norris attained world wide fame with the success of his own locomotive design. The engine was named the *George Washington,* used anthracite coal as fuel, and was first placed in service on the Philadelphia and Columbia Railroad. Norris was associated with Stephen H. Long, the army topographical engineer and explorer who was instrumental in selecting the route for the Baltimore and Ohio Railroad.

View of the Erie Canal at Little Falls on the Mohawk River, Little Falls, New York, 1830. Engraving by Fenner, Sears, & Co. from a drawing by W. G. Wall.

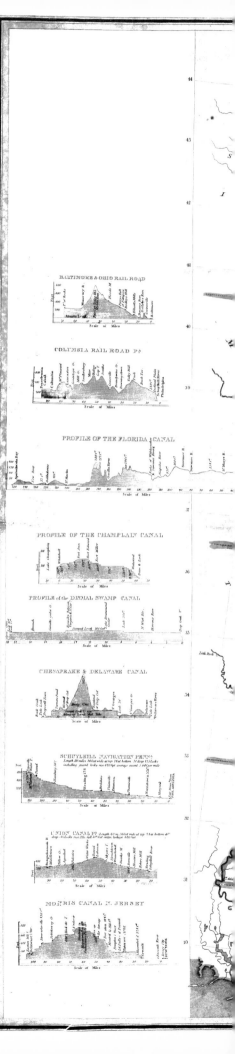

MAP

OF THE

RAILROADS AND CANALS

FINISHED, UNFINISHED AND
IN CONTEMPLATION
IN THE

UNITED STATES

Drawn and Engraved for

D.K. MINOR EDITOR OF THE RAILROAD JOURNAL

BY WILLIAM NORRIS

ERIE CANAL AT THE LITTLE FALLS

PROFILE OF THE OHIO CANAL

PROFILE OF THE PENNSYLVANIA CANAL

PROFILE OF THE CHESAPEAKE & OHIO CANAL

PROFILE OF THE ERIE CANAL, N.Y.

MASSACHUSETTS RAIL ROAD

EXPLANATION

Railroads   Canals

Finished
Making
Chartered
Contemplated
Proposed Ship Canal

Scale of Miles

Pacific Routes

1849

19. Whitney, Asa (1797-1872) [Map without title showing the railroad route to Santa Fe and San Diego; the central route through South Pass and on to San Francisco and "Puget's Sound," and the "Whitney Route" from Prairie du Chien to "Puget's Sound," and connecting railroads east of the Mississippi]. New York: Miller's Lith., 1849. 38 × 46 cm (15 × 18 in).

At top of map: "No. 2." Relief shown by hachures. Includes distance chart showing distances via northern route, southern route, Galveston route, and St. Louis route.

From the author's *A Project for a Railroad to the Pacific.*

Uncolored outline map of North America showing proposed railroad routes within the present limits of the United States.

This copy annotated in black ink to show an alternate route to Lake Erie. It apparently portrays part of the Parkersburg, West Virginia, line and runs north to Sandusky, Ohio.

Asa Whitney, a man with a vision, was a successful New York dry-goods merchant who was active in the 1830s in trade with the Orient. As early as 1830 he recognized the importance of an overland trade route to the Far East. By 1845 he was ready to tell the world about his novel and ingenious idea in his article entitled, "Memorial of Asa Whitney of the City of New York, praying a grant of land, to enable him to construct a railroad from Lake Michigan to the Pacific Ocean"

"Across the Continent." Currier & Ives, 1868.

(28th Congress, 2nd Session, Senate Doc. 69, Serial 451, January 28, 1845):

> Your memorialist begs respectfully to represent to your honorable body, that by rivers, railroads, and canals, all the States east and north of the Potomac connect directly with the waters of the great lakes.
>
> That there is a chain of railroads in projection, and being built, from New York to the southern shore of Lake Michigan, which, crossing all the veins of communication through all the States south and east of the Ohio river, will produce commercial, political, and national results and benefits, which must be seen and felt throughout our vast Confederacy. Your memorialist would further represent to your honorable body, that he has devoted much time and attention to the subject of a railroad from Lake Michigan, through the Rocky Mountains, to the Pacific Ocean.
>
> He recognized that no private citizen could finance such an enterprise alone, but he did not think of forming a corporation. And so he hit upon the idea of land grants, a novel idea when applied to such a grandiose project.

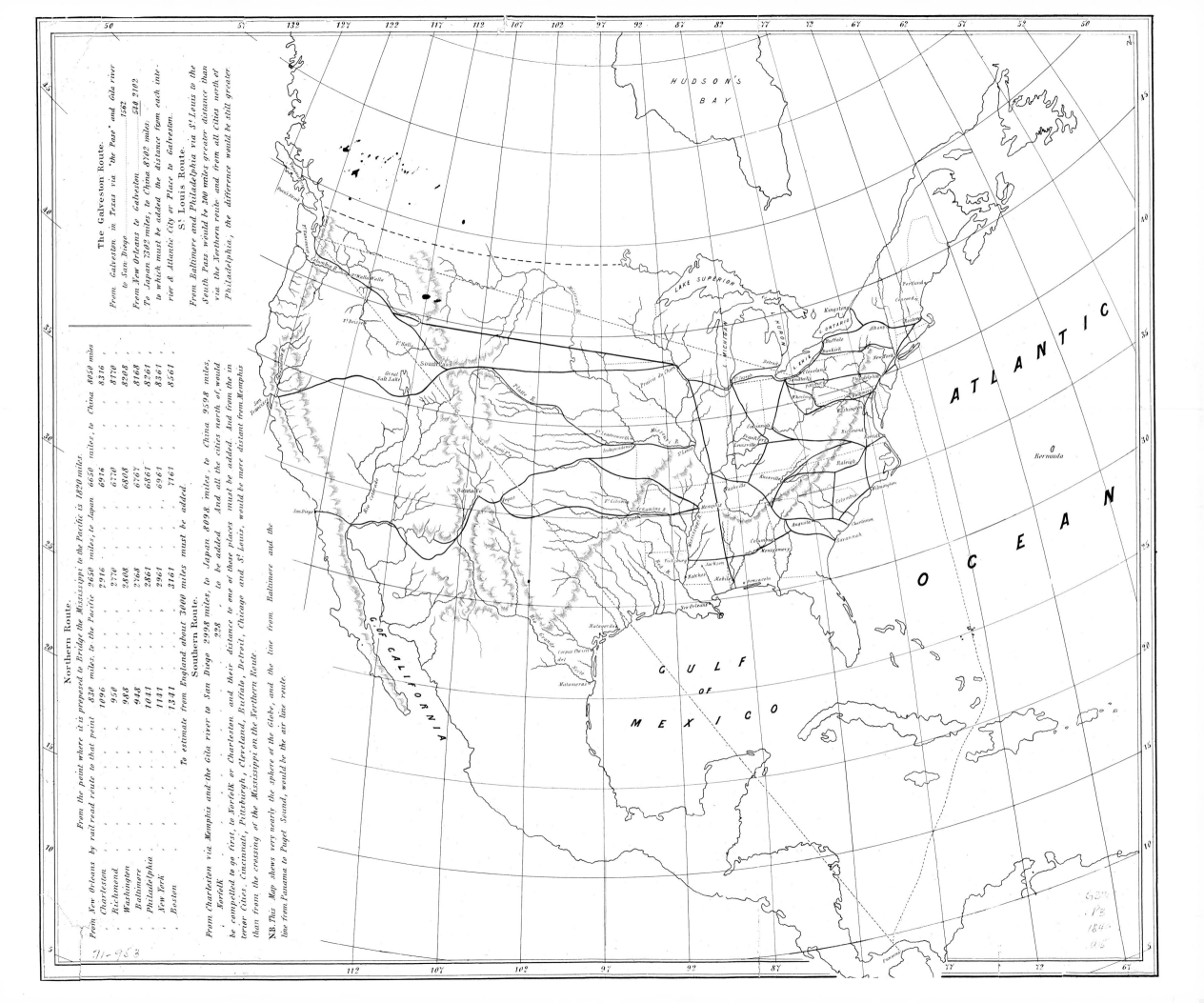

Northern Route.

From the point where it is proposed to Bridge the Mississippi to the Pacific is 1829 miles.

From New Orleans by rail road route to that point 830 miles, to the Pacific 2650 miles, to Japan 6650 miles, to China 8050 miles.

Charleston	1096	2916	6716	8316
Richmond	950	2770	6770	8770
Washington	988	2808	6808	8208
Baltimore	948	2768	6767	8168
Philadelphia	1041	2861	6861	8261
New York	1141	2961	6961	8361
Boston	1341	3161	7161	8561

To estimate from England about 3000 miles must be added.

Southern Route.

From Charleston via Memphis and the Gila river to San Diego 2998 miles, to Japan 8098 miles, to China 9598 miles.

From Norfolk 228 to be added. And all the cities north of Norfolk, to go first, to Norfolk or Charleston, and their distance to one of these places must be added. And from the interior Cities, Cincinnati, Pittsburgh, Cleveland, Buffalo, Detroit, Chicago and St. Louis, would be more distant from Memphis than from the crossing of the Mississippi on the Northern Route.

N.B. This Map shews very nearly the sphere of the Globe, and the line from Baltimore and the line from Panama to Puget Sound, would be the air line route.

The Galveston Route.

From Galveston in Texas via "the Pass" and Gila river to San Diego. 1562

From New Orleans to Galveston. 540 2102

To Japan 7302 miles, to China 8702 miles: to which must be added the distance from each interior & Atlantic City or Place to Galveston.

St. Louis Route.

From Baltimore and Philadelphia via St. Louis to the South Pass would be 300 miles greater distance than via the Northern route: and from all cities north of Philadelphia, the difference would be still greater.

Northern Route

1853

20. Johnson, Edwin F. Map of the proposed Northern Route for a railroad to the Pacific. 1853. Lith of E. C. Kellogg & Co., Hartford, Conn. 52 × 83 cm (21 × 32½ in).

Published in *American Railroad Journal, Steam Navigation, Commerce, Mining, Manufacturers,* Henry V. Poor, Editor. Published weekly, at No. 166 Nassau St., New York; Second Quarto series Vol. IX, No's. 45-52. (To illustrate a series of articles by Edwin F. Johnson on "Railroad to the Pacific-Northern Route. Its General Character, Relative Merits, etc.")

Uncolored outline map of the continental United States showing drainage, state boundaries, major cities, and names of states. Under each state, population figures are given. Western states show topography by hachures and spot heights. Some major rail lines are shown in the northeastern states. Besides the "Northern Route" the map also indicates four more southerly proposed routes west of the Mississippi River. Completed major eastern railroads are shown as solid lines and projected connections are indicated by dashed lines. Some roads and explorers' routes are shown as dotted lines. The 40°F isothermal line in the north is also indicated as a dotted line.

Edwin Ferry Johnson (1803-1872) was one of the foremost railroad engineers of his day and was an early advocate of a transcontinental railroad. As early as 1826 he suggested a line to run from the Hudson River westward. Johnson became the chief engineer of the Northern Pacific Railroad.

James J. Hill's first engine, *Wm. Crooks,* on the Great Northern Railroad, Glacier Park Station, Montana.

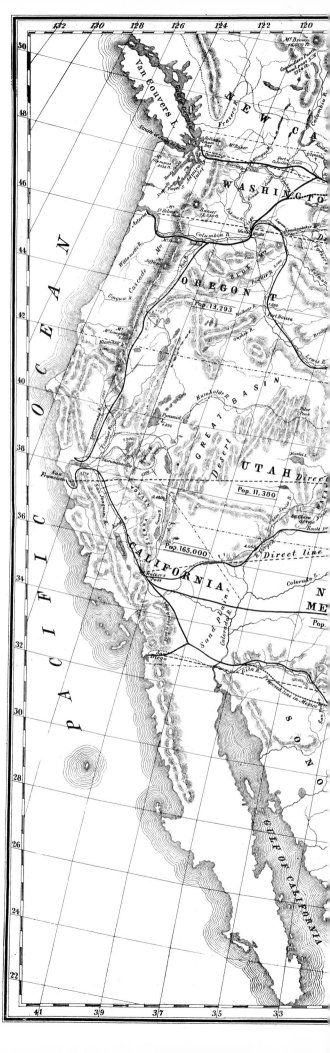

Map
OF THE
Proposed **NORTHERN ROUTE** for a
Railroad to the
PACIFIC,
by Edwin F. Johnson, C.E.
1853.

Scale in Statute Miles.

United States

1854

21. Poor, Henry Varnum. Map of all the railroads in the United States in operation and progress. Published by H. V. Poor, editor of the American Railroad Journal. D. McLellan, Lithographer. New York [1854] 90 × 102 cm (35½ × 40 in).

Colored map covering the eastern United States and including the states and territories adjacent to the west bank of the Mississippi River. Shows drainage and relief by hachures. Identifies railroads in operation, in progress, and projected.

The map was lithographed and hand colored by David McLellan for Henry V. Poor, the longtime editor of the *Manual of Railroads*. David McLellan and his brother James operated a lithographic printing establishment a few doors down from Poor's Publishing House on Spruce Street in New York City until 1860. Thereafter the printing of Poor's maps was continued by the famous map firm of George W. Colton.

Henry Poor and his brother John Alfred Poor were heavily involved in railroading. Henry was a noted journalist and economist and a founding member of the American Geographical Society. His brother, a lawyer and railroad official, is best known for securing the charter for completing, in 1871, the European and North American Railway Company, which connected Maine railroads with those of lower Canada.

United States

1859

22. Lloyd, James T. Lloyd's American railroad map of the United States showing the three proposed roads and the overland mail route to the Pacific, by J. T. Lloyd. N[ew] Y[ork] Engd. by Rae Smith, 1859. 65 × 92 cm (24 × 36 in).
Note: "Drawn & engraved at Rae Smith's . . . N.Y. from materials furnished to the 36th Congress March 1859 by G. K. Warren Lt. U.S. Top. Eng. for the passage of the Pacific Railroad bill."

Outline map of the continental United States showing drainage, relief by hachures, state boundaries, major cities, forts, railroads and proposed railroads.

Portraits of twenty-eight railroad presidents are reproduced in the border: John Robin McDaniel, Jacob Strader, J. D. De Frees, John Caldwell, C. A. Brown, J. Edgar Thomson, Thos. D. Walker, E. Hobbs, R. N. Rice, S. S. L'Hommedieu, Wm. Case, George Palmer, P. A. Hall, Henry C. Lord, A. G. Jaudon, Edwin Robinson, E. H. Gill, W. T. Joynes, J. B. Warring, S. L. Fremont, John L. Helm, John Ross, A. S. Crothers, E. Gest, Erastus Corning, L. M. Hubby, W. H. Clements, John T. Levis.

Of interest to historians of cartography is the railroad executive J. Edgar Thomson, whose portrait appears in the center at the top of this map. He was a financier and pioneer in railroad engineering who became president of the Pennsylvania Railroad in 1852. He served with the Georgia Railroad from 1832 until 1847 and was responsible for drawing the first commercial map of the Georgia Railroad in 1839. He was the son of John Thomson, who is credited with drawing the first American railroad survey in 1809.

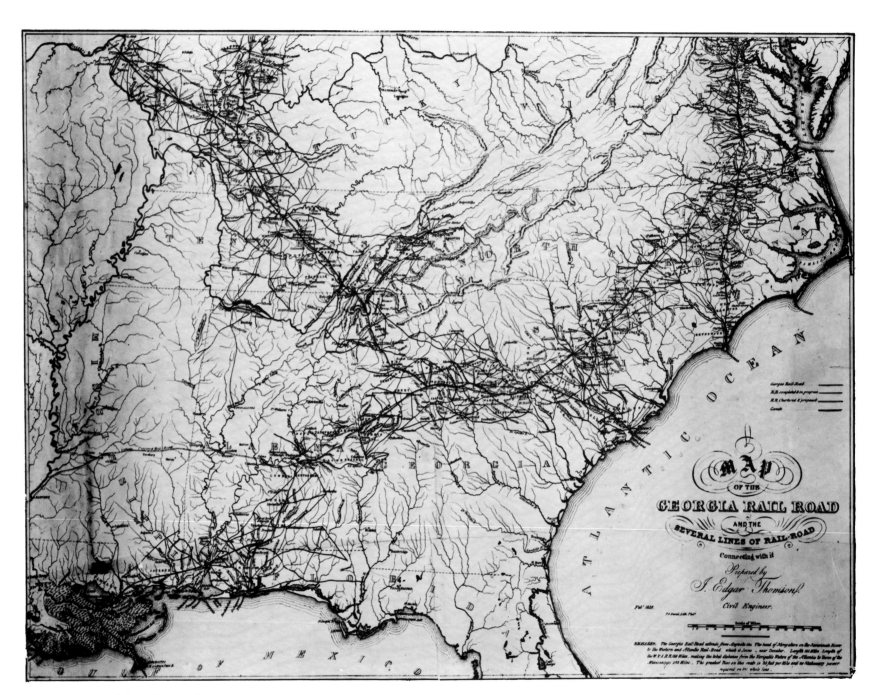

J. Edgar Thomson's commercial map of the Georgia Railroad, 1839.

United States

1875

23. Watson, Gaylord. Centennial American Republic and railroad map of the United States and of the Dominion of Canada. Compiled from latest official sources. [New York, 1875] 98 × 129 cm (37 × 51 in).

Shows drainage, cities and towns, and the railroad network with names of lines. Includes distance chart from New York City to important cities in the United States and the World. Includes population statistics for U.S. cities.

This hand-colored map was published specifically for the celebration of the centennial of the United States. It is decorated with a portrait of George Washington and pictures of Independence Hall, Philadelphia, the U.S. Capitol, and the main building of the centennial exhibition in Philadelphia. The title cartouche represents an industrial and pastoral scene in the East, separated by railroad and telegraph lines from a scene in the Wild West.

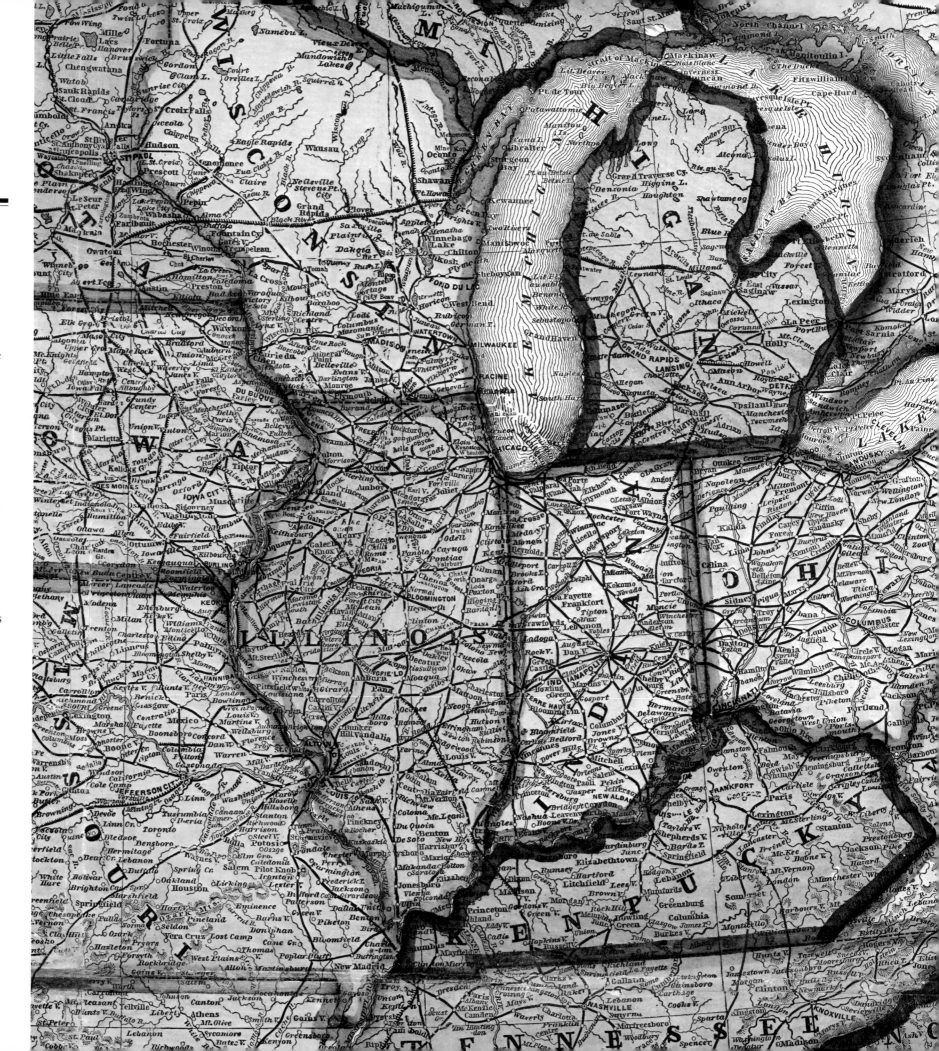

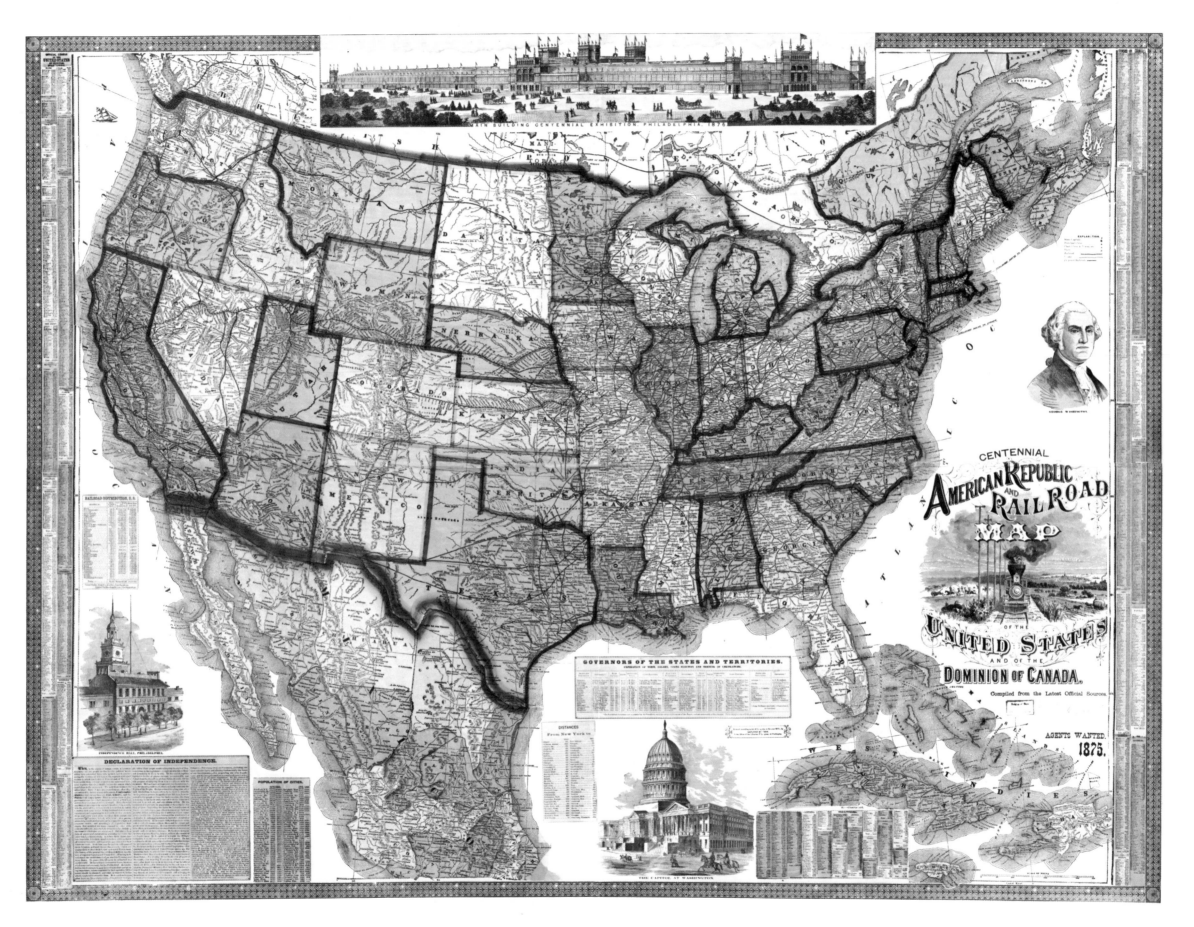

CENTENNIAL
American Republic
AND
RAIL ROAD
MAP
OF THE
UNITED STATES
AND OF THE
DOMINION OF CANADA.

Compiled from the Latest Official Sources.

AGENTS WANTED.
1875.

United States

1876

24. Neuman, Louis E. Watson's new illustrated county rail road and distance map of the United States and Dominion of Canada. Compiled from the latest government surveys. 1876. Published by Gaylord Watson, New York, and R. A. Tenney, Chicago, 1876. 87 × 143 cm (37½ × 56 in).

Portion of an uncolored map of the United States, eastern Canada, northern Mexico, and Cuba. The map shows the railroad network in great detail, with mileage between stations. Includes counties, cities and towns, forts, trading posts, railroad stations, and junction points. Names major railroad lines, shows relief by hachures, names important land features, and includes river drainage systems. Indicates progress of railroad construction west of the Mississippi River.

A beautiful scenic "Panorama of the Country Between New York and San Francisco" appears across the top center of the map, traversed by trains from east and west. Vignettes of the U.S. Capitol, Mount Vernon, the White Mountains, Yosemite Valley, and sequoia trees decorate the map. Includes a list of governors, population statistics by cities and states, and a table of the railroad distribution in the United States by miles of road, cost, and earnings.

This is an important map for the study of North American railroads. Unfortunately the map was printed by a wax engraving process which has rendered some names illegible.

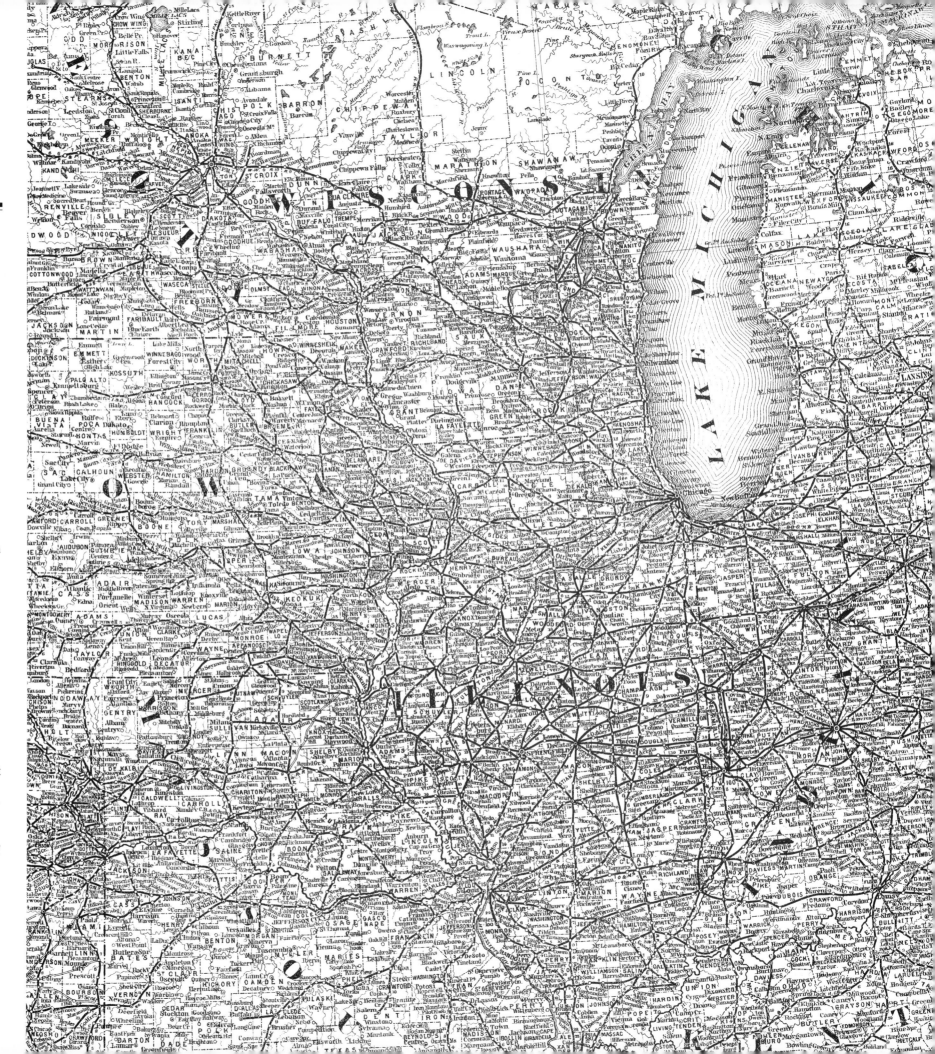

Pacific Railroads

1883

25. U.S. Bureau of Statistics (Dept. of Commerce and Labor) Map exhibiting the several Pacific railroads prepared for the report on the internal commerce of the United States by the Bureau of Statistics. [Chicago] Rand, McNally & Co., 1883. 68 × 107 cm (26½ × 42½ in).

A detailed map of the continental United States, southern Canada, and northern Mexico. Indicates drainage, relief by hachures, international boundaries, cities, towns, railroad stations, forts, roads, the railroad network, and the Pacific railroads colored by hand to distinguish the lines. The Canadian Pacific is colored orange, the Northern Pacific is green, the Union Pacific and connecting lines are red, and the Central and Southern Pacific and connecting lines are blue. Mexican connections are colored yellow. The remaining railroad network appears in solid black lines with names of railroads, or their initials, printed along the lines.

"Across the Continent on the Pacific Railroad. — Dining Saloon of the Hotel Express Train." Wood engraving in *Frank Leslie's Illustrated Newspaper,* January 15, 1870.

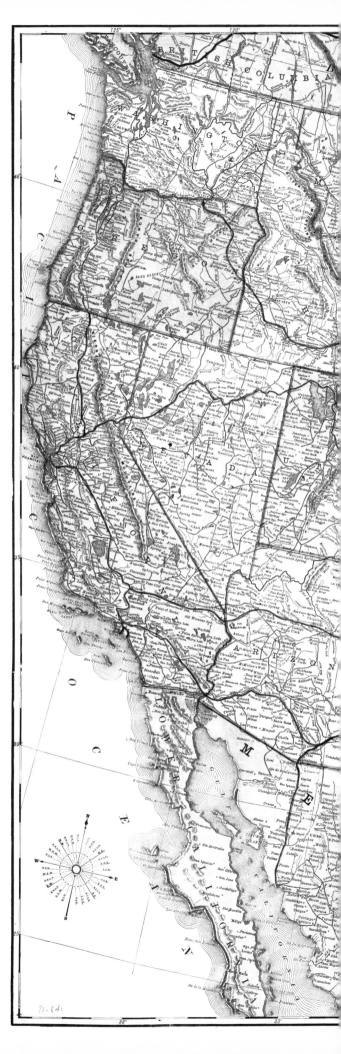

MAP

EXHIBITING THE SEVERAL

PACIFIC RAILROADS

PREPARED FOR THE REPORT

ON THE

INTERNAL COMMERCE OF THE UNITED STATES

BY THE

CHIEF OF THE BUREAU OF STATISTICS.

RAND, McNALLY & CO.

1883

EXPLANATION:

CANADIAN PACIFIC ....

NORTHERN PACIFIC ....

UNION PACIFIC AND CONNECTING LINES ....

CENTRAL AND SOUTHERN PACIFIC AND CONNECTING LINES .....

Suspension bridge, Niagara Falls,
built by John A. Roebling, 1855.

Eastern States

1856

26. Ensign, Bridgman & Fanning. Ensign, Bridgman
& Fanning's rail road map of the Eastern States. New
York, 1856. 44 × 65 cm (17 × 24½ in).

A handsomely designed and executed
lithographed and hand-colored map of New
England, part of eastern Canada, New York,
Pennsylvania, New Jersey, Delaware, most of
Maryland, and part of Virginia. Shows
drainage, some relief by hachures, place
names, and state boundaries.

A view of the Canadian side of Niagara
Falls appears in the upper left of the map. A
"Plan of the New England States on an
Enlarged Scale" is inset on the right side of
the main map. The completed railroad network represents actual railroad track with
linear cross-hatched lines, and railroads under
construction are shown as solid thin lines.
Many names of railroads appear on the lines
and others are keyed by number to a list of
lines.

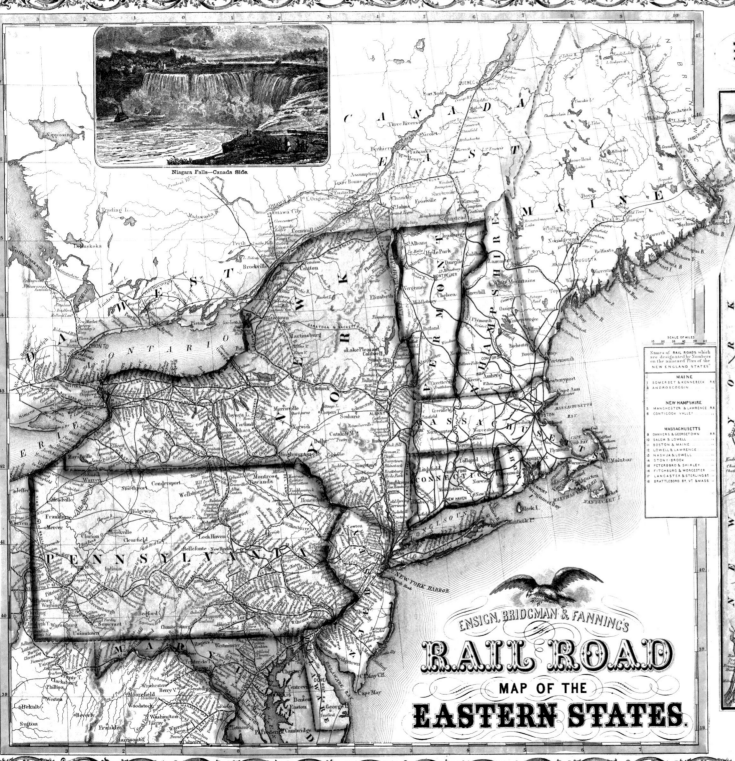

Niagara Falls—Canada Side.

ENSIGN, BRIDGMAN & FANNING'S

RAIL ROAD
MAP OF THE
EASTERN STATES.

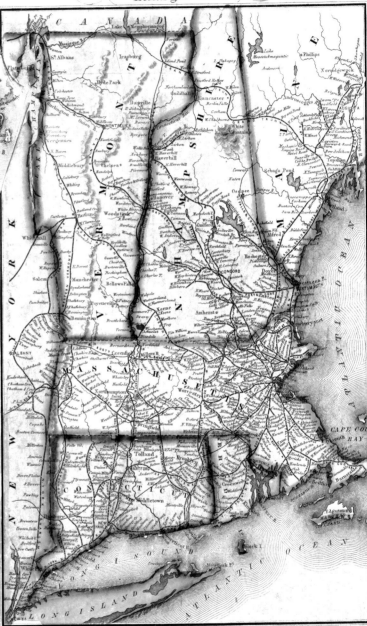

Plan of the
NEW ENGLAND STATES,
on an
Enlarged Scale.

SCALE OF MILES

Names of RAIL ROADS which
are designated by Numbers
on the annexed Plan of the
NEW ENGLAND STATES.

MAINE
1 SOMERSET & KENNEBECK   R.R.
2 ANDROSCOGGIN

NEW HAMPSHIRE
3 MANCHESTER & LAWRENCE RR.
4 CONTICOOK VALLEY

MASSACHUSETTS
5 DANVERS & GEORGETOWN   R.R.
6 SALEM & LOWELL
7 BOSTON & MAINE
8 LOWELL & LAWRENCE
9 NASHUA & LOWELL
10 STONY-BROOK
11 PETERSBRO & SHIRLEY
12 FITCHBURG & WORCESTER
13 LANCASTER & STERLINGRD.
14 BRATTLEBORO &c. VT. & MASS.

Published by
ENSIGN, BRIDGMAN & FANNING
156 William St. New York 1856.

Railroads Tributary to Philadelphia

1851

27. Ellet, Charles. Jr. Map of the western railroads tributary to Philadelphia, with their rival lines. Prepared under the direction of Charles Ellet Jr., Civil Engineer. Philadelphia by W[ellington] Williams, Map Engraver, 1851. 40 × 80 cm (16½ × 31 in).

Lightly hand-colored map covering the area from Jefferson City, Missouri, to New Haven, Connecticut, and from Oswego, New York, to Blakely, North Carolina. Railroads tributary to Philadelphia are indicated by solid black lines; those tributary to New York and Baltimore are indicated by dashed lines. Distances in miles between major centers are given in the top left of the map. Ellet notes the following on the map:

> The Railroads upon this Map are either completed or in rapid progress of construction and little doubt is entertained that within the next 3 years all those important lines of communication will be opened for trade and travel. As they are now arranged they show the natural course of the vast trade of the Great West and the diversion of it towards the large competing cities of the seaboard.

A typical mid-nineteenth century, commercially produced regional map by the distinguished civil engineer and Civil War naval officer, who designed and built suspension bridges and advocated flood control of western rivers. Charles Ellet, Jr., built the Virginia Central Railroad across the Blue Ridge mountains in 1854. In the book *Coast and Harbour Defences* (1855), he proposed the construction and use of "ram-boats," with massively built prows carrying an iron ram that revived the tactics of ancient galleys. In 1862 he led a fleet of nine ram-boats down the Mississippi and won the surrender of Memphis. During this action he was mortally wounded.

Railroad bridge over Wissahickon, near Manayunk, Pennsylvania, 1835. From a lithograph by Charles Fenderich.

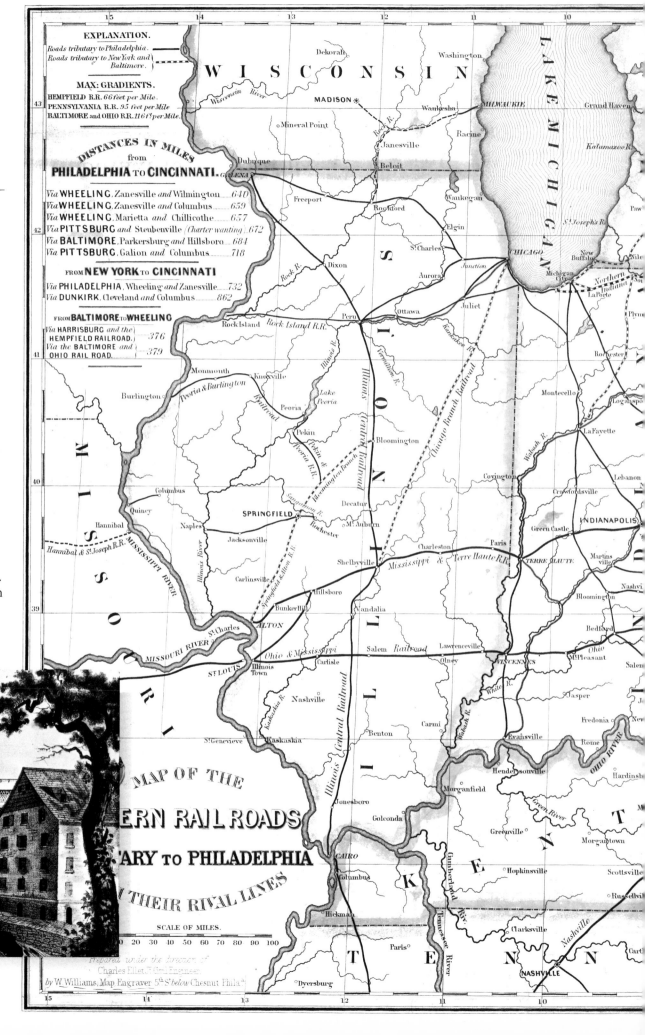

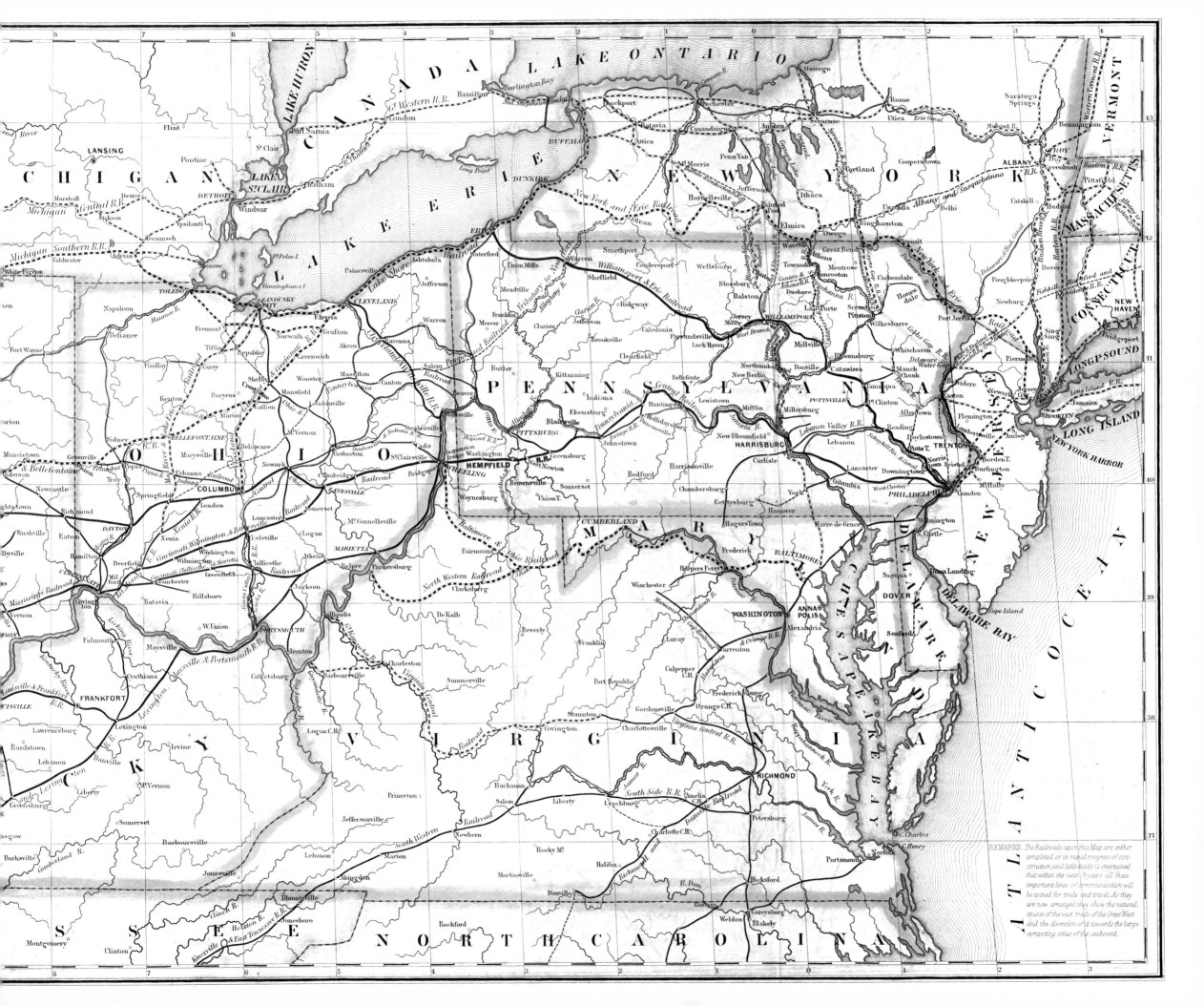

Eastern United States

1860

28. Colton, George Woolworth. New York, New Jersey, Pennsylvania, Delaware, Maryland, Ohio and Canada, with parts of adjoining states. New York, 1860. 68 × 90 cm (26½ × 35 in).

At head of title: "G. Woolworth Colton's series of railroad maps, No. 3."

"Printed for the History of the Railroads of the United States by H. V. Poor."

Shows state, county, and township boundaries, outlined in color, and indicates mileage between stations. Railroad names are indicated along the lines. Completed lines are in solid black and those under construction appear as black dashed lines. State capitals, principal cities, county towns, stations, and railroad junction points and terminals are indicated. The vicinities of terminal points, New York and Philadelphia, appear in insets on an enlarged scale.

A full-size facsimile edition of this map is appended to the reprint edition of Henry V. Poor's *History of Railroads* . . . (New York: Augustus M. Keller, 1970).

The original map is one of the first of many maps drawn and published by G. W. Colton for Henry V. Poor. Colton took over publication of this series of maps from David and James McLellan.

Depot at Harrisburg, Pennsylvania.

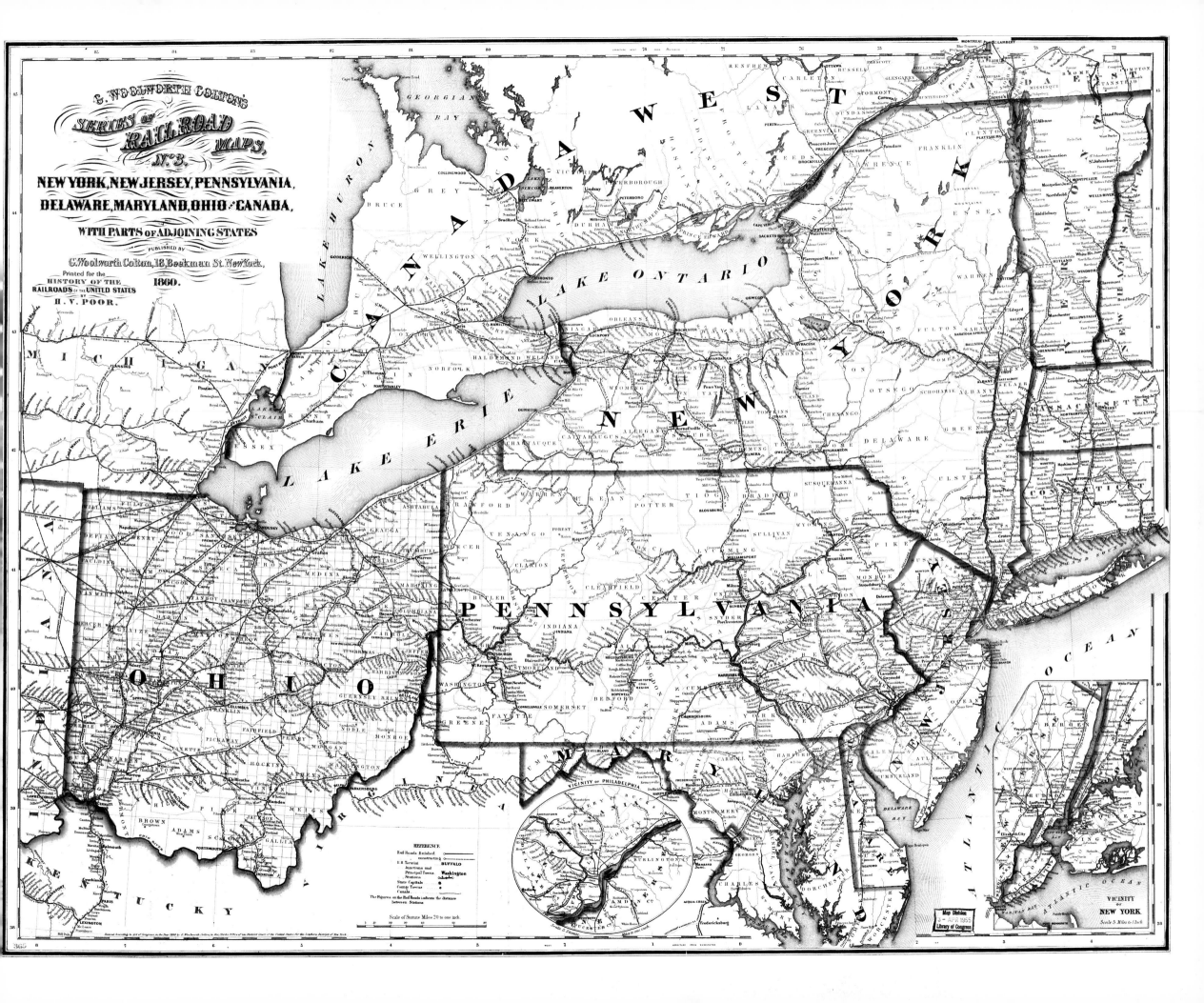

G. WOOLWORTH COLTON'S
SERIES OF
RAILROAD MAPS,
No. 3.
NEW YORK, NEW JERSEY, PENNSYLVANIA,
DELAWARE, MARYLAND, OHIO & CANADA,
WITH PARTS OF ADJOINING STATES
PUBLISHED BY
G. Woolworth Colton, 18 Beekman St. New York.
Printed for the
HISTORY OF THE
RAILROADS OF THE UNITED STATES
BY H. V. POOR.
1860.

Border and Southern States

1861

The map shows a detailed drainage network and names rivers and creeks, state capitals, county seats, village post offices, and railroad stations, and indicates relief by hachures. Canals are shown in Pennsylvania, Maryland, Virginia, and North Carolina. The detailed railroad network includes the names of railroad lines. An inset map of southern Florida, at a reduced scale, appears at the lower right of the map. Color is used to distinguish states.

This map was published on the eve of the Civil War, and later editions were widely distributed to show the progress of the war.

29. Hall, Edward S. Lloyd's new military map of the border & southern states. Drawn by Edward S. Hall. New York, H. H. Lloyd & Co. 1861. 78 × 106 cm (31 × 41 in).

At top of map: "H. H. Lloyd & Co's. new military map of the southern and border states."

Seventeen-thousand-pound mortar, the *Dictator*, Petersburg, Virginia, July 25, 1864.

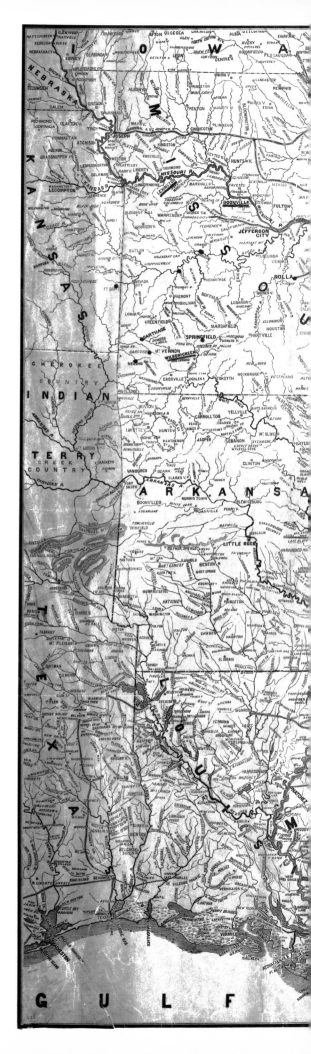

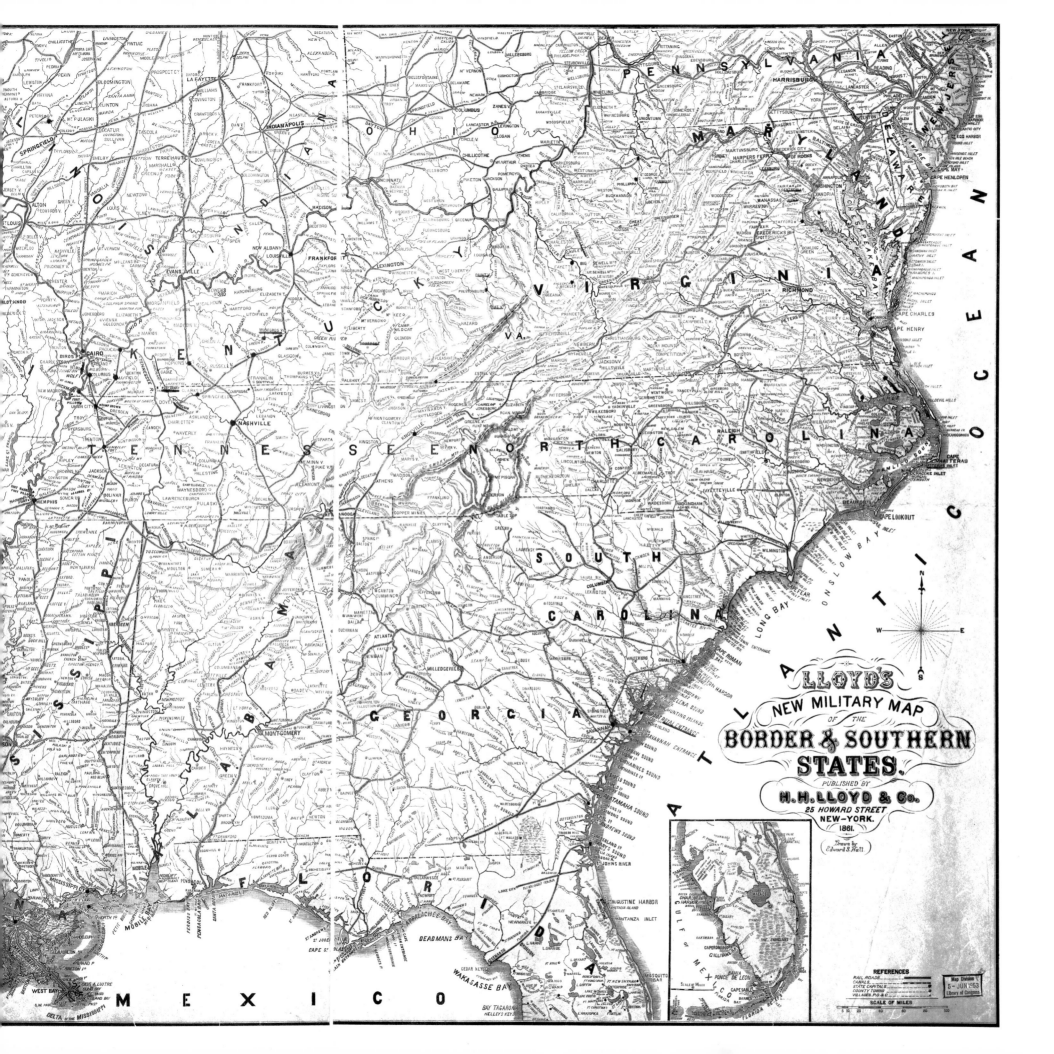

LLOYD'S
NEW MILITARY MAP
OF THE
BORDER & SOUTHERN
STATES.
PUBLISHED BY
H. H. LLOYD & Co.
25 HOWARD STREET
NEW-YORK.
1861.

Drawn by
Edward S. Hall

REFERENCES
RAIL ROADS
CANALS
STATE CAPITALS
COUNTY TOWNS
VILLAGES, P.O. &C.

SCALE OF MILES

Military Railroads

1866

30. Bien, Julius. Map of United States military rail roads, showing the rail roads operated during the war from 1862-1866, as military lines, under the direction of Bvt. Brig. Gen. D. C. McCallum, Director and General Manager. Lith of J. Bien, N.Y. 1866. 64 × 97 cm (25 × 38½ in).

General colored map of the U.S. Southeast showing the major drainage network, relief by hachures, cities, towns, forts, railroad stations, and junction points. The railroad network is printed in black, and each state is distinguished by color. Railroads under construction are shown by parallel dashed lines, and surveyed routes are in single dashed lines. The military railroads are hand colored to distinguish the three different gauges. The 5-foot gauge is in blue, the standard gauge is in red, and the 5.5-foot gauge is in yellow. The yellow line appears only on the Memphis and Little Rock Railroad, from Little Rock to the White River.

This map was made under the authority of Daniel Craig McCallum, an architect, builder, and railroad engineer who was appointed on February 11, 1862, to take charge of all the military railroads in the country.

Julius Bien (1826-1909), born and educated in Hesse-Cassel, Germany, came to America to escape retribution for his involvement in the revolutionary movement of 1848.

In 1849 he started his business in New York with one hand lithographic press. By the time of his death in 1909, his mapmaking firm was the leading establishment of its kind in the country, employing two hundred persons and operating fifteen steam lithographic presses and a number of copper plate presses.

He was instrumental in printing, designing, and publishing thousands of maps and a number of atlases for the U.S. government. He printed Edward Freyhold and G. K. Warren's famous map, which became the standard map of the West for twenty-five years. His activities included the equipping of a field map printing unit used in the Civil War by Gen. William T. Sherman in his march to the sea. He was also instrumental in establishing scientific standards for American cartography.

Herman Haupt, chief of U.S. military rail transportation, directs repair work on the Orange and Alexandria Railroad, Devereux Station, 1863. The engine in the photograph was named for him.

Major General D. C. McCallum.

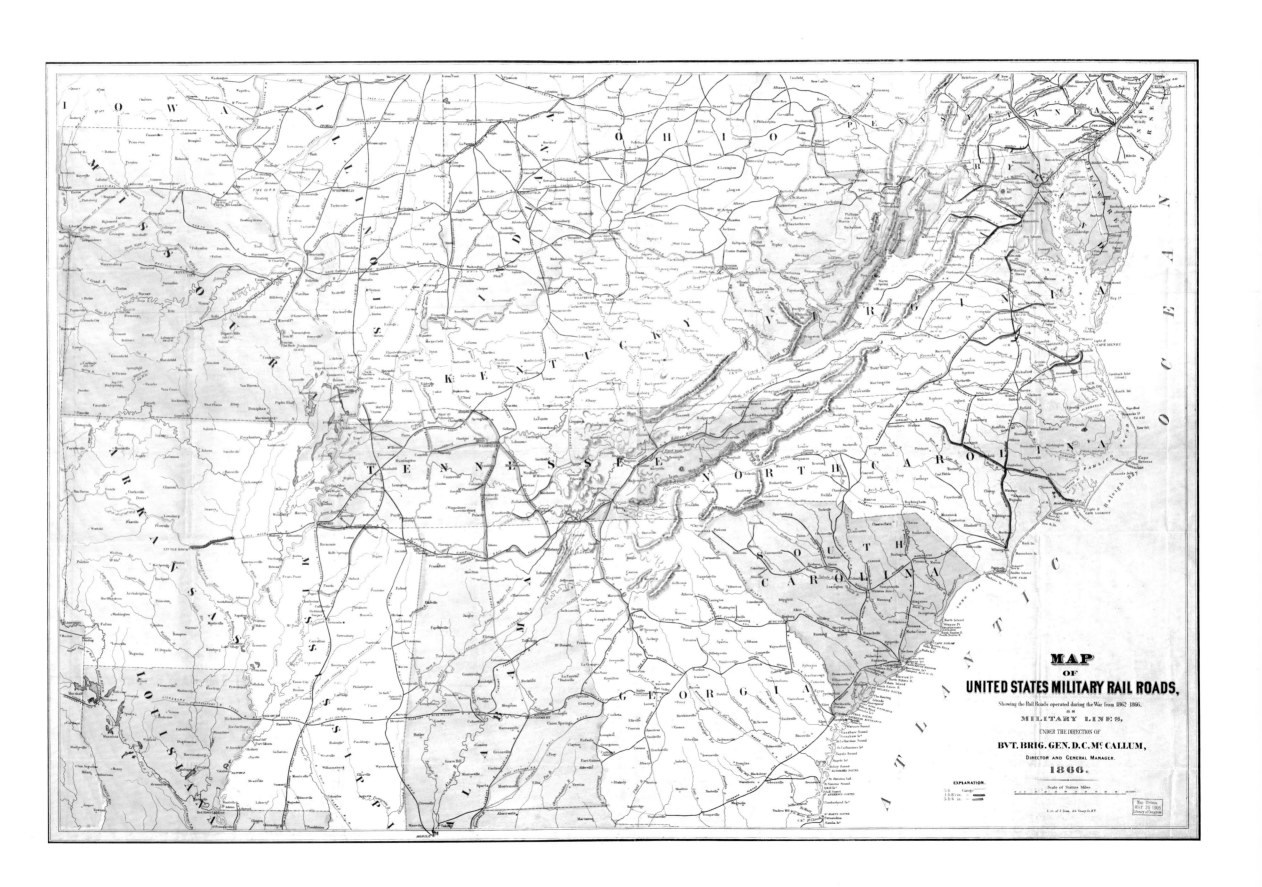

MAP
OF
UNITED STATES MILITARY RAIL ROADS,

Showing the Rail Roads operated during the War from 1862-1866,

AS

MILITARY LINES,

UNDER THE DIRECTION OF

BVT. BRIG. GEN. D. C. McCALLUM,

DIRECTOR AND GENERAL MANAGER.

1866.

EXPLANATION.

Scale of Statute Miles

Routes to Pike's Peak

1859

31. McGowan, D. Map of the United States west of the Mississippi showing the routes to Pike's Peak, overland mail route to California and Pacific rail road surveys. To which are added the new state & territorial boundaries, the principal mail & rail road routes with all the arrangements & corrections made by Congress up to the date of its issue. Compiled and drawn from U.S. land & coast surveys and other reliable sources, by D. McGowan and Geo. H. Hildt. St. Louis, Leopold Gast & Bro., 1859. 58 × 72 cm (23 × 28 in).

Detailed general map delicately colored by hand and framed in decorative borders. It shows drainage and names rivers, indicates relief by hachures and names physical features, shows indian tribes, forts, cities and towns, routes to Pike's Peak and its gold regions, mail routes, mail stations, divisions of the overland mail route, state boundaries and the proposed state of Jefferson. Pacific railroad surveys and the completed railroads west of the Mississippi River, in the state of Missouri, are also indicated. An excellent example of a commercially produced promotional map to encourage immigration.

An interesting seven-page booklet entitled *Map exhibiting the routes to Pike's Peak,* not originally intended to be published with the map, was provided as a guide to the map and in helping the prospective traveler obtain proper provisions for the journey.

First page of D. McGowan's guide to the gold fields entitled *Map exhibiting the routes to Pike's Peak,* published to accompany the 1859 "Map of the United States West of the Mississippi . . . ."

MAP
OF THE
United States West of the Mississippi
Showing the Routes to
PIKE'S PEAK
Overland Mail Route to California
and
PACIFIC RAIL ROAD SURVEYS.
To which are added the new State & Territorial Boundaries, the principal Mail & Rail Road Routes
with all the arrangements & corrections made by Congress up to the date of its issue.
Compiled and drawn from U.S. Land & Coast Surveys
and other reliable Sources,
by
D. McGowan C.E. & U.S.
and
Geo. H. Hildt C.E.

Leopold Gast & Bro. lith. St. Louis, Mo.

Scale English Statute Miles.

Division of Maps
Library of Congress

Explanation:
Route to Pikes Peak
Mail Routes
Rail Road Surveys
Mail Stations
Divisions of Overland Mail Route
State Boundaries
Proposed Territorial Boundaries
Forts

Railway Mail Service

1898

32. Galbraith, Frank H. Galbraith's railway mail service maps. Iowa. Chicago, McEwen Map Co., 1897. c1898. 8 sheets, each 70 × 54 cm (21 × 28 in).

Northeastern portion of the map of Iowa, one of eight large-scale hand-colored manuscript maps of the midwestern states showing routes and post offices of the Railway Mail Service. Designed by Chicago railway mail clerk Frank H. Galbraith to help employees of the Railway Mail Service quickly locate counties and post offices. The maps were rented for practicing or prospective workers who numbered over six thousand and traveled over a million miles a year on the rails sorting mail. A printed title cartouche accompanied by a list of counties for each of the states by McEwen Map Company of Chicago is pasted on the maps.

Pictorial representation in caricature, which suggest post office names, illustrate the maps. Dogwood Post Office, for example, is identified by a picture of a dog, Elizabeth by a queen, Starlight by a star, and Worth by a dollar sign.

"The Fast Mail." Lithograph by J. A. Burch, 1875.

GALBRAITH'S
Railway Mail Service

MAPS.
—IOWA—

Copyright, 1897, by Frank H. Galbraith, Chicago, Ill.

Published by McEwen Map Co.,
1473 W. MONROE STREET.
CHICAGO,   -   ILLINOIS.

IOWA.

Frisco Lines

1912

33. Parker Engraving Company. Frisco Lines. St. Louis, 1912. 72 × 58 cm (28 × 23 in).

An example of a clear and legible early twentieth-century railroad map covering the midwestern and southwestern states from Chicago, Illinois, to Brownsville, Texas, indicating major rivers, cities and towns, railroad stations, and the railroad network. Lines of the St. Louis & San Francisco Railroad and auxiliary lines are shown in red, those of the Chicago & Eastern Illinois Railroad are in blue, the Gulf Coast lines are in green, and the Houston & Texas Central Railroad is in brown. Connecting lines, with their initials, are in light black lines. Dashed lines represent railroads under construction.

"The Cool Route from Texas to the Northern Summer Resorts." Lithograph for the Frisco Line, The Strobridge Lith. Co., 1898.

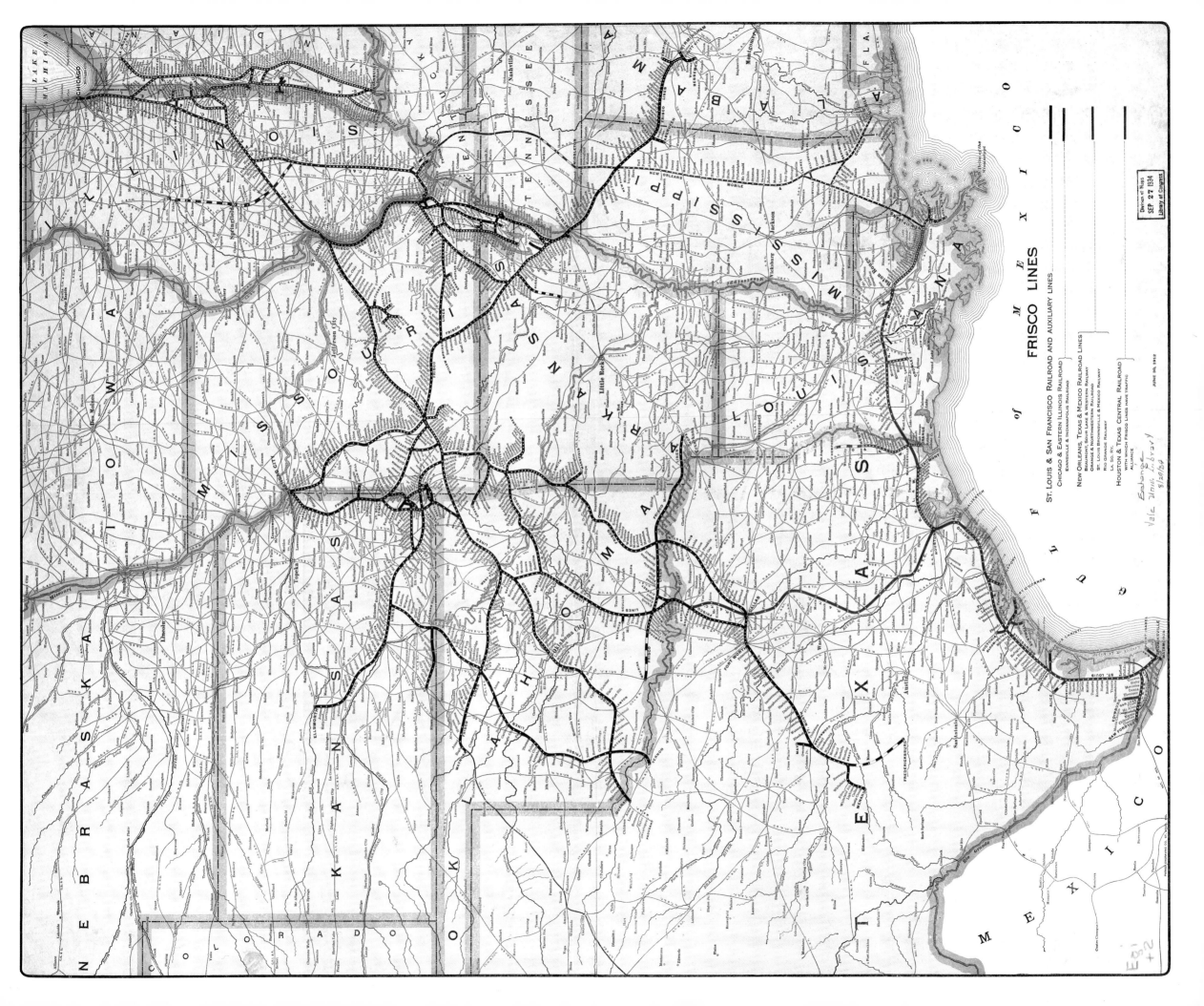

FRISCO LINES

ST. LOUIS & SAN FRANCISCO RAILROAD AND AUXILIARY LINES
CHICAGO & EASTERN ILLINOIS RAILROAD
EVANSVILLE & INDIANAPOLIS RAILROAD

NEW ORLEANS, TEXAS & MEXICO RAILROAD LINES
BEAUMONT, SOUR LAKE & WESTERN RAILWAY
ORANGE & NORTHWESTERN RAILROAD
ST. LOUIS, BROWNSVILLE & MEXICO RAILWAY
RIO GRANDE RAILWAY
LA. SO. RY.

HOUSTON & TEXAS CENTRAL RAILROAD
WITH WHICH FRISCO LINES HAVE TRAFFIC
ALLIANCE

Santa Fe Route

1888

34. Rand McNally and Company. The Santa Fe Route and connections 1888. Chicago, 1888. 39 × 63 cm (16 × 25 in).

Typical colored railroad map of the southwestern United States and northern Mexico showing relief by brown hachures, drainage pattern in blue, cities and towns, railroad stations, Indian reservations, state boundaries, and a schematically presented railroad network emphasizing the Santa Fe system in red. Displays elevation profiles from Kansas City to points in California and to Mexico City. Shows connections to the Mallory Steamship Line leaving Galveston, Texas, for New York City.

Passengers boarding the California Limited, Sante Fe Railroad. Photograph by George R. Laurence Co., May 15, 1905.

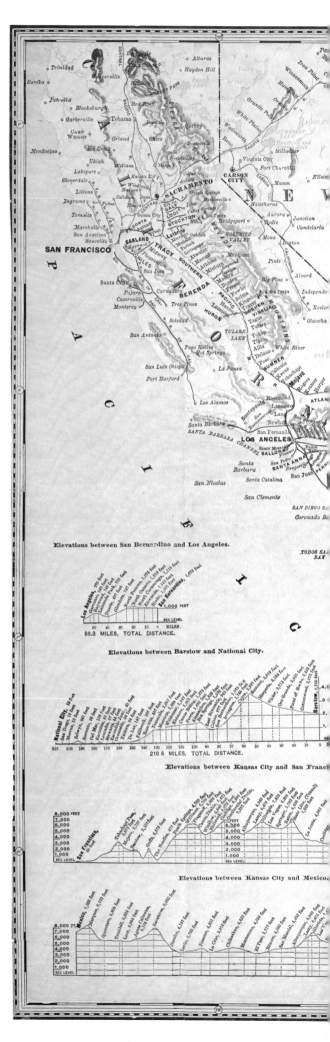

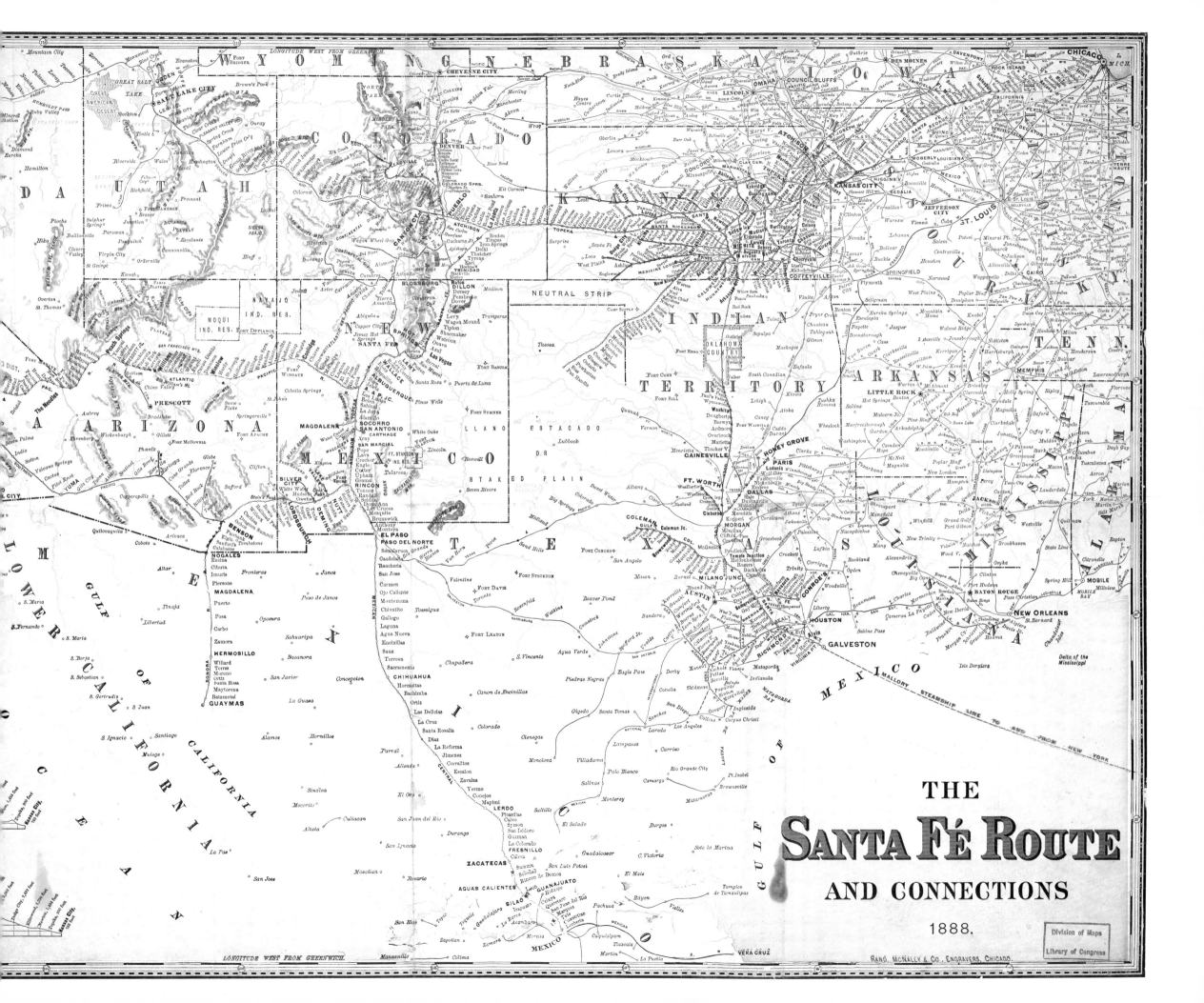

THE
SANTA FÉ ROUTE
AND CONNECTIONS
1888.

RAND, MCNALLY & CO., ENGRAVERS, CHICAGO.

LONGITUDE WEST FROM GREENWICH.

Central California

1860

35.   Elliott, S. G. Map of central California showing the different rail road lines completed & projected. 1860. Published by G. W. Welch, Nevada. Lith. of Britton & Co., San Francisco. 72 × 59 cm (29 × 23 in).

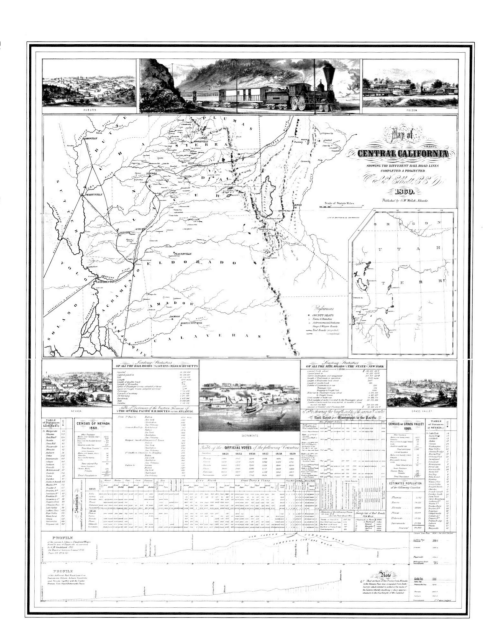

An uncolored locally lithographed promotional map of the Sacramento Valley in central California, west of Lake Bicler (Tahoe), showing drainage, relief by hachures, county seats, towns, ranches, stage and wagon roads, and completed and projected railroads.

This map contains pictures of Auburn, Folsom, Nevada City in California, Sacramento, Grass Valley, and a railroad train of the period, together with statistical data on railroads, agriculture, distances, population, and voting strength of counties. Profiles of several routes over the Sierra Nevada are shown at the lower left.

The aim of the map was to promote the desire of Nevada City to obtain the projected transcontinental railroad line, which is shown on this map with the title "Central Pacific RR," leading from Auburn to Illinoistown, thence by way of Grass Valley to Nevada City and up to South Yuba past "Eureka South" and over the crest of the Sierra Nevada near Henness Pass to the "Little Truckee Lakes." The route above Illinoistown (the present Colfax), which was actually followed by the Central Pacific after Theodore D. Judah's surveys, is not shown, though a road from Forest Hill over Truckee Pass past "Starvation Camp" on "Big Truckee" (Donner) Lake appears.

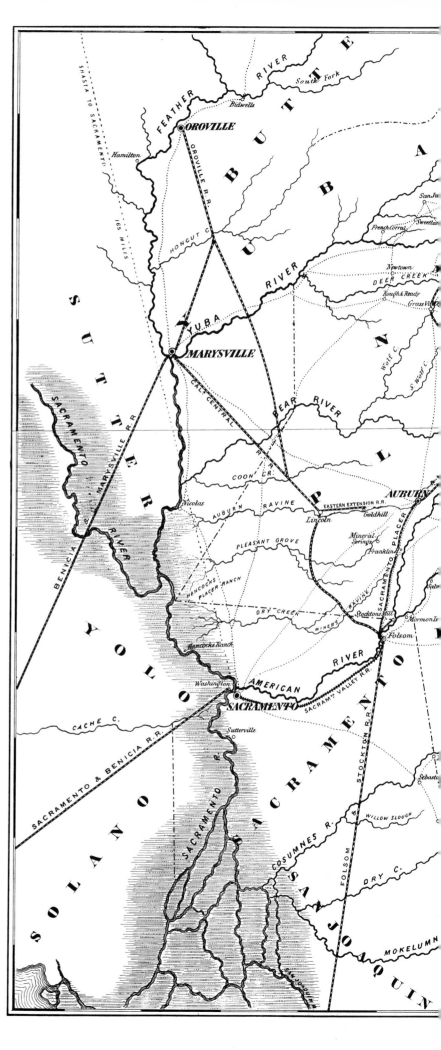

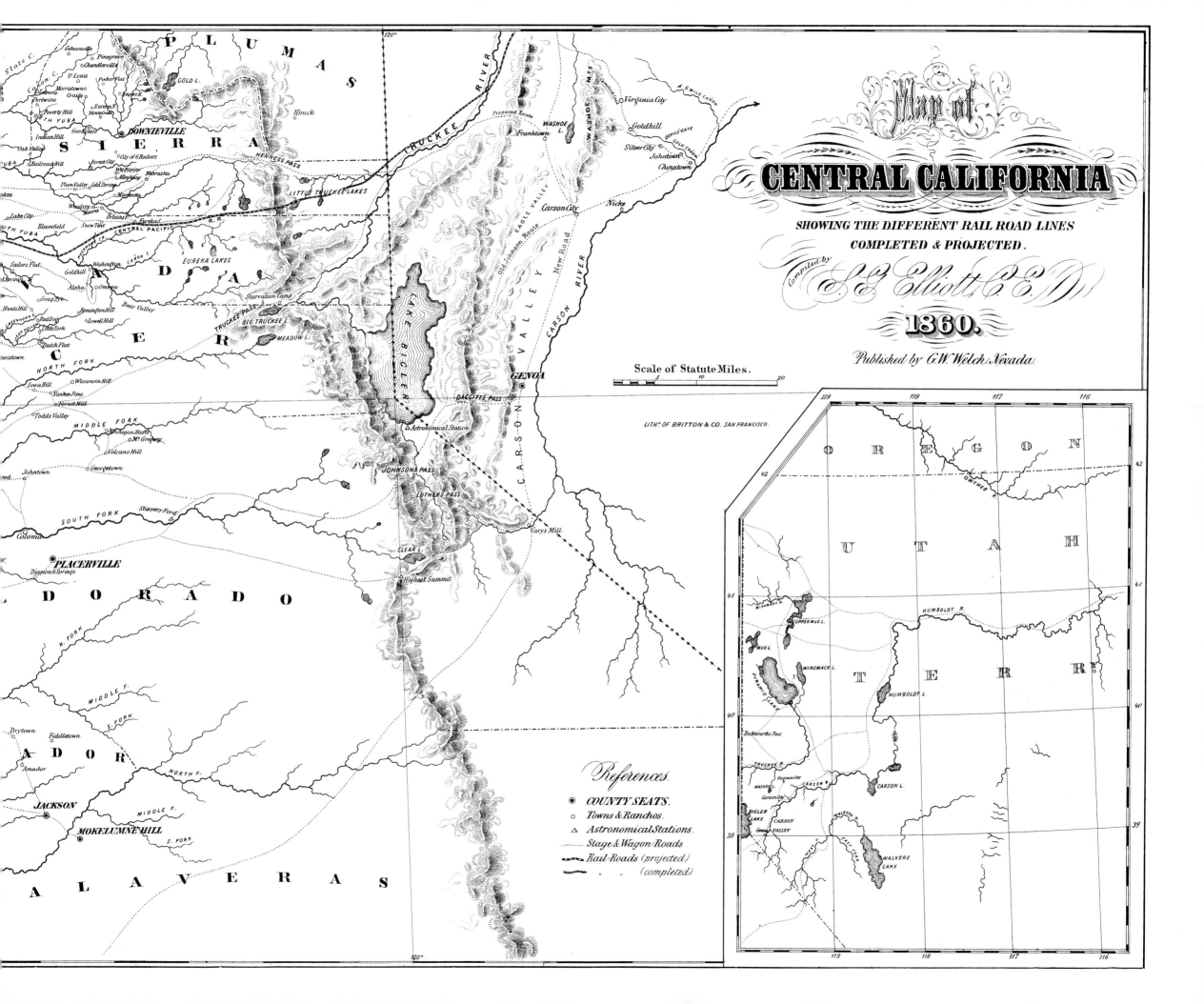

Map of
CENTRAL CALIFORNIA

SHOWING THE DIFFERENT RAIL ROAD LINES
COMPLETED & PROJECTED.

Compiled by
S. G. Elliott, C. E.

1860.

Published by G.W. Welch, Nevada.

Scale of Statute Miles.

LITH.º OF BRITTON & CO. SAN FRANCISCO.

References.
⊙ COUNTY SEATS.
○ Towns & Ranchos.
△ Astronomical Stations.
········· Stage & Wagon Roads
▰▰▰ Rail-Roads (projected)
✛✛✛ " " (completed)

Flagler System

1914

36. Matthews-Northrup Works. Map of the peninsula of Florida and adjacent islands. Florida East Coast Railway. Flagler System. Buffalo, 1914. 101 × 40 cm (40 × 16 in).

Detailed general map of Florida showing water areas in blue and county boundaries in yellow, and overprinted in red to show the Flagler railroad system. Other railroads are indicated in black solid lines, and canals are depicted in black and white lines. Unfinished railroads and regular steamship lines appear as dashed lines. Portrays cities and towns, forts, township and range lines, and the path of the Gulf Stream. Famous resort hotels, built by Henry M. Flagler, points of interest, and lighthouses are also shown in red. Identifies the Deep Lake Company's electric railroad in the southern Everglades. Includes inset "Map of Florida and the West Indies" and a "Map of Cuba," which is folded under and not shown in this illustration.

Henry Morrison Flagler (1830-1913) was an associate of John D. Rockefeller in the Standard Oil Company and became one of the first of a long line of retired millionaires who came to Florida to play and remained to work. At the age of fifty-three he visited St. Augustine, where he was struck with the lack of modern facilities for visitors. He gained control of the Jacksonville-St. Augustine Line to bring in materials for his Ponce de Leon Hotel, the first of a series of hotels which he built at points from St. Augustine to Key West. In 1888 he acquired a narrow-gauge road running from Tocoi Junction to East Palatka and a logging railroad extending from East Palatka to Daytona. With these as a nucleus, he laid rails southward in a system that became known as the Florida East Coast Railway. Train service was established to New Smyrna in 1892, to Fort Pierce in January 1894, and to Palm Beach three months later. By 1896, continuous rail facilities had been completed from Jacksonville to Miami, a distance of 366 miles. Not until 1912, a year before his death, did Flagler complete the last and most spectacular extension of the Florida East Coast Railway, connecting the Florida Keys en route to Key West by overseas bridges. After the Labor Day hurricane of 1935, when thirty-eight miles of this track were destroyed, the "overseas" railroad was rebuilt as a highway.

H. M. Flagler's special first train crossing Long Key Viaduct, Long Key, Florida. Photograph by J. N. Chamberlain, Miami, Florida, April 8, 1909.

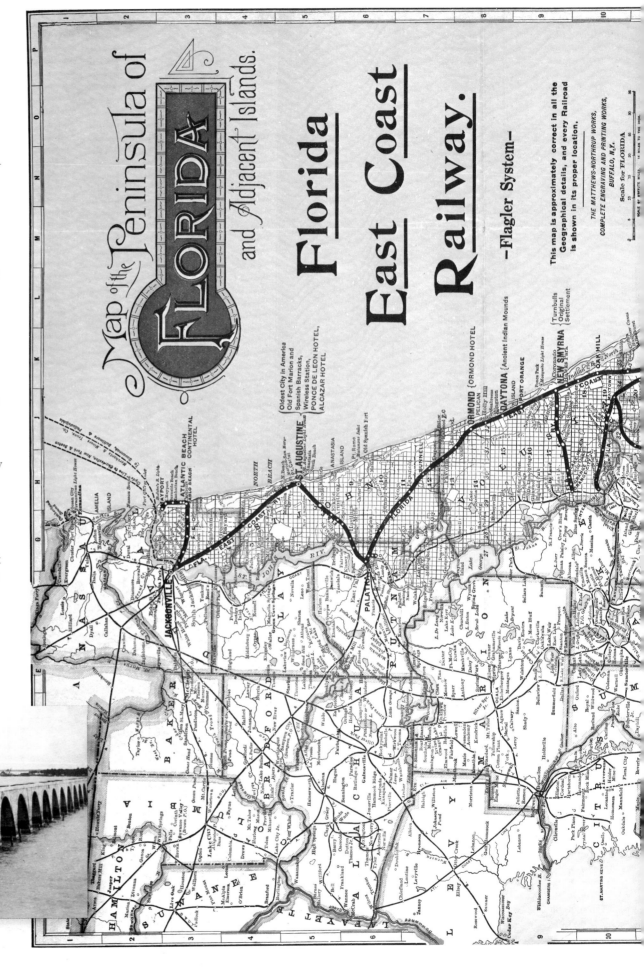

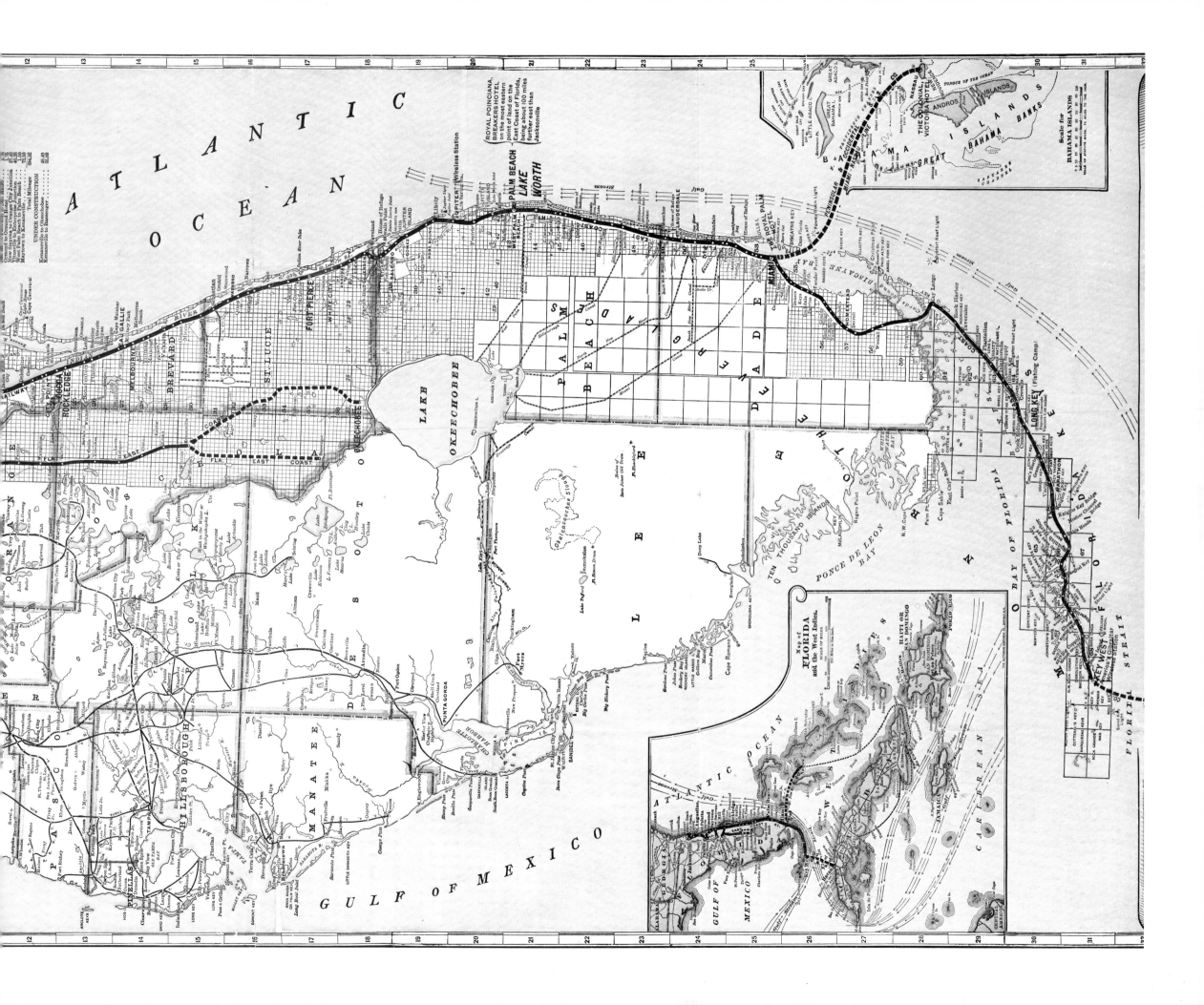

The "West Point," the Second Locomotive built in the United States for actual service on a Railroad.

The "West Point" was built at the West Point Foundery Works, in New York City, for the South Carolina Railroad, forwarded to Charleston by ship Lafayette, and after several experimental trials, in February, 1831, made the first excursion trip, as above, on Saturday afternoon, March 5, 1831.
(See extract from *Charleston Courier*, page 154.)

First trip on *The West Point*, March 5, 1831. Wood engraving in William H. Brown's *History of the First Locomotive in America* (1877).

Northeastern States

1849

37. Disturnell, John. Traveller's map of the middle, northern, eastern states and Canada showing all the railroad, steamboat, canal and principal stage routes. New York, 1849. 48 × 59 cm (19 × 24 in).

Detailed uncolored guide map covering the northeastern portion of the United States. The map includes a list of "Canal, Rail Road and Steamboat Routes" and a view of the Niagara Falls area showing the proposed ship canal and railroads. This view was drawn by William G. Williams of the U.S. Topographical Corps, an associate engineer for the Louisville, Cincinnati, and Charleston Railroad in the 1830s. The entire map was lithographed by the distinguished New York lithographer James Ackerman, who was noted for his hand-colored lithographs of flowers for book illustrations.

John Disturnell (1801-1877), a native of Lansingburg, New York, was a noted publisher and compiler of maps, guidebooks, gazetteers and resort directories. Editions of this map appeared in his popular series of guides entitled *Disturnell's Guide Through the Middle, Northern, and Eastern States*.

First trip on the Mohawk and Hudson, August 9, 1831. Lithograph based on a black paper silhouette cut out from a sketch on the spot by William H. Brown.

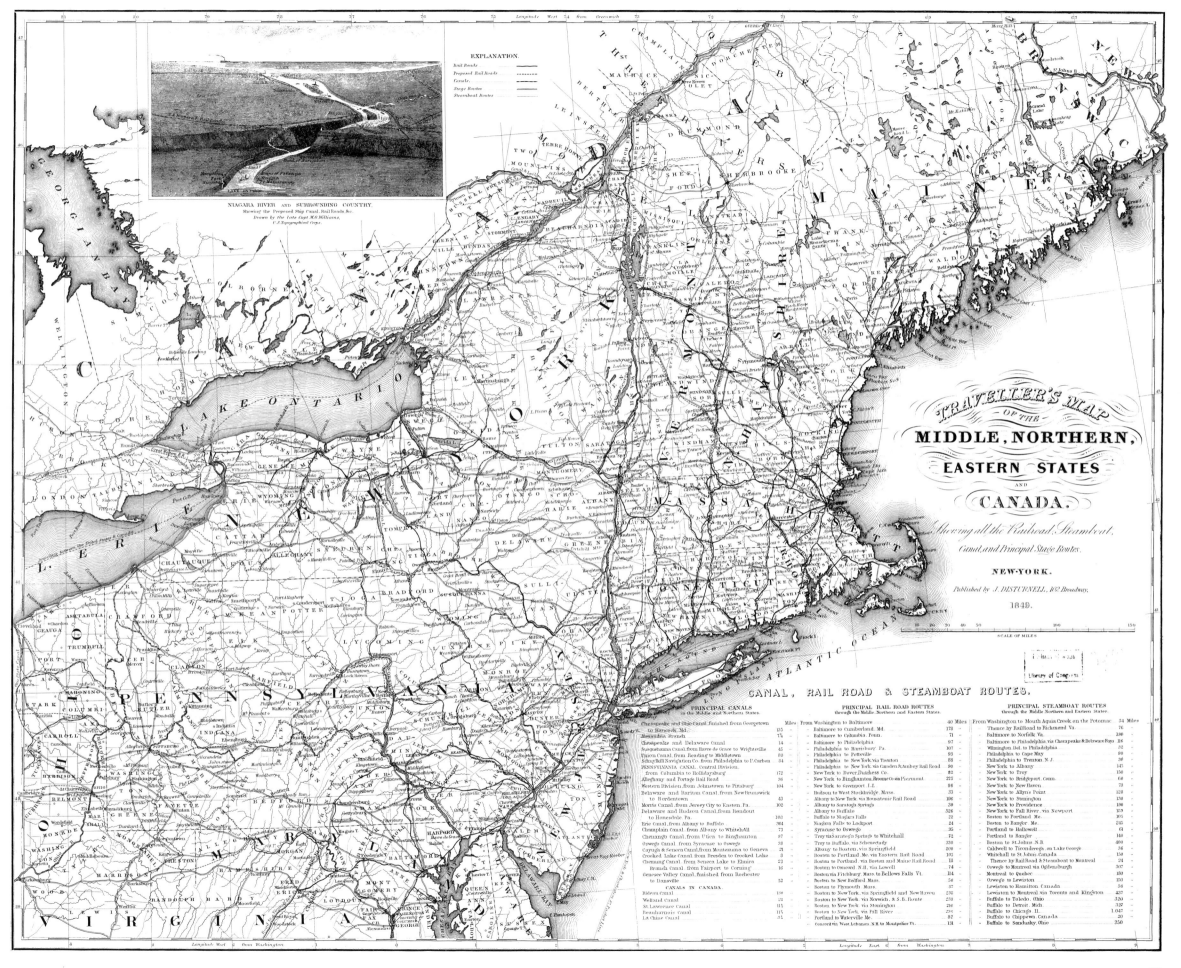

EXPLANATION.

Rail Roads
Proposed Rail Roads
Canals
Stage Routes
Steamboat Routes

NIAGARA RIVER AND SURROUNDING COUNTRY.
Showing the Proposed Ship Canal, Rail Roads, &c.
Drawn by the late Capt. W.G. Williams,
U.S. Topographical Corps.

TRAVELLER'S MAP
OF THE
MIDDLE, NORTHERN,
EASTERN STATES
AND
CANADA.
Showing all the Railroad, Steamboat,
Canal, and Principal Stage Routes.
NEW-YORK.
Published by J. Disturnell, 102 Broadway.
1849.

SCALE OF MILES

CANAL, RAIL ROAD & STEAMBOAT ROUTES.

PRINCIPAL CANALS
in the Middle and Northern States.

	Miles
Chesapeake and Ohio Canal, finished from Georgetown to Hancock, Md.	135
Alexandria Branch	7¼
Chesapeake and Delaware Canal	14
Susquehanna Canal, from Havre de Grace to Wrightsville	45
Union Canal, from Reading to Middletown	82
Schuylkill Navigation Co. from Philadelphia to P. Carbon	54
PENNSYLVANIA CANAL, Central Division. from Columbia to Hollidaysburg	172
Allegheny and Portage Rail Road	36
Western Division, from Johnstown to Pittsburg	104
Delaware and Raritan Canal, from New Brunswick to Bordentown	43
Morris Canal, from Jersey City to Easton, Pa.	102
Delaware and Hudson Canal, from Rondout to Honesdale, Pa.	108
Erie Canal, from Albany to Buffalo	364
Champlain Canal, from Albany to Whitehall	73
Chenango Canal, from Utica to Binghamton	97
Oswego Canal, from Syracuse to Oswego	38
Cayuga & Seneca Canal, from Montezuma to Geneva	21
Crooked Lake Canal, from Dresden to Crooked Lake	8
Chemung Canal, from Seneca Lake to Elmira	23
Branch Canal, from Fairport to Corning	16
Genesee Valley Canal, finished from Rochester to Dansville	52

CANALS IN CANADA

	Miles
Rideau Canal	130
Welland Canal	28
St Lawrence Canal	11½
Beauharnois Canal	11½
La Chine Canal	8½

PRINCIPAL RAIL ROAD ROUTES
through the Middle, Northern and Eastern States.

	Miles
From Washington to Baltimore	40
Baltimore to Cumberland, Md.	178
Baltimore to Columbia, Penn.	71
Baltimore to Philadelphia	97
Philadelphia to Harrisburg, Pa.	107
Philadelphia to Pottsville	93
Philadelphia to New York, via Trenton	88
Philadelphia to New York, via Camden & Amboy Rail Road	90
New York to Dover, Duchess Co.	82
New York to Binghamton, Broome Co. via Piermont	225
New York to Greenport, L.I.	96
Hudson to West Stockbridge, Mass.	33
Albany to New York, via Housatonic Rail Road	196
Albany to Saratoga Springs	39
Albany to Buffalo	326
Buffalo to Niagara Falls	22
Niagara Falls to Lockport	24
Troy via Saratoga Springs to Whitehall	72
Troy to Buffalo, via Schenectady	330
Albany to Oswego	200
Albany to Boston, via Springfield	200
Boston to Portland, Me. via Eastern Rail Road	105
Boston to Portland, via Boston and Maine Rail Road	111
Boston to Concord, N.H., via Lowell	74
Boston via Fitchburg, Mass. to Bellows Falls Vt.	114
Boston to New Bedford, Mass.	54
Boston to Plymouth, Mass.	37
Boston to New York, via Springfield and New Haven	235
Boston to New York, via Norwich, & S.B. Route	233
Boston to New York, via Stonington	235
Boston to New York, via Fall River	236
Portland to Waterville, Me.	82
Concord via West Lebanon, N.H. to Montpelier Vt.	131

PRINCIPAL STEAMBOAT ROUTES
through the Middle, Northern and Eastern States.

	Miles
From Washington to Mouth Aquia Creek on the Potomac	54
Thence by Railroad to Richmond Va.	76
Baltimore to Norfolk Va.	190
Baltimore to Philadelphia via Chesapeake & Delaware Bays	106
Wilmington, Del. to Philadelphia	32
Philadelphia to Cape May	86
Philadelphia to Trenton, N.J.	24
New York to Albany	145
New York to Troy	150
New York to Bridgeport, Conn.	62
New York to New Haven	78
New York to Allyns Point	130
New York to Stonington	130
New York to Providence	200
New York to Fall River, via Newport	185
Boston to Portland Me.	105
Boston to Bangor, Me.	245
Portland to Hallowell	40
Portland to Bangor	140
Boston to St Johns N.B.	400
Caldwell to Ticonderoga, on Lake George	36
Whitehall to St Johns Canada	24
Oswego to Montreal via Ogdensburgh	307
Montreal to Quebec	180
Oswego to Lewiston	150
Lewiston to Hamilton Canada	56
Lewiston to Montreal via Toronto and Kingston	437
Buffalo to Toledo, Ohio	320
Buffalo to Detroit, Mich.	332
Buffalo to Chicago, Ill.	1,047
Buffalo to Chippewa, Canada	20
Buffalo to Sandusky, Ohio	250

Old Colony

1891

38. Rand, Avery Supply Company. Map of the Old Colony Railroad and connections. Boston, 1891. 38 × 22 cm (16 × 8½ in).
    From: Manual of Old Colony Resorts. Containing List of Hotels and Boarding Houses on the Old Colony system. Boston, 1891.

Recreational map which advertises the resorts, accommodations, and excursions served by this company. The service of the Old Colony system is indicated in red and covers all of southeastern Massachusetts, including the ocean coastline from South Boston to Newport and Providence, Rhode Island. Shows New Hampshire connections in blue.

This railroad was incorporated in March and organized on June 25, 1844. The first part of the line was opened to traffic between South Boston and Plymouth on November 10, 1845.

MANUAL

OF

OLD COLONY RESORTS.

CONTAINING LIST OF

HOTELS AND BOARDING HOUSES

ON THE

OLD COLONY SYSTEM.

EXCURSION, COMMUTATION, SEASON TICKET RATES, AND GENERAL INFORMATION.

PUBLISHED BY
PASSENGER DEPARTMENT OLD COLONY RAILROAD.
1891.

RAND AVERY SUPPLY CO., BOSTON.

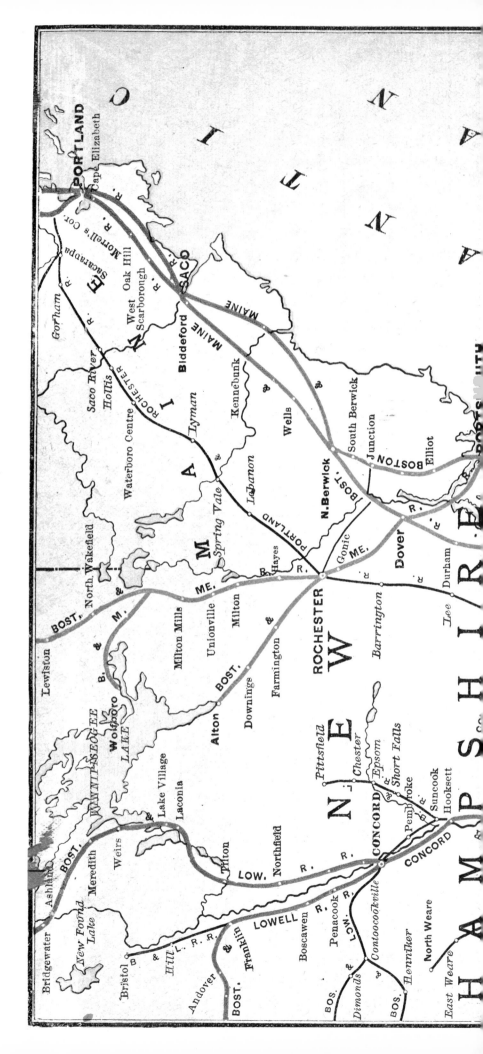

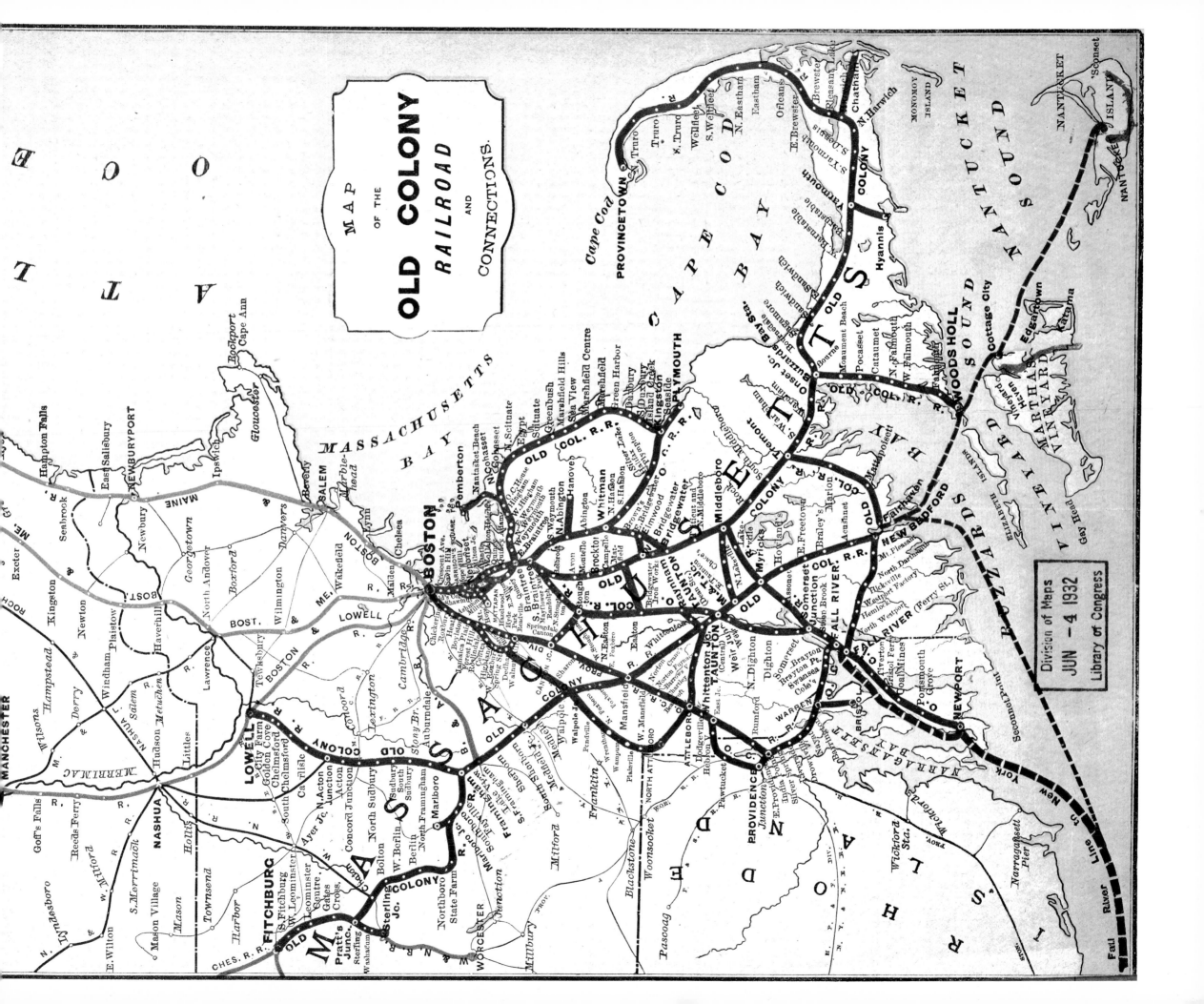

Delaware and Hudson

1909

39. Northrup, William P. Map of Delaware & Hudson Co's railroad and connecting lines. Buffalo: Matthews-Northrup Works, 1909. 22 × 19 cm (15 × 8½ in).

From: *Delaware and Hudson Time Tables. Spring Schedules.*

Accompanied by a colored pictorial transportation and tourist map of the Lake Champlain area which commemorates the 300th anniversary of Samuel de Champlain's discovery of the lake. The maps show drainage and mountains by color shading, the major railroad network in red, canals by black dashed lines, and roads by parallel black lines. Also accompanied by illustrations and descriptions of the area's summer resort scenes from the brochure.

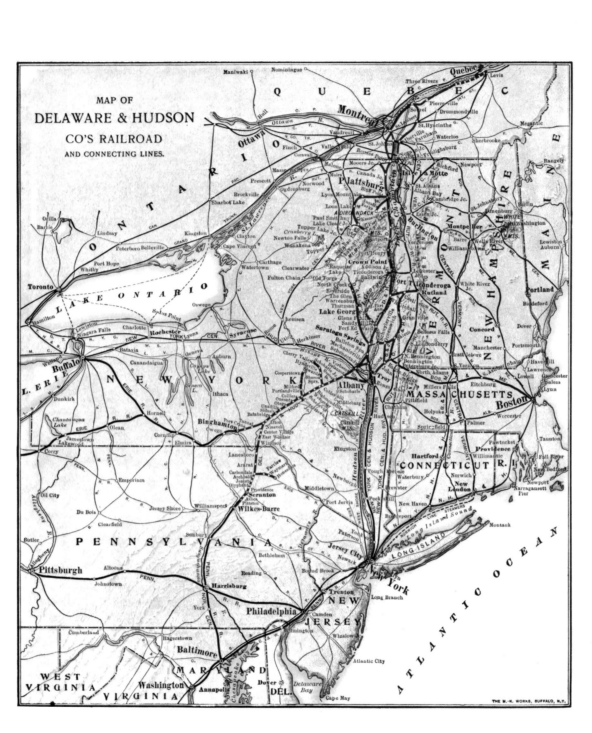

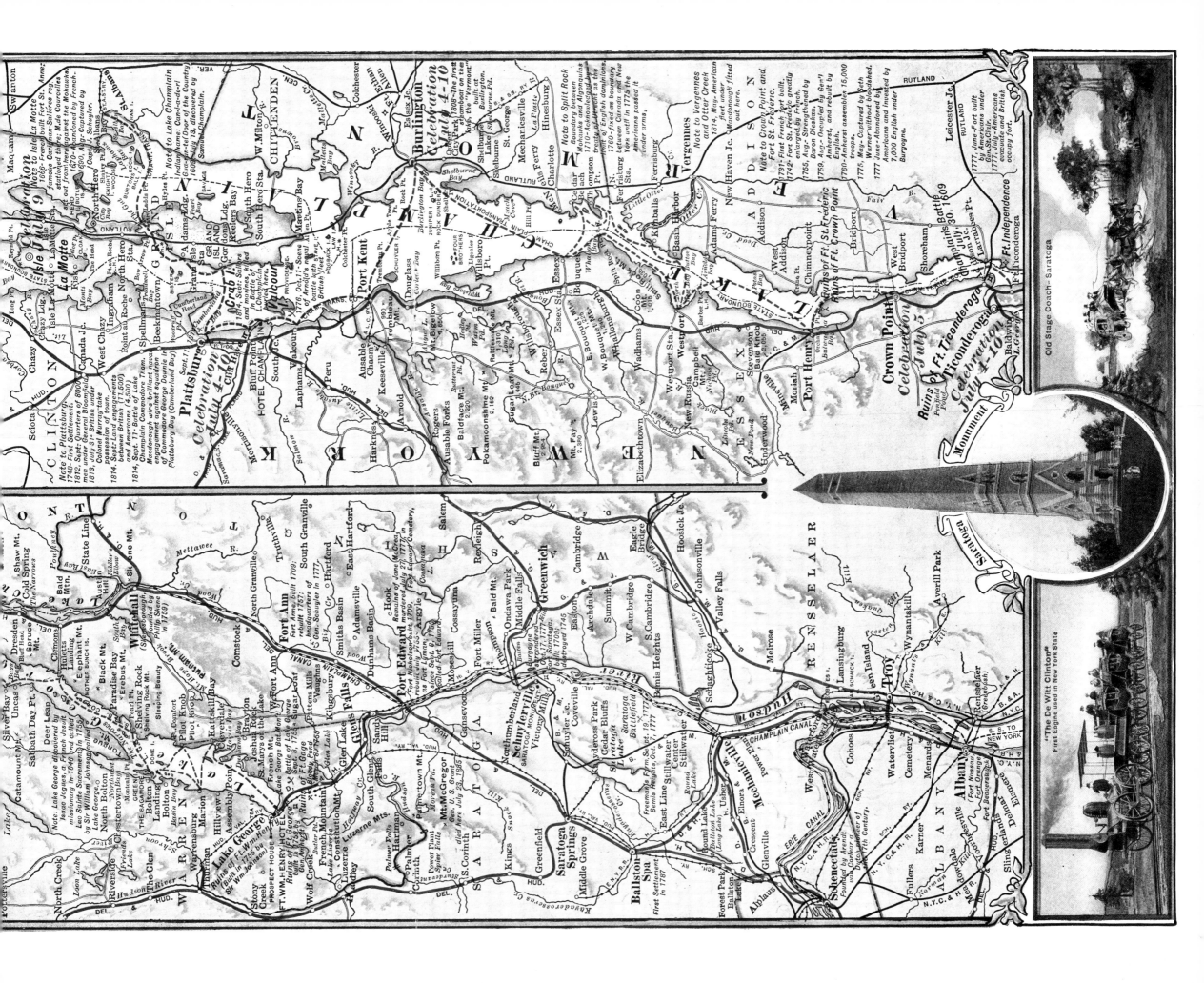

Old Stage Coach - Saratoga

"The De Witt Clinton"
First Engine used in New York State

Erie Railway

1882

40. Taunton, S. D. L. Topographical Map of summer resort regions, reached by the Erie Railway, New York, 1882. 48 × 33 cm (19 × 13 in).

A colorful and interesting summer resort and hunting and fishing map of parts of New York, New Jersey, and Pennsylvania. Indicates rivers and lakes in blue, relief by black hachures, and names of geographic features. Shows cities and towns, counties distinguished by color, canals, roads, the Erie Railroad system, and connecting lines. The map is overprinted in red to show fishing areas for bass, trout, and pickerel, and hunting areas for bear, deer, grouse, quail, and woodcock. An advertising notice appears below the title of the map:

In presenting this MAP and GUIDE to the public, the Erie Railway Company has kept in view the fact that people seeking sojourning places in the country, especially desire to avoid all localities subject to MALARIAL INFLUENCES. The ERIE is peculiarly fortunate in the ANTI-MALARIAL CHARACTER OF THE COUNTRY THROUGH WHICH IT PASSES. The pure air, rapid waters, and high elevations of the RAMAPO, DELAWARE and NEVERSINK valleys, and the back regions of ULSTER, SULLIVAN,

ORANGE, PIKE, WAYNE and DELAWARE counties, are persistent foes to the diseases that have become so prevalent in other parts of the country. MALARIA CANNOT ORIGINATE in the above localities, and physicians are annually sending patients afflicted with malarial affections to the above HEALTH-RENEWING RESORTS ALONG THE ERIE.

Cascade Bridge on the New York and Erie Railroad near Lanesboro, Susquehanna County, Pennsylvania, 1857.

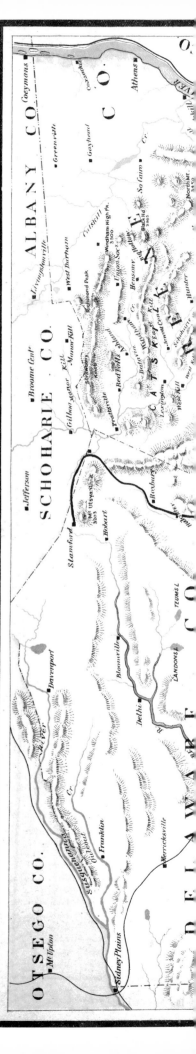

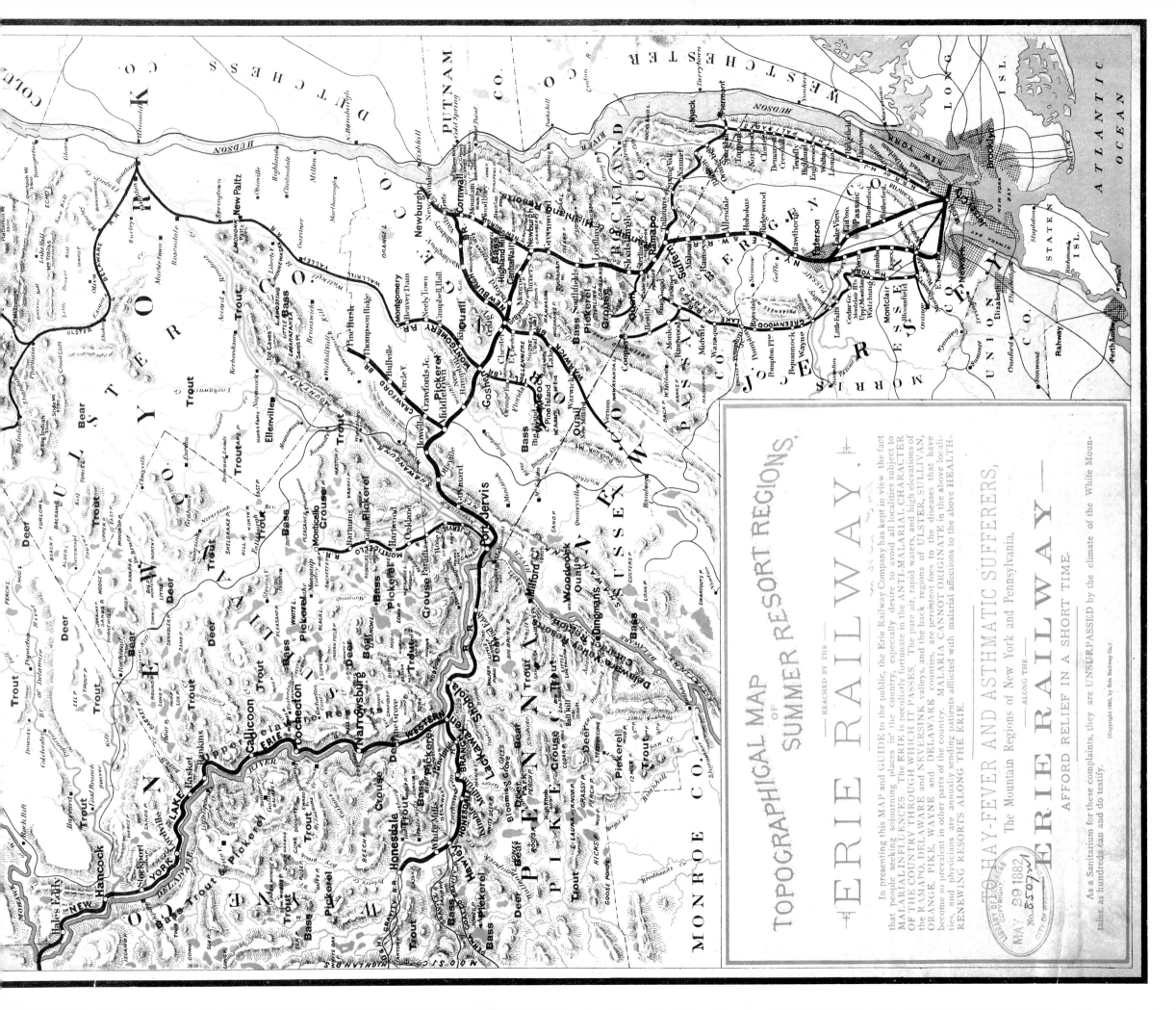

TOPOGRAPHICAL MAP
OF
SUMMER RESORT REGIONS,

— REACHED BY THE —

ERIE RAILWAY.

In presenting this MAP and GUIDE to the public, the Erie Railway Company has kept in view the fact that people seeking sojourning places in the country, especially desire to avoid all localities subject to MALARIAL INFLUENCES. The ERIE is peculiarly fortunate in the ANTI-MALARIAL CHARACTER OF THE COUNTRY THROUGH WHICH IT PASSES. The pure air, rapid waters, and high elevations of the RAMAPO, DELAWARE and NEVERSINK valleys, and the back regions of ULSTER, SULLIVAN, ORANGE, PIKE, WAYNE and DELAWARE counties, are persistent foes to the diseases that have become so prevalent in other parts of the country. MALARIA CANNOT ORIGINATE in the above localities, and physicians are annually sending patients afflicted with malarial affections to the above HEALTH-RENEWING RESORTS ALONG THE ERIE.

TO HAY-FEVER AND ASTHMATIC SUFFERERS,
The Mountain Regions of New York and Pennsylvania,
— ALONG THE —

ERIE RAILWAY —

AFFORD RELIEF IN A SHORT TIME.

As a Sanitarium for these complaints, they are UNSURPASSED by the climate of the White Mountains, as hundreds can and do testify.

(Copyright 1882, by Erie Railway Co.)

New York Central and Hudson River

1893

41. Daniels, George H. The New York Central &
Hudson River R.R. and connections. Buffalo: Matthews-
Northrup Co., c 1893. 40 × 100 cm (16 × 39½ in).
   Across top of map: ''The health and pleasure
resorts of New York and New England . . .''
   On the verso: ''America's great resorts via New
York Central & Hudson River R.R.''
   Note: ''Only four-track railroad in the World. This
is Americas great four-track trunk line between the east
and west. It is the direct line to Niagara Falls, along the
historic Hudson River and through the beautiful Mohawk
Valley. It is the most comfortable route between the east
and Chicago, the 'World's Fair City.' ''

A fine example of the wax-engraving
lithographic process for mass producing
detailed maps. A combination of a commercial railroad map and a bird's-eye-view map
specifically designed as a resort publication to
attract summer tourist trade to the Chicago
World's Fair of 1893. Covers points in the
northeastern, midwestern, and Great Lakes
regions, and part of maritime Canada. Includes the area between the Atlantic Ocean
and the Mississippi River. Shows a view of
Grand Central Station in New York City.
There are many interesting resorts pictured
and described on the verso of the map.

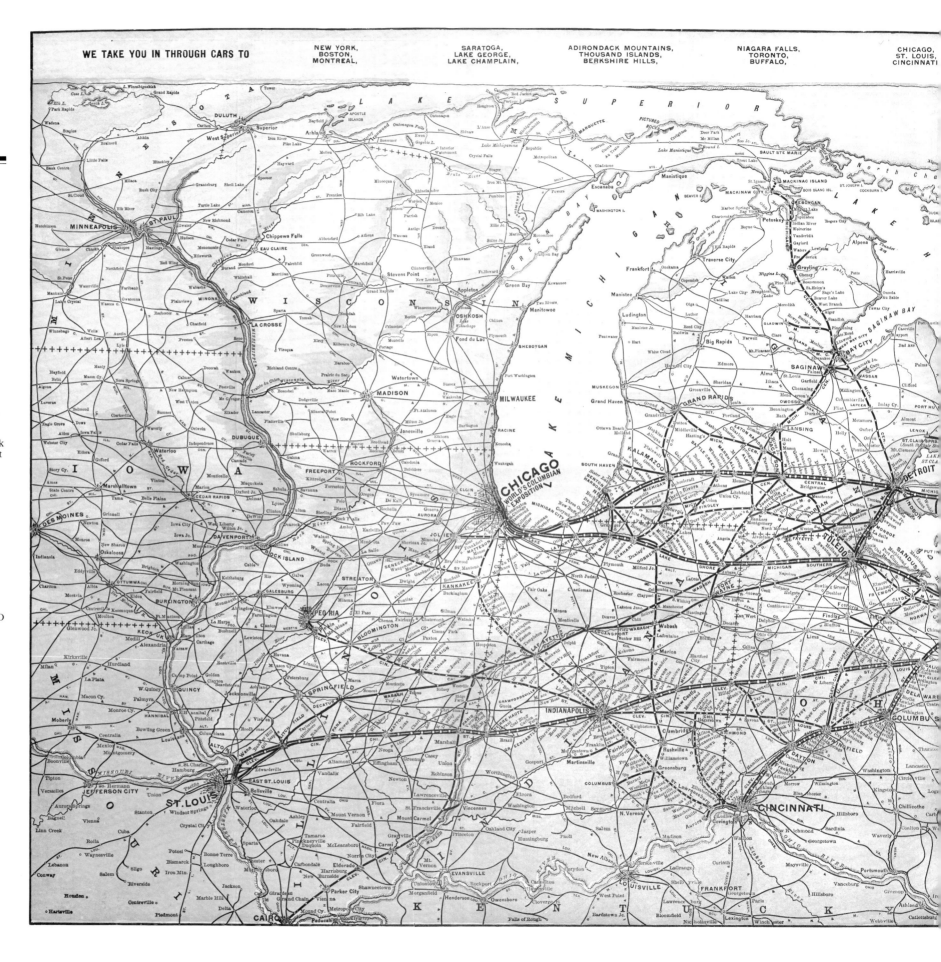

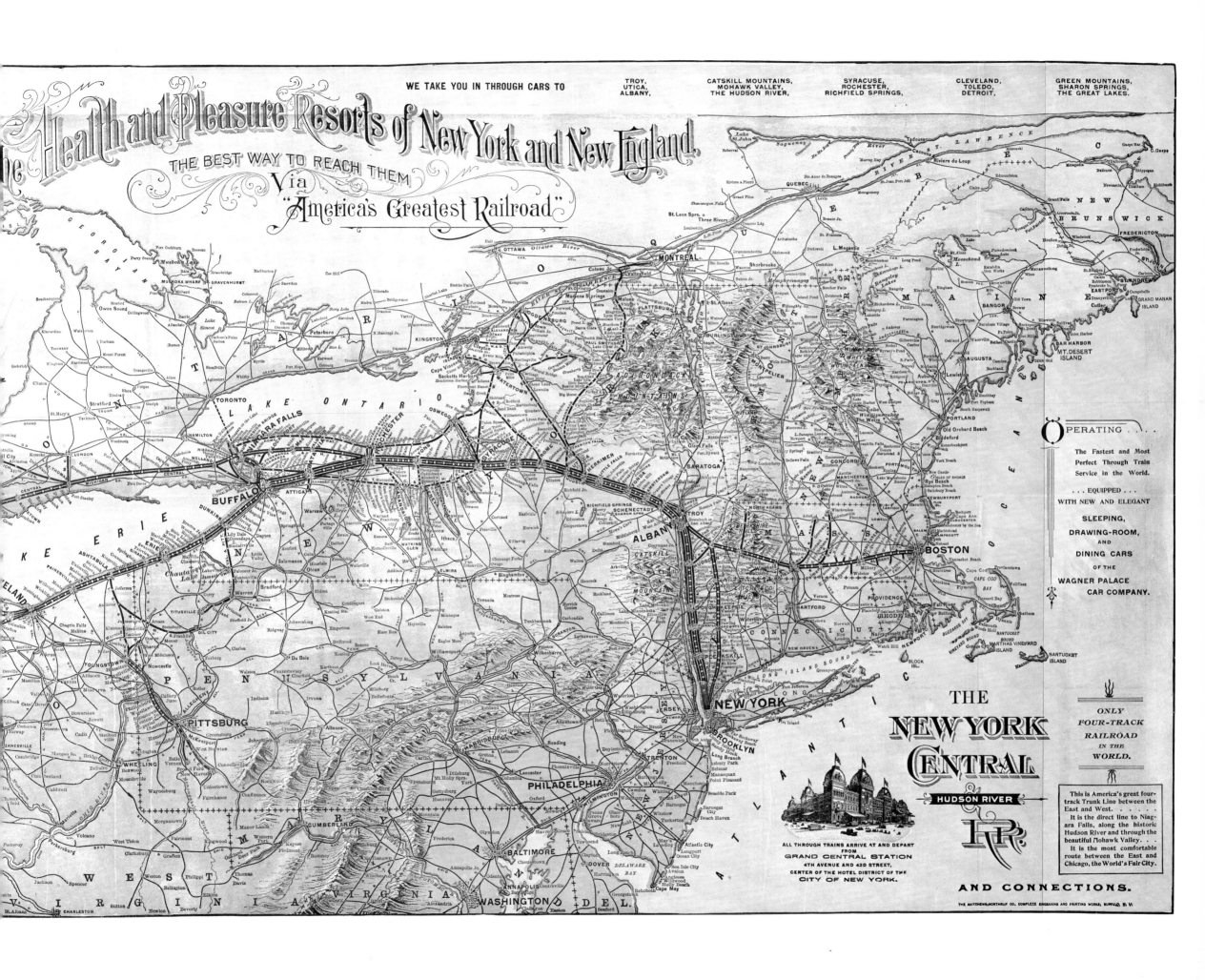

WE TAKE YOU IN THROUGH CARS TO

TROY,
UTICA,
ALBANY,

CATSKILL MOUNTAINS,
MOHAWK VALLEY,
THE HUDSON RIVER,

SYRACUSE,
ROCHESTER,
RICHFIELD SPRINGS,

CLEVELAND,
TOLEDO,
DETROIT,

GREEN MOUNTAINS,
SHARON SPRINGS,
THE GREAT LAKES.

The Health and Pleasure Resorts of New York and New England,

THE BEST WAY TO REACH THEM

Via "America's Greatest Railroad"

OPERATING . . .

The Fastest and Most
Perfect Through Train
Service in the World.

. . . EQUIPPED . . .
WITH NEW AND ELEGANT

SLEEPING,

DRAWING-ROOM,

AND

DINING CARS

OF THE

WAGNER PALACE
CAR COMPANY.

ONLY
FOUR-TRACK
RAILROAD
IN THE
WORLD.

THE

NEW YORK

CENTRAL

HUDSON RIVER

ALL THROUGH TRAINS ARRIVE AT AND DEPART
FROM
GRAND CENTRAL STATION
4TH AVENUE AND 42D STREET,
CENTER OF THE HOTEL DISTRICT OF THE
CITY OF NEW YORK.

AND CONNECTIONS.

This is America's great four-
track Trunk Line between the
East and West . . . . . .
It is the direct line to Niag-
ara Falls, along the historic
Hudson River and through the
beautiful Mohawk Valley . . .
It is the most comfortable
route between the East and
Chicago, the World's Fair City.

THE MATTHEWS-NORTHRUP CO. COMPLETE ENGRAVING AND PRINTING WORKS, BUFFALO, N. Y.

Washington and Atlantic

1883

Map of the middle Atlantic states showing relief by hachures, drainage, cities and towns, coal and iron ore deposits in West Virginia and western Maryland, and the railroad network with emphasis on the main line. Connections to the mining areas, steamer lines, and the Chesapeake and Ohio Canal are also indicated.

42. Colton (G. W. and C. B.) and Company. Map showing the route of the Washington and Atlantic Railroad and its connections. New York, 1883. colored. 62 × 80 cm (25 × 31½ in).

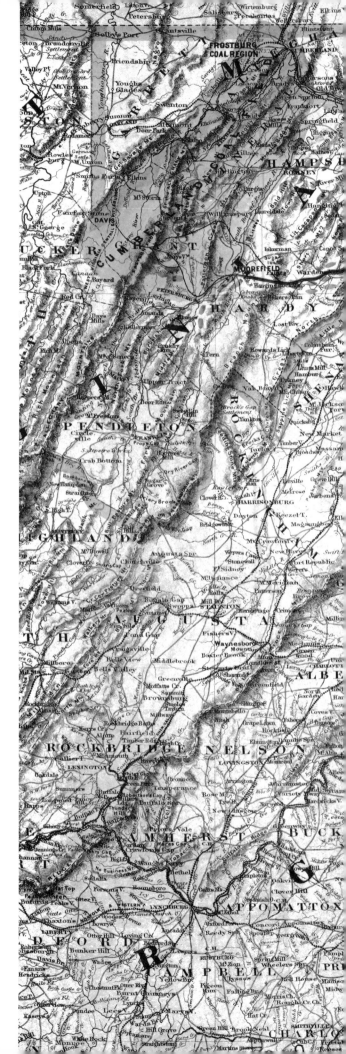

"Maryland Heights, from Harper's Ferry, with the Canal and River." From *Photographic Views of the Baltimore and Ohio Railroad and its Branches* (Baltimore: Cushings & Bailey; Hagadorn Brothers, 1872).

Map showing the Route of the

WASHINGTON AND ATLANTIC

RAILROAD

AND ITS CONNECTIONS.

SCALE OF STATUTE MILES, 12 TO ONE INCH.

Central of Georgia

1899

43. Central of Georgia Railway Company. Map of Central of Georgia Ry. and connections. St. Louis: Woodward & Tiernan Printing Company, 1899. Colored map 97 × 78 cm (38 × 31½ in).
  At top of map: Winter Camps of the U.S. Army. Savannah Line composed of the Central of Georgia Railway and Ocean Steamship Company and connections.

Perspective colored map distributed by the railroad company for families of soldiers who were stationed in the area after the signing of the Treaty of Paris (December 10, 1898), which ended the Spanish-American War. The map embraces the southeastern United States and Cuba and includes an inset map of Puerto Rico. Shows major drainage pattern, relief by hachures and color shading, cities and towns, roads, steamship routes, the railroad network with names of lines, and the main lines in heavy red color. U.S. camps are identified by small flags. The map includes a distance table and a table of military organization for "Troops in the Division of Cuba, January, 1899." A list of military departments is also included. The verso of the map includes descriptions of Cuba and its major cities and provinces.

Landing of American troops in Cuba. Photograph by William Dinwiddie, 1898.

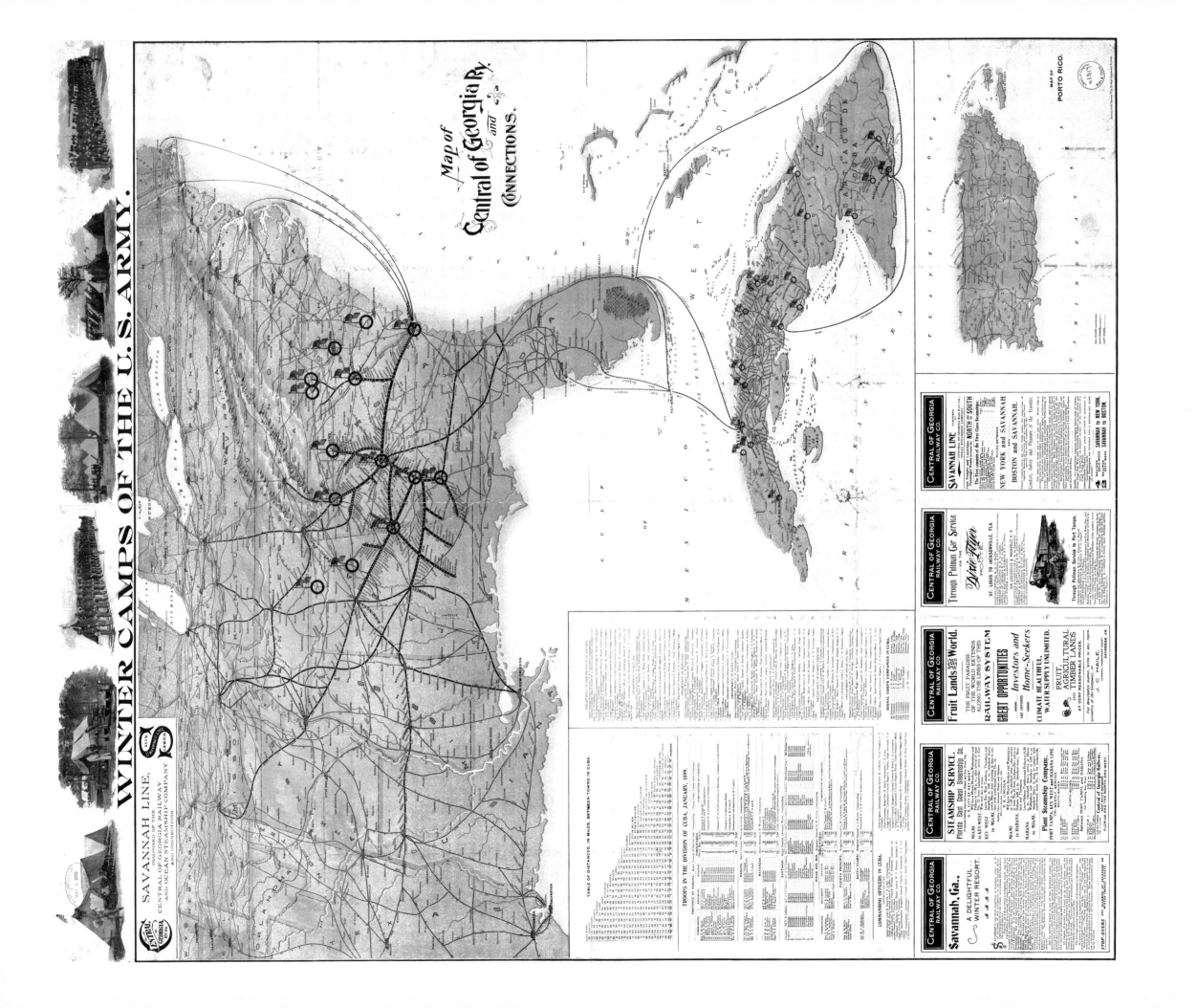

Chicago, Milwaukee, and St. Paul Railway

1874

44. Rand McNally and Company. [Map of the Chicago, Milwaukee, and St. Paul Railway]. Chicago, 1874. 35 × 45 cm (13½ × 17½ in).

Colored and illustrated map of the north-central states showing drainage, cities and towns, railroad stations, and the railroads with lines labeled. Emphasis is on the main lines, which are shown in heavy black. Projected or unfinished railroad lines appear as linear cross-hatched lines, normally associated with complete railroad lines. Incorporated in 1863 as the Milwaukee and St. Paul Railway, the word Chicago was added to the name in 1874.

In the borders of the map are picturesque scenes of the country traversed by the railroad, as well as a list of railroad stations in the Middle West. On the verso are timetables and ticket information and a small "Map of the Business District of Chicago," which locates railroad depots (see this page).

This is a typical artistic timetable map developed for distribution to the public in railway guides and as pocket maps. Soon after the distribution of this type of railroad map, the distorted schematic railroad map was devised. These new maps were made to show the importance of a particular railroad by the intensity of the line symbol, distortion of scale, and manipulation of particular lines to portray them favorably in relation to competing lines.

The geographic inaccuracy in railroad maps led George H. Heafford, general passenger agent for the Missouri Pacific, to note in 1878 that, "If this World could be made over according to some of our ideas, I have not the faintest doubt but that the railroads we represent would all be the straightest and shortest lines between every prominent city in the country." An 1879 Rand McNally booklet confirms that

map "designing" to other than a railroad official, might seem a peculiar phrase, but the majority of railroad maps have some "peculiar designs" hidden under the careful pencil of the draughtsman. It requires a faculty only acquired by experience and a perfect knowledge of the railroad system of the country, to "design" a good railroad advertising map.

The various friendly interests must be shown to best advantage, and the rival interests disposed of in a manner that "no fellow can find out." The drawing of a good map is a matter of considerable difficulty, but the "designing" of a good map involves the exercise of tact and ingenuity. Probably more *original* map projections have been made in our map drawing room than have ever been produced in the United States.

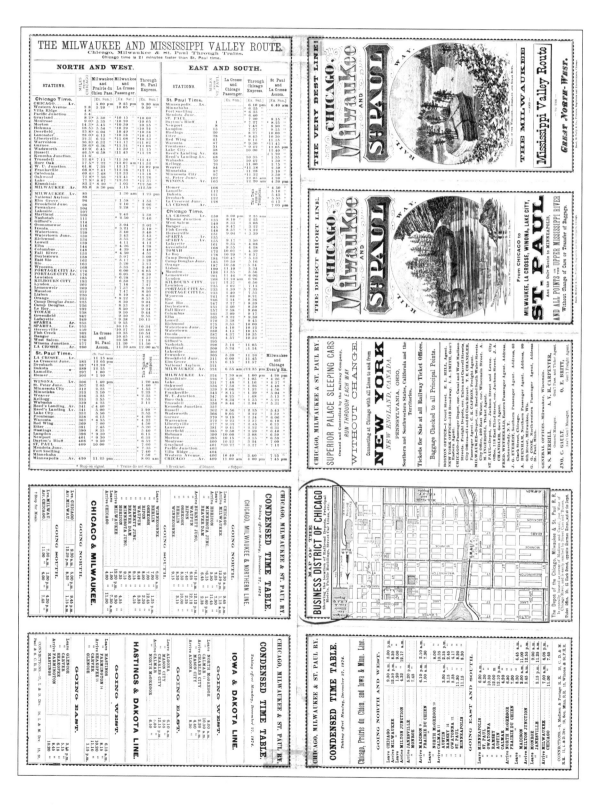

FORT SNELLING, MINN.

DELLS OF THE WISCONSIN.—INKSTAND & SUGAR BOWL.
On the Line of the Chicago, Milwaukee & St. Paul Railway.

TEMPLAR ROCK, LAKE PEPIN.
Reached only by the Chicago, Milwaukee & St. Paul Railway.

STATIONS
ON THE LINES OF THE
Chicago, Milwaukee & St. Paul
RAILWAY.

WISCONSIN.

Ackerville.	Fall River.	Lowell.	Reed's Corners.
Allen's Grove.	Fish Creek.	Lyndon.	Richfield.
Arena.	Fisk's.	Lyons.	Richwood.
Arlington.	Fox Lake.	Madison.	Rio. Ripon.
Avoca.	Fox Lake Junc.	Marshall.	Rolling Prairie.
Bangor.	Franksville.	Mauston.	Rubicon.
Beaver Dam.	Genesee.	Mazomanie.	Rush Lake.
Beloit.	Germantown.	McFarland.	Salem.
Berlin.	Granville.	Middleton.	Schleisingerville.
Black Earth.	Greenfield.	Milton.	Schwartzburg.
Blue River.	Hanover.	Milton Junc.	Sparta.
Boscobel.	Hartford.	Milwaukee.	Springfield.
Brandon.	Hartland.	Minnesota Junc.	Spring Green.
Bridgeport.	Helena.	Monroe.	Stoughton.
Brodhead.	Herseyville.	Morrison.	Sun Prairie.
Brookfield Junc.	Horicon Junc.	Muscoda.	Tomah Junc.
Burlington.	Hubbellton.	Nashotah.	Truesdell.
Burnett Junc.	Iron Mountain.	North Prairie.	Union Grove.
Cambria.	Iron Ridge.	Oakwood.	Waterloo.
Camp Douglas.	Ixonia.	Oconomowoc.	Watertown.
Clinton.	Janesville.	Omro.	Watertown Junc.
Columbus.	Juda.	Orange.	Waukau.
Cross Plains.	Kansasville.	Orford.	Waukesha.
Darien.	Kilbourn City.	Oshkosh.	Waupun.
Deansville.	Kinnikinic.	Palmyra.	Wauwatosa.
De Forest.	La Crosse.	Pardeeville.	Wauzeka.
Delavan.	Lafayette.	Pewaukee.	Western Union J.
Dover.	Lake.	Pickett's.	Whitewater.
Doylestown.	Lemonweir.	Portage.	Windsor.
Eagle.	Leroy.	Poynette.	Winneconne.
Edgerton.	Lewiston.	Prairie du Chien.	Winona Junc.
Elba.	Lima.	Racine.	Woodland.
Elkhorn.	Lisbon.	Racine Junc.	Woodman.
Elm Grove.	Lone Rock.	Randolph.	Wyocena.

STATIONS
ON THE LINES OF THE
Chicago, Milwaukee & St. Paul
RAILWAY.

MINNESOTA.

Adams.	Etter.	Lansing.	Red Wing.
Auburn.	Faribault.	Medford.	Rosemount.
Aurora.	Fairfield.	Mendota.	Shakopee.
Austin.	Farmington.	Minneapolis.	St. Paul.
Benton.	Frontenac.	Minnehaha.	St. Paul Junc.
Blooming Prai.	Glencoe.	Minneiska.	Vermillion.
Carver.	Hastings.	Minnesota City.	Wabasha.
Castle Rock.	Homer.	Newport.	Wacouta.
Chaska.	Kellogg.	Northfield.	Weaver.
Dahlgren.	La Crescent Jc.	Owatonna.	Winona.
Dakota.	Lake City.	Prior Lake.	Young America.
Dresbach.	Lamoille.	Ramsey.	
Dundas.	Langdon.	Reed's Landing.	

ILLINOIS.

Chicago.	Florence.	Libertyville.	Savanna.
Dakotah.	Freeport.	Morton.	Shannon.
Davis.	Grayland.	Mount Carroll.	Shirland.
Deerfield.	Gurnee.	Rock City.	Wadsworth.
Durand.	Lanark.	Rockton.	

IOWA.

Algona.	Clear Lake.	Lime Springs.	Nor. McGregor.
Beulah Junc.	Connover.	Luana.	Ossian.
Brit.	Cresco.	Lyle.	Plymouth.
Calmar.	Decorah.	Mason City.	Postville.
Carpenter.	Floyd Crossing.	McGregor.	Ridgeway.
Castalia.	Fort Atkinson.	Monona.	Rudd.
Charles City.	Garner.	New Hampton.	Wesley.
Chester.	Lawler.	Nora Junction.	
Chickasaw.	Leroy.	Nora Springs.	

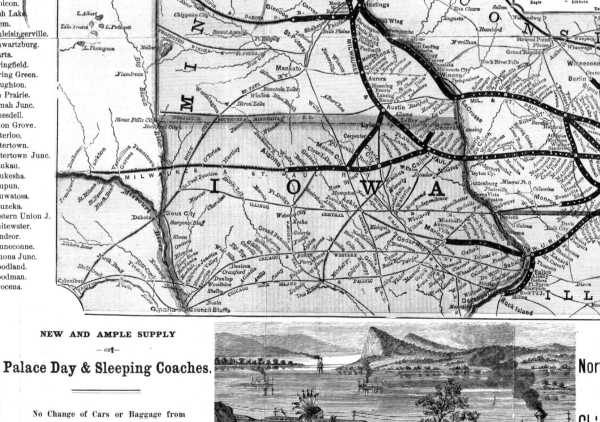

JAWS OF THE DELLS.

THE MAIDEN'S ROCK, ON LAKE PEPIN.

VIZOR LEDGE, EAST OF STAND ROCK.

Northern Pacific

1883

45. Rand McNally and Company. New and correct map of the lines of the Northern Pacific Railroad and Oregon Railway & Navigation Co. [Chicago, 1883]. 39 × 110 cm (15½ × 43 in).
 Signed in ms: "Wm H Brewer October 1883."

A fine example of a commercial railroad map of northern United States and part of Canada showing relief by hachures, drainage, cities and towns, and railroads. Shaded area shows land grants. Main lines indicated by heavy black and red.

This map was designed to attract settlers to the area along the line and in the northwest. It advertises homes, farms, and grazing land for sale, and gives information for settlers. On the verso of the map there is detailed timetable information and illustrations of railroad sleeping and dining cars.

An uncolored facsimile edition of this map was published by Rand McNally and Company in celebration of their centennial in 1956.

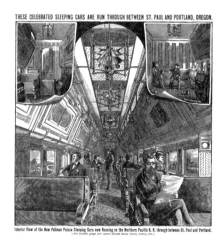

THESE CELEBRATED SLEEPING CARS ARE RUN THROUGH BETWEEN ST. PAUL AND PORTLAND, OREGON.

Interior View of the New Pullman Palace Sleeping Cars now Running on the Northern Pacific R. R. through between St. Paul and Portland.

This is our Pacific Express, with Pullman and Dining Cars attache
running through to Portland witho

New **&** Correct Map

OF THE

LINES OF THE

Northern Pacific

RAILROAD **AND**

OREGON RAILWAY & NAVIGATION CO.

hich leaves St. Paul at 8.00 p.m., every day in the week, *Wm H Brewer*

hange of Cars in <u>4</u> days.

October 1883

Denver and Rio Grande

1898

46. Hooper, S. K. Map of the Denver & Rio Grande Railroad. Showing its connections to the Klondike gold fields. Chicago: Poole Bros., 1898. 20 × 40 cm (7½ × 15½ in).

From a folder entitled *The Klondike Gold Fields as Reached Via the Denver & Rio Grande Railroad "Scenic Line of the World."*

This colored map depicts the western United States and shows in red and blue the company's lines in Colorado, northern New Mexico, and Utah. Connecting lines in other states are shown in black. A reduced scale map, inset in the left side of the main map, shows connections from Chicago to steamship lines in the Pacific Northwest, Alaska, and the Northwest Territories in Canada.

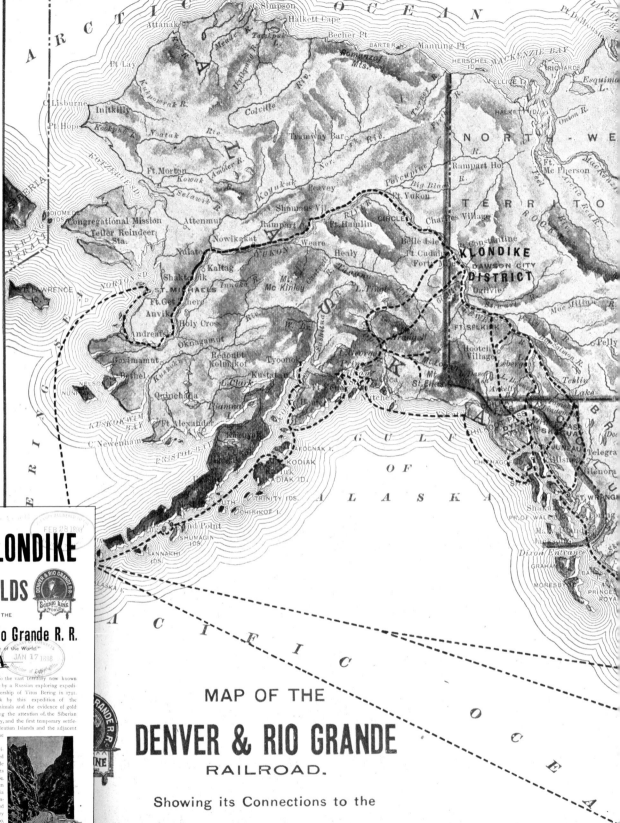

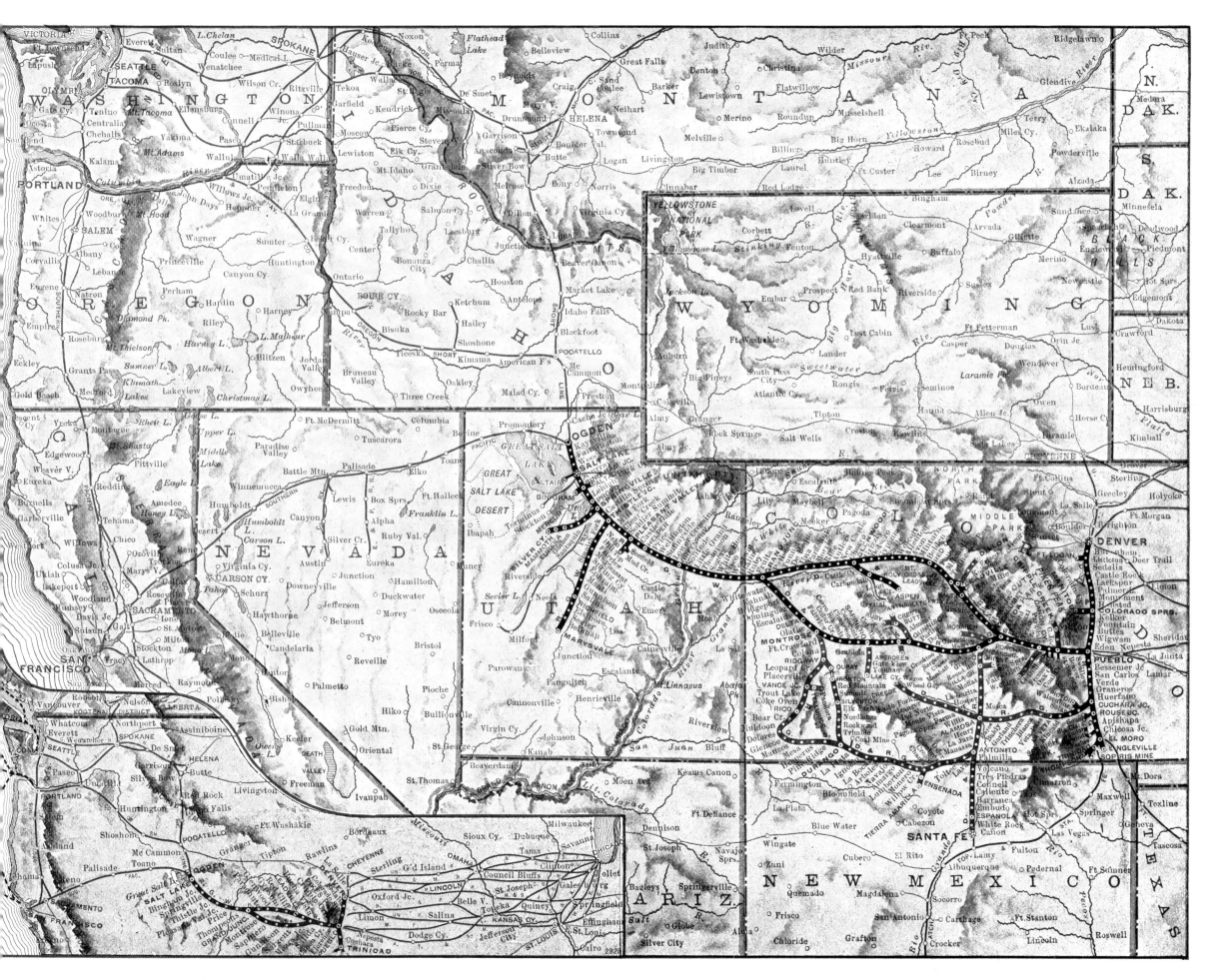

93

Oregon Railroad and Navigation Company

1897

47. Poole Brothers. Oregon Railroad & Navigation Company's Map of Alaska and the Klondike mining country. Chicago, 1897. 56 × 46 cm (22 × 18 in).

A shipping and transportation map of Alaska, northwest Canada, and the Pacific Northwest showing water areas in blue, geographic features, cities and towns, steamship lines, and trails in black. The main lines of the Oregon Railroad appear in red on the inset map, and connections are in solid black lines. The map identifies trails and waterways for reaching the gold fields, both through the inland passage via Skagway and by the ocean route to St. Michael, near the delta of the Yukon River. St. Michael became the deepwater port where cargo and the gold seekers were transferred to stern-wheelers for the long journey upriver to the Klondike.

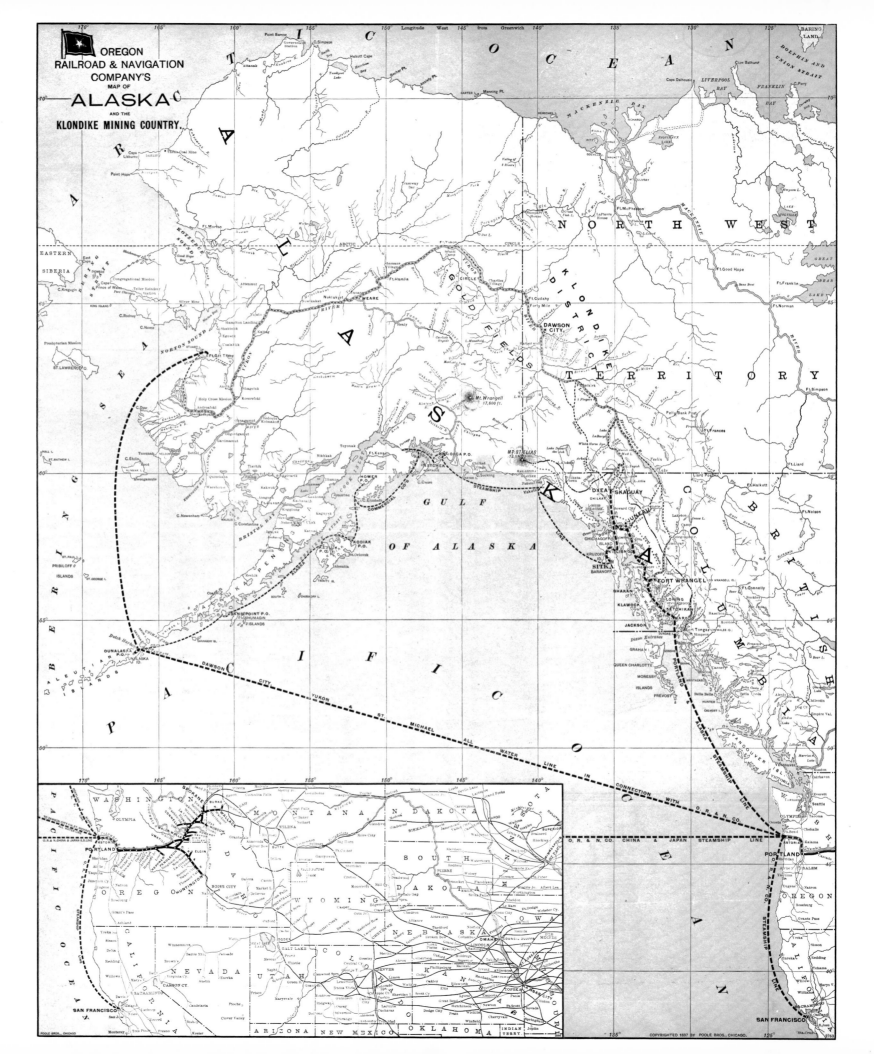

Chicago-New York Electric Air Line

1907

48. Clapp, O. W. Map of the Chicago-New York Electric Air Line. St. Louis, 1907. 8 × 21 cm. On sheet measuring 57 × 30 cm (22 × 11 in).

Outline sketch map of the northeastern United States illustrating an unusual advertisement for promoting stock certificates issued by this railroad company. This interurban line, chartered in 1905, had twenty-five miles of track in operation by 1912 between Laporte and Westville, Indiana, and had control of other interurban lines in northern Indiana. The goal of the company was to connect the commerce of the East Coast and the Midwest with a fast straight line known as the Air Line distance, having few curves and grades. In this broadside and in its monthly periodical, *Air Line Notes,* the company promoted public ownership of its stock. Unfortunately, with the advent of the motor bus after World War I the interurbans declined in popularity and ended competition for the steam railroads.

This grandiose project for building a double-track electric railroad in a straight line was to have no grade crossings with other railroads. The promoters proposed to haul standard passenger trains behind streamlined electric locomotives at an average speed of 75 miles per hour. They would have offered ten-hour service at a flat $10 fare on a route of only 742 miles, more than 150 miles shorter than any existing steam railroad. Although it appeared to be a fraudulent scheme, scholars believe that it was a sincere but misguided effort to build such a line.

The principal promoter of this project was Alexander C. Miller, an experienced railroad man who had spent twenty years as an operating official of the Chicago Burlington & Quincy. Miller had conceived the idea of the Air Line — presumably for the New York Central — which after three hours' fast running out of New York was farther from Chicago, its destination, than it had been when it started.

Although electric interurbans were not originally in the scope of this atlas, we have included this particular map to show an interesting example of the use of railroad maps in promotional advertising.

Denver and Rio Grande

1883

49. Rand McNally and Company. Denver and Rio Grande Railway System, 1883. Chicago, 1883. 46 × 60 cm (17½ × 24 in).

A detailed colored railroad map of central and western Colorado, eastern Utah, and northern New Mexico showing relief by hachures, mountain passes, rivers, cities and towns, mining areas, stage roads, and railroads in operation, under construction, and projected. Includes an inset of the southwestern states which shows railroad connections with the major lines to the east and north.

This map was distributed by the Colorado Loan and Trust Company of Denver as promotional literature to encourage settlement of the San Luis Park area of southern Colorado. It describes the climate, soils, geography, and the agricultural and irrigation opportunities of the region. There is also information on the map on how to obtain government lands.

THE COLORADO LOAN AND TRUST COMPANY

DENVER, COL.,

OFFERS TO SETTLERS IN

THE SAN LUIS PARK,

HOW TO OBTAIN GOVERNMENT LAND

ELEVATIONS

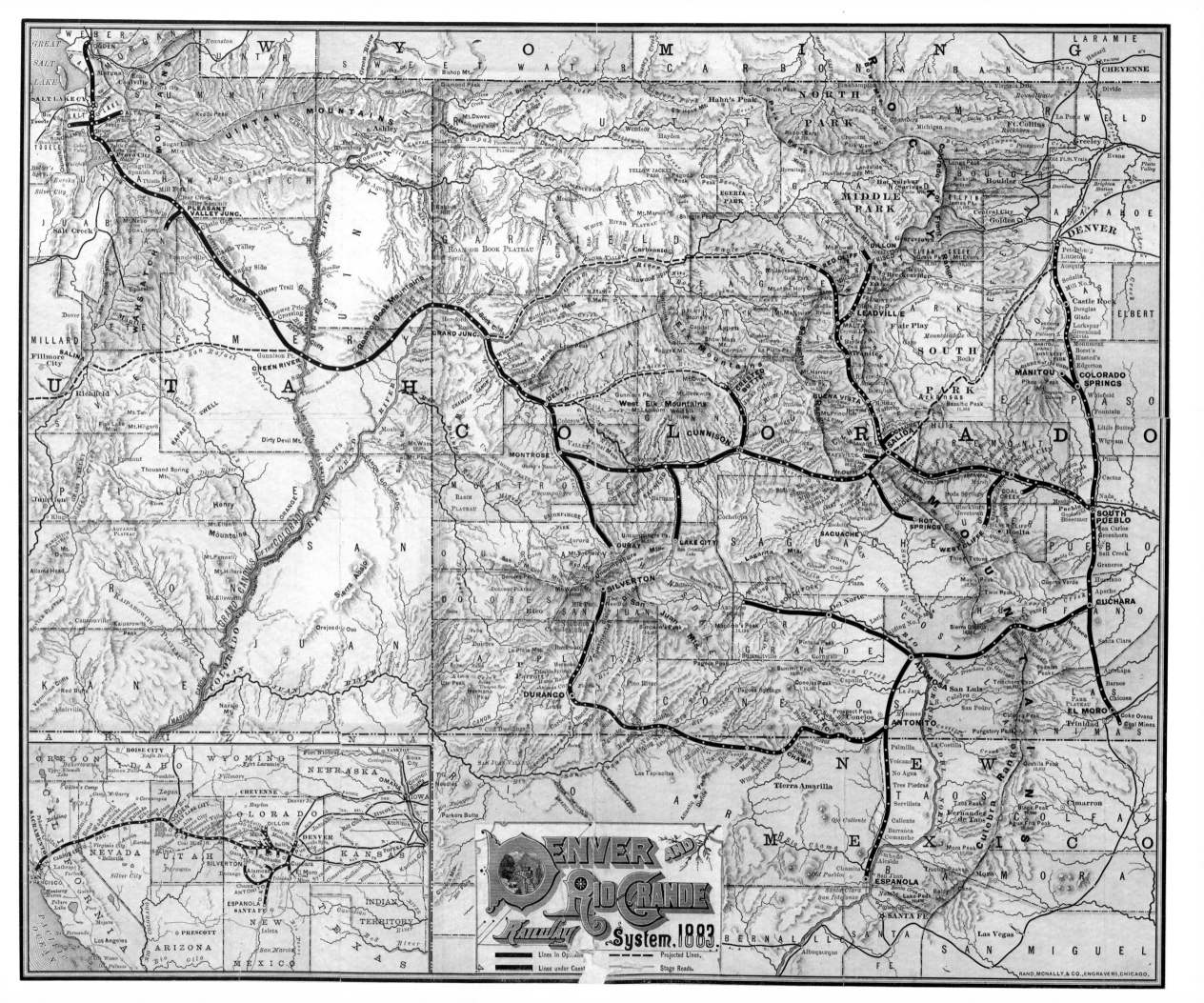

DENVER AND RIO GRANDE RAILWAY System, 1883.

Lines In Operation.   Projected Lines.
Lines under Const.   Stage Roads.

RAND, MCNALLY, & CO., ENGRAVERS, CHICAGO.

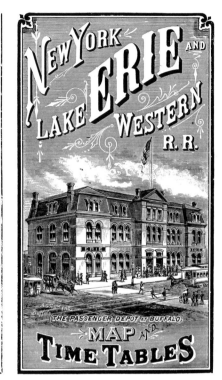
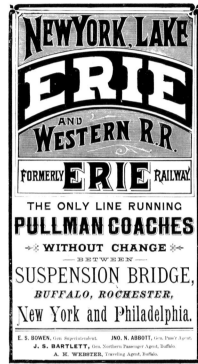

Erie Railway

1880

50. Erie Railway Company. New York, Lake Erie and Western R.R. Formerly Erie Railway. Map and time tables. Buffalo, 1880. Title from verso. 2 maps on one sheet, 31 × 53 cm (12 × 21 in).

A popular uncolored timetable map distributed by the railroad's passenger ticket office. One map shows the railroad network, emphasizing the Erie Railway in the northeastern states, and the other map depicts parts of New York City showing the location of the Hudson River and East River piers. Indicates ferry connections and coastwise steamer timetables. On the sides and the verso of the map, numerous services and timetables are shown.

The Erie Railway Company was reorganized in 1861 from the bankrupt New York and Erie Railroad, which was incorporated in 1832 (see entry 5). The new company gained sound financial footing during the Civil War before it became the subject of a tremendous financial battle. Daniel Drew, Jay Gould, and James Fisk became allies and from 1866 to 1868 — with the aid of unauthorized stock issues, political chicanery, and incessant litigation — outmaneuvered Cornelius Vanderbilt to keep control of the Erie Railway Company. Drew lost his control to Gould, who during his presidency (1868-72) ruined the Erie Railway Company. After further financial trickery, the Erie Railway Company went bankrupt and was reorganized (1878) as the New York, Lake Erie and Western Railway Company. This map represents the new reorganization which by 1880 had branch lines connecting to Chicago.

Jay Gould, who was responsible for the demise of this railroad company, began his career in the mid-1850s as a surveyor and mapmaker in Ulster County, New York.

NEW ENTERPRISE!

to second and **third** class passengers **from the West**, coming to New York, or passing
oute to Europe, we have now arranged for a

SPECIAL OMNIBUS TRANSFER,

r of our Jersey City Depot (the arriving place of through trains from the West), to convey pas-
ge direct to Steamships, Hotels, Boarding Houses, or wherever they may be consigned—thus
protection, and freedom from contact with the "sharpers" who seek to prey upon strangers ar-
he Erie Company will perform this service with its own omnibuses, in charge of trusty servants,
exceed fifty cents for the transfer of a passenger and ordinary baggage; families or parties at
ice. A transfer Agent of the Company will board each incoming train from the West an hour
al in Jersey City, and tender to passengers the facilities above announced.
ansfer service above referred to will be entirely distinct from the regular "first-class" transfer
ntinues as heretofore.

EUROPEAN PASSENGERS
—AND—
BUSINESS MEN

Will save five miles of tedious city transfer by entering New York on the Erie Railway.

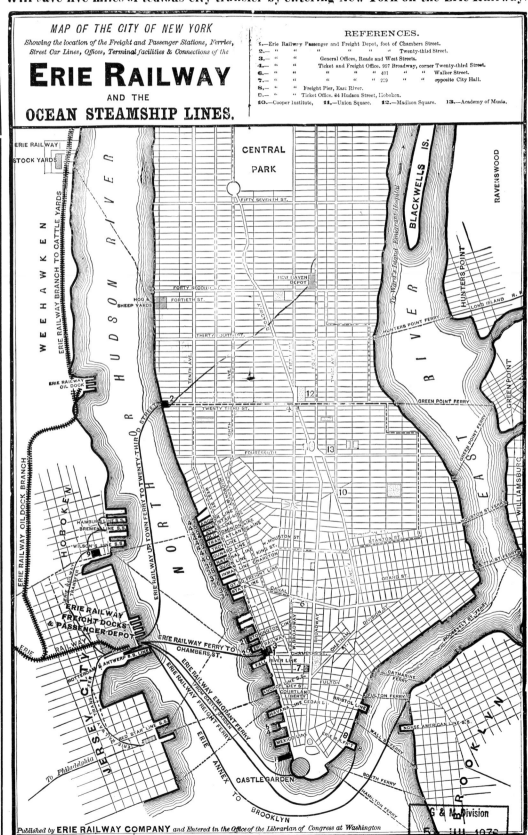

MAP OF THE CITY OF NEW YORK

Showing the location of the Freight and Passenger Stations, Ferries,
Street Car Lines, Offices, Terminal facilities & Connections of the

ERIE RAILWAY
AND THE
OCEAN STEAMSHIP LINES.

REFERENCES.

1.—Erie Railway Passenger and Freight Depot, foot of Chambers Street.
2.—   "   "   "   "   Twenty-third Street.
3.—   "   General Offices, Reade and West Streets.
4.—   "   Ticket and Freight Office, 957 Broadway, corner Twenty-third Street.
5.—   "   "   "   401   "   Walker Street.
6.—   "   "   "   229   "   opposite City Hall.
7.—   "   "   "
8.—   "   Freight Pier, East River.
9.—   "   Ticket Office, 24 Hudson Street, Hoboken.
10.—Cooper Institute.   11.—Union Square.   12.—Madison Square.   13.—Academy of Music.

Published by **ERIE RAILWAY COMPANY** and Entered in the Office of the Librarian of Congress at Washington

White Pass and Yukon

1919

51. Poole Brothers. Map of Alaska, British Columbia and Yukon Territory showing connections of the White Pass & Yukon Route, with gold fields of Atlin, White Horse, Klondike and Yukon River points to Cape Nome. Chicago, Kennedy, Del., 1919. 3 maps on one sheet measuring 61 × 51 cm (24 × 20 in).

Colored map of the northwestern part of North America indicating the steamer connections to the White Pass and Yukon in red, showing the "U.S. Military Reserve" centered on St. Michael, Alaska. The enlarged inset maps show the rail line in red, completed from Skagway to White Horse, its northern terminus. From there a red line shows a trail to Ft. Selkirk, Yukon, where it meets the Dalton trail at the Yukon River.

This narrow gauge superbly scenic 110 mile railroad was built by Michael J. Heaney, an Irish contractor. It took two years to build and put the first locomotive into service at Skagway, Alaska, in July 1898, the northernmost point for an engine in North America.

The line is still in operation for tourist and freight. In earlier days it had a lake steamer connection (see map) from Caribu (Carcross) to Atlin. An exerpt from the 1915 Poole Brothers brochure *Alaska and the Yukon Territory* describes the excursions as follows:

The trip from Skaguay, by rail, over the summit of White Pass to White Horse, is one of the most interesting rides imaginable. Nowhere is there more awe-inspiring scenery than on this trip. One of the features of the railway trip is the twenty-seven-mile ride along the winding shores of Lake Bennett, made

famous by the trials and tribulations of the gold-seekers of '97 and '98, who stampeded to the Yukon in search of gold.

At Caribou, sixty-eight miles from Skaguay, connection is made with the steamer to Atlin, on the east shore of Lake Atlin — "one of the beauty spots of the world." In the opinion of the many tourists who have visited Lake Atlin, there is nothing in all their travels that will compare with it for beauty and grandeur — not even the famed lakes of Switzerland and Italy.

Returning to Caribou the trip, by rail, is continued past historic Miles Canon and White Horse Rapids, of Klondike memory, to White Horse, the head of navigation on the upper Yukon River.

Today two trains, starting in opposite directions, climb over the precipitous Coast Range, through White Pass, elevation 2888 feet, meeting at Lake Bennett, the halfway point, where the trains can pass each other and the passengers can partake of a traditional meal that is served at the spacious inn.

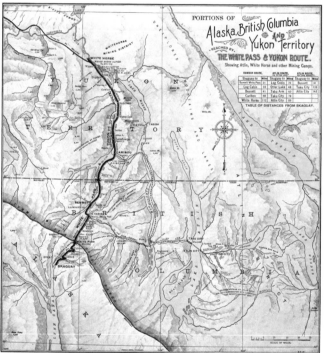

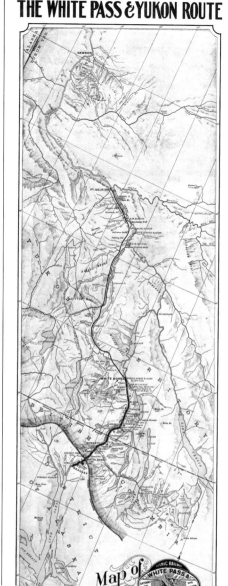

Alaska, Klondike gold rush, 1902. First train over the White Pass and Yukon.

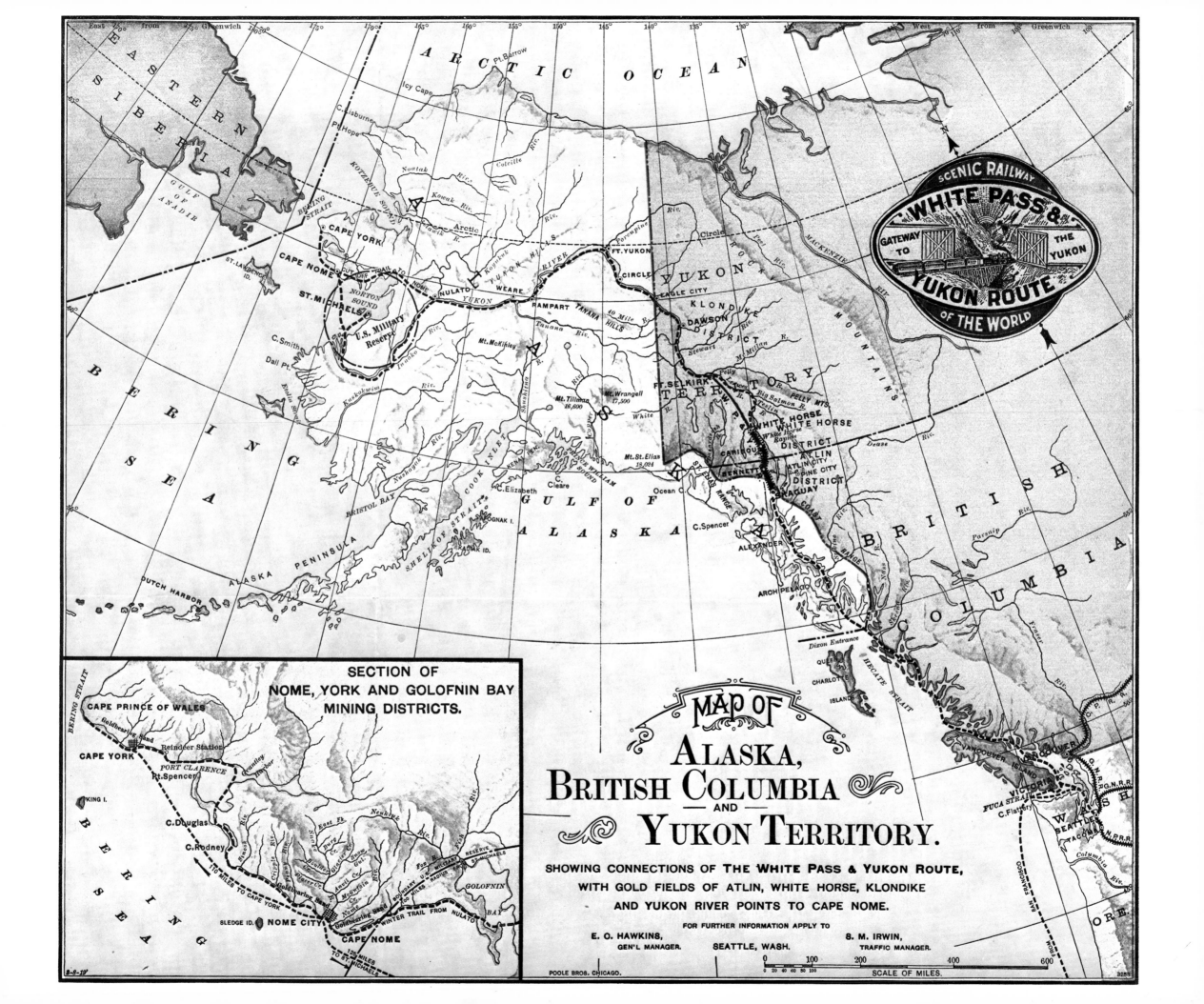

MAP OF
ALASKA,
BRITISH COLUMBIA
AND
YUKON TERRITORY.

SHOWING CONNECTIONS OF THE WHITE PASS & YUKON ROUTE,
WITH GOLD FIELDS OF ATLIN, WHITE HORSE, KLONDIKE
AND YUKON RIVER POINTS TO CAPE NOME.

FOR FURTHER INFORMATION APPLY TO

E. O. HAWKINS,
GEN'L MANAGER.

SEATTLE, WASH.

S. M. IRWIN,
TRAFFIC MANAGER.

POOLE BROS. CHICAGO.

SCALE OF MILES.

SECTION OF
NOME, YORK AND GOLOFNIN BAY
MINING DISTRICTS.

SCENIC RAILWAY
WHITE PASS &
GATEWAY TO
THE YUKON
YUKON ROUTE
OF THE WORLD

Atchison Topeka and the Santa Fe

1880

52. Woodward, Tiernan & Hale. A geographically correct county map of states traversed by the Atchison Topeka and the Santa Fe Railroad and its connections. St. Louis [1880]. 37 × 78 cm (13½ × 20 in).

Detailed map of the central United States showing relief by hachures, drainage, counties, cities and towns, roads, wagon trails, and the railroad network.

This line was chartered by the state of Kansas in 1859, but it was not until the spring of 1871 that the first seventy-five miles were extended to Newton, Kansas. A branch line was built from there to the southern Kansas cattle town of Wichita (see also entry 73), which assured its success as an important cattle shipping point. Ten years later most of the trail herds headed for Dodge City, another shipping point on this famous railroad line. The line also connected with the Denver and Rio Grande and the Union Pacific railroads.

A bird's-eye-view of the plains stretches across the top of the map and depicts the Arkansas River, the Rocky Mountains, in the west, a cattle drive, a buffalo hunt, cattle towns, and railroad connections.

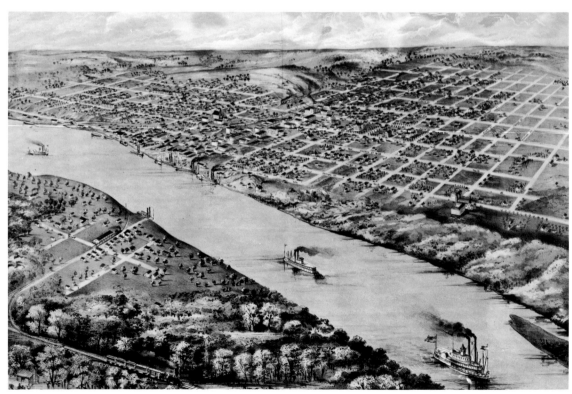

Bird's-eye-view of Atchison, Kansas, 1869.

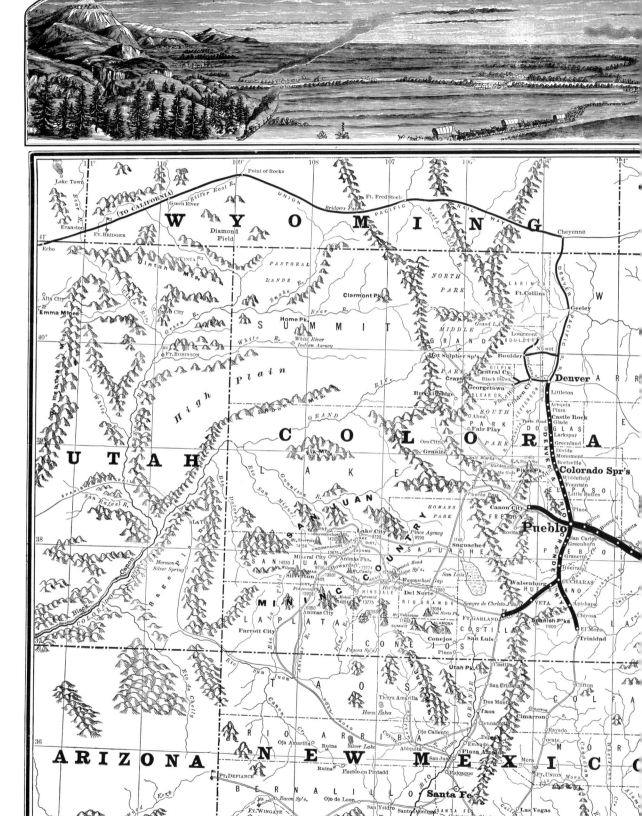

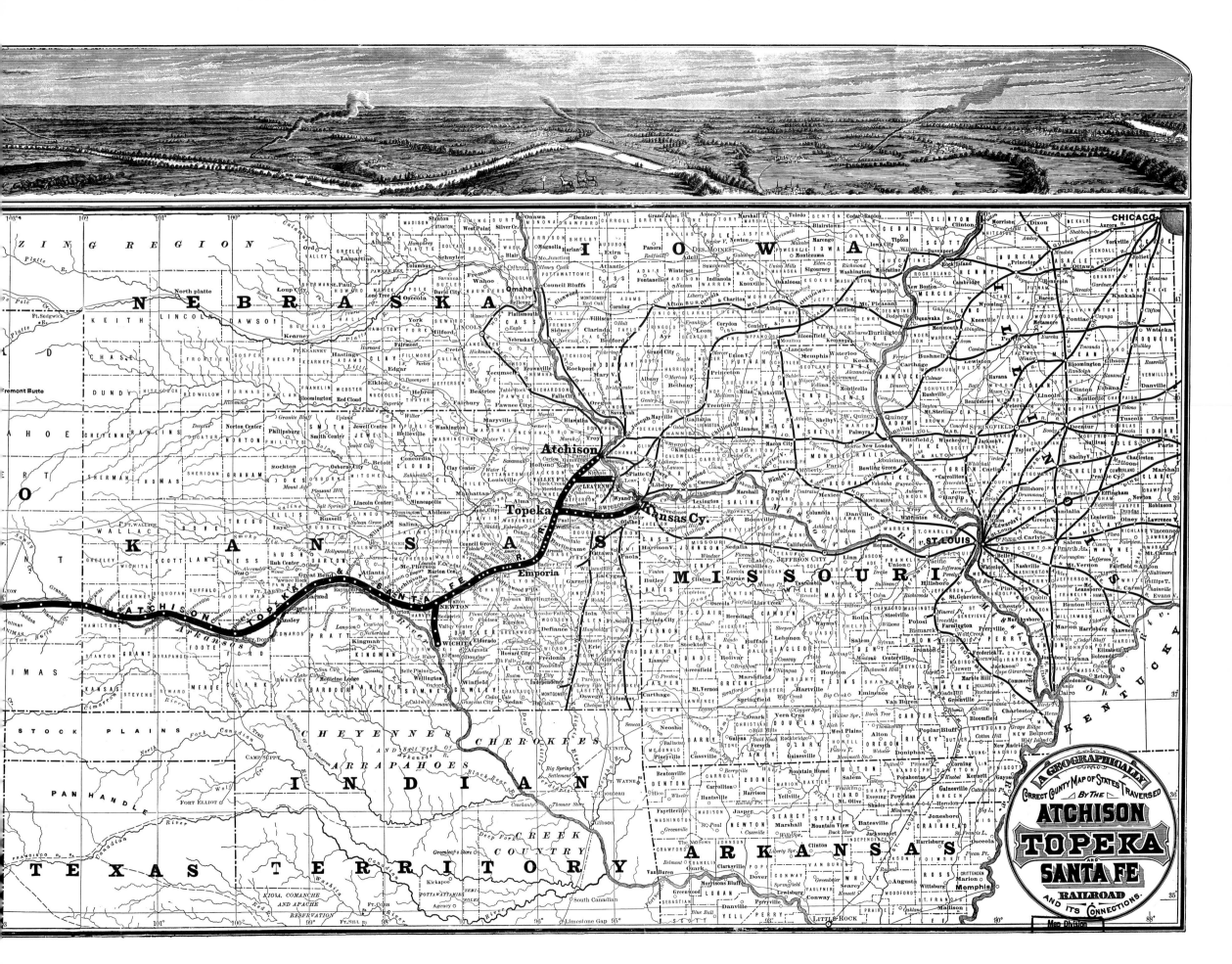

Baltimore and Ohio

1876

53. Rand McNally and Company. General map of
the Baltimore and Ohio Rail Road & its connections. The
great national route between the east and west. [Chicago,
1876] 34 × 51 cm (13½ × 20 in).

Typical colored railroad map giving pro-
minence to the main lines. Depicts part of the
eastern United States, showing relief by
hachures, major drainage, state boundaries,
cities and towns, and the railroad network,
with names of railroads, and an inset of the
transcontinental lines. The verso of the map
includes detailed timetable information.

"Bridge over the Ohio River at
Bellaire." From *Photographic
Views of the Baltimore and Ohio
Railroad and its Branches*
(Baltimore: Cushings & Bailey;
Hagadorn Brothers, 1872).

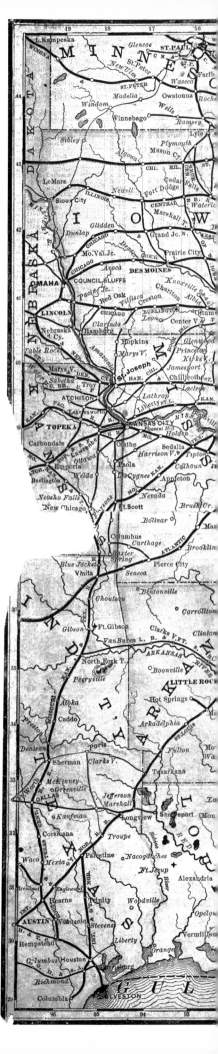

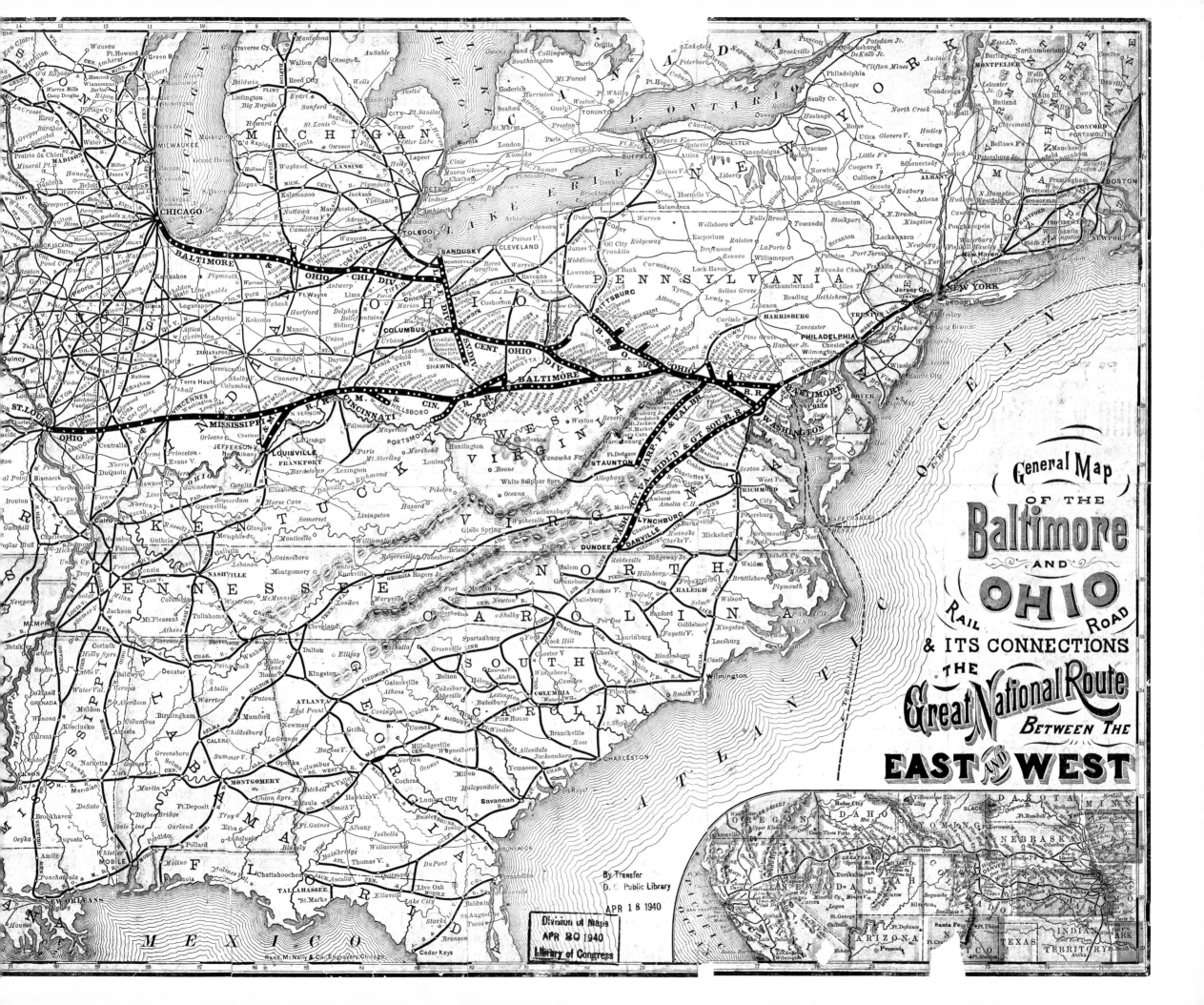

General Map
OF THE
Baltimore
AND
OHIO
Rail Road
& ITS CONNECTIONS
THE
Great National Route
BETWEEN THE
EAST AND WEST

Rand, McNally & Co. Engravers, Chicago.

Delaware and Hudson

1885

54. American Bank Note Company. Map of the Delaware and Hudson Canal Company's railroads & connections — [The Saratoga Line]. New York, 1885. The map as shown measures 40 × 50 cm (16 × 20 in).

This typical uncolored railroad timetable map of the northeastern United States and part of Canada depicts the Saratoga Line as the shortest route between New York and Montreal, via the Hudson Valley and the Lake Champlain lowland. Wagon and stage roads link the smaller communities with the railroad stations. Major railroads are named along the lines. The map includes detailed timetable information on the sides and on the verso.

In this illustration the right-hand side of the map has been folded over to reveal the cover title, logo, and timetable information for Boston.

Saratoga Springs. Broadway, north from Grand Union, 1889. Photograph by S. R. Stoddard, Glens Falls, New York.

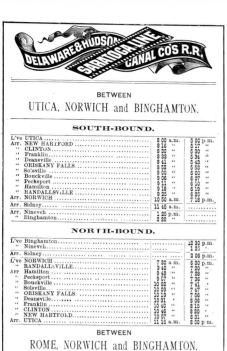

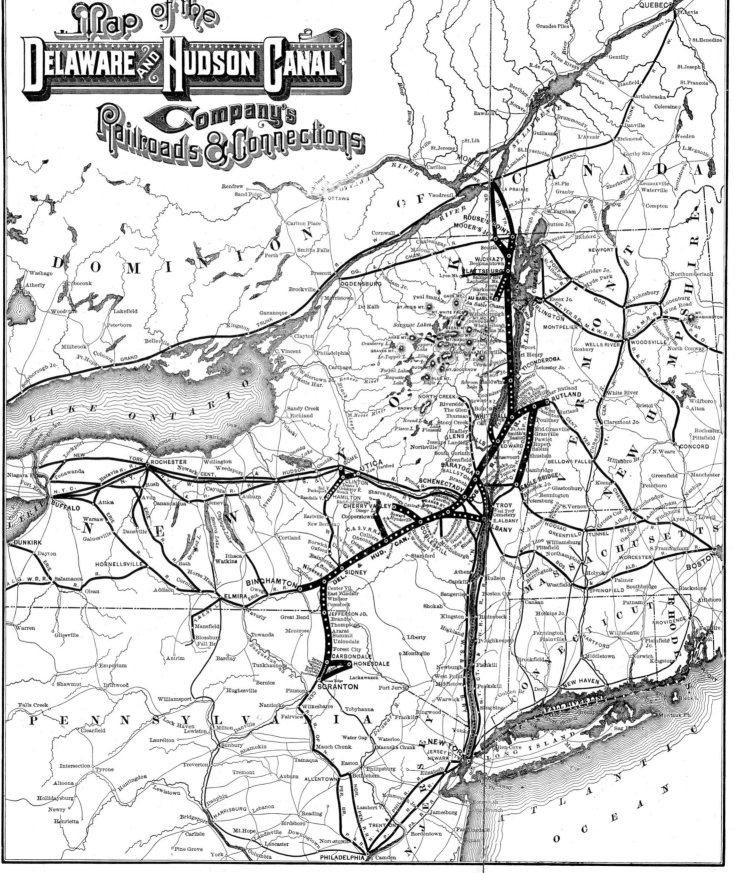

Map of the DELAWARE AND HUDSON CANAL Company's Railroads & Connections

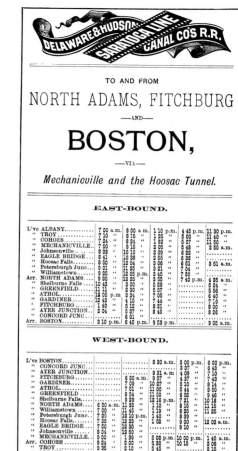

Denver and Rio Grande

1873

55. Von Motz, Albert. Map of the Denver and Rio Grande Railway and connections. Comp. & Drawn by Alb. von Motz, Colorado Springs, [1873]. 61 × 28 cm (24 × 11 in).

This map, made for free distribution, covers western Colorado and New Mexico and shows relief by hachures, drainage, cities, towns, counties, and mining areas, identifying individual minerals such as gold, silver, and coal. It also shows roads and trails and completed and proposed railroad lines. General information for tourists is given on the verso of the map.

The Denver and Rio Grande Railway was incorporated on October 27, 1870, and the right of way for construction was granted by an Act of Congress in 1871. The line was conceived by the Civil War general William J. Palmer as a narrow-gauge line from Denver, Colorado, to Mexico City, Mexico. The adoption of a narrow gauge was made because of the expected difficulty of construction in the central Rocky Mountains. The route was projected along the Rio Grande del Norte. Soon the course was diverted westward through the Royal Gorge to tap the Leadville mining district. In 1883 the narrow-gauge line was completed between Denver and Ogden, Utah,

with branches reaching wherever mining activities demanded transportation. The narrow gauge was supplanted in 1890 as the line became a part of several transcontinental systems. Until the early 1950s, over six hundred miles of narrow track remained in southwest Colorado, the longest in the United States. These lines served as models for similar operations in the world, but today only fragments remain as tourist lines.

The achievements of the Denver and Rio Grande railway in mountain climbing and canyon threading entitle it to its popular name, ''The Scenic Line of the World.'' Five times it crosses the main ranges of the Rocky Mountains, at elevations that range from nine thousand to over eleven thousand feet: La Veta Pass, Cumbres, Tennessee Pass, Marshall Pass, and Fremont Pass. To gain these heights a grade of over two hundred feet was necessary for about one hundred miles of the route. A journey over these passes abounds in interest. Two of the grandest of Rocky Mountain canyons, the Grand canyon of the Arkansas and the Black canyon of the Gunnison, together with a score of lesser ones, are traversed by this railroad.

Gen. William Jackson Palmer (1836-1909) was a distinguished Union cavalry officer and railroad executive. After the war, he served as an official of the Union Pacific Railroad's Eastern Division, which became the Kansas Pacific and later merged into the Union Pacific. In 1870, he became president of the Denver and Rio Grande and completed its line westward by 1883. During the 1880s, he organized and constructed Mexican railroads, and two lines from Mexico City to the border were completed by 1890.

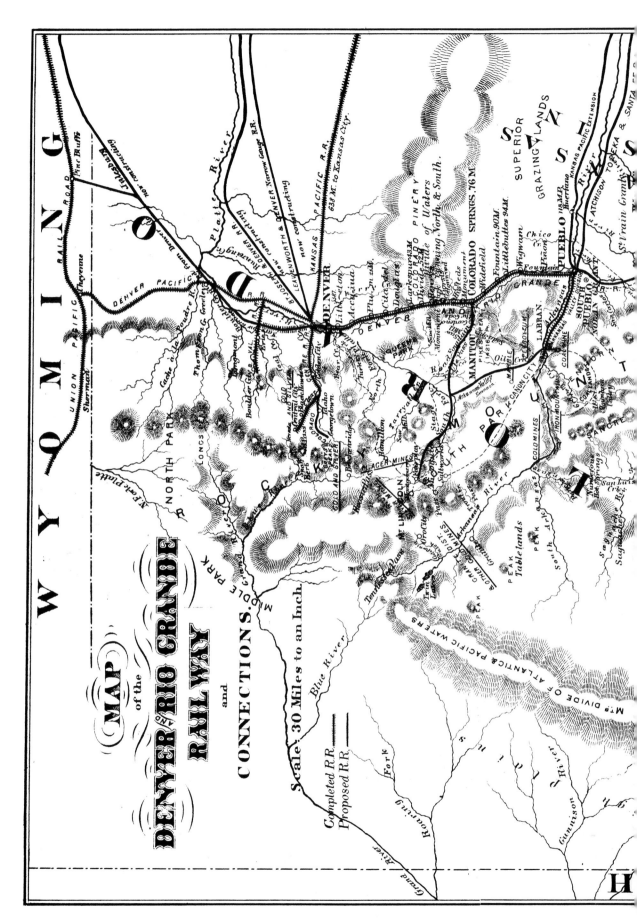

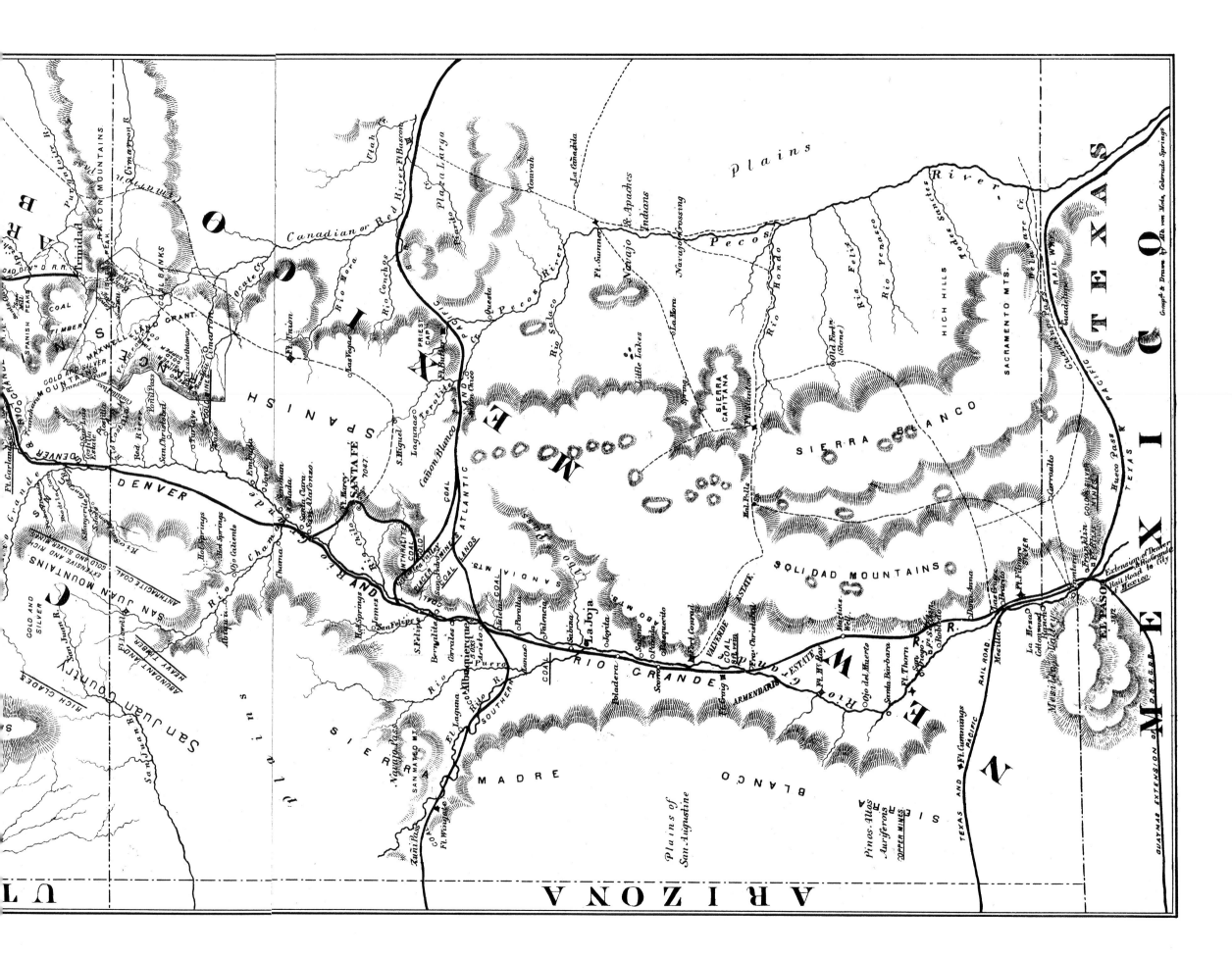

109

Great Northern

1890

56.   Poole Brothers. Great Northern Railway and proprietory lines. Chicago, 1890. 42 × 82 cm (17 × 32 in).

From the *First Annual Report of the Great Northern Railway Company* (St. Paul: The Pioneer Press, 1890) reflecting for the first time the official name change.

This colored map, first of a series to appear in future annual reports, shows the progress of the company in the north-central and northwestern states. It indicates topography, drainage, cities and towns, forts, railroad stations, and terminal points. The company's network is in red and proprietary lines are in blue and green. Dashed lines show work in progress. Connecting lines and lines in Canada are shown in solid black lines. It is interesting to observe that in North Dakota the company's tracks end short of the Canadian border. American shippers had to transfer their goods to Canadian lines. On this copy of the map, the 1890 population census figures have been added in red ink to all counties in North Dakota.

The Great Northern was founded by James J. Hill, the famous Canadian railroad executive. Under his guidance the vast system of over eight thousand miles of rails prospered without land grants or government aid. It managed to weather all financial storms and maintained an uninterrupted dividend record.

In 1878 Hill purchased the St. Paul and Pacific Railroad. The following year the properties were reorganized as the St. Paul, Minneapolis & Manitoba Railway Company. By 1881 the Manitoba company was operating 695 miles of track. The rails reached as far west as Devils Lake, North Dakota, in 1885, and two years later penetrated Montana, where connection was made with other lines operating to the Pacific Northwest.

On September 18, 1889, the name of the old Minneapolis & St. Cloud Railroad Company (chartered by the state of Minnesota in 1856 and acquired by the Hill interests in 1881) was changed to Great Northern Railway Company. In February 1890 the Great Northern took over properties of the St. Paul, Minneapolis & Manitoba, and by the end of the year was operating 3,260 miles.

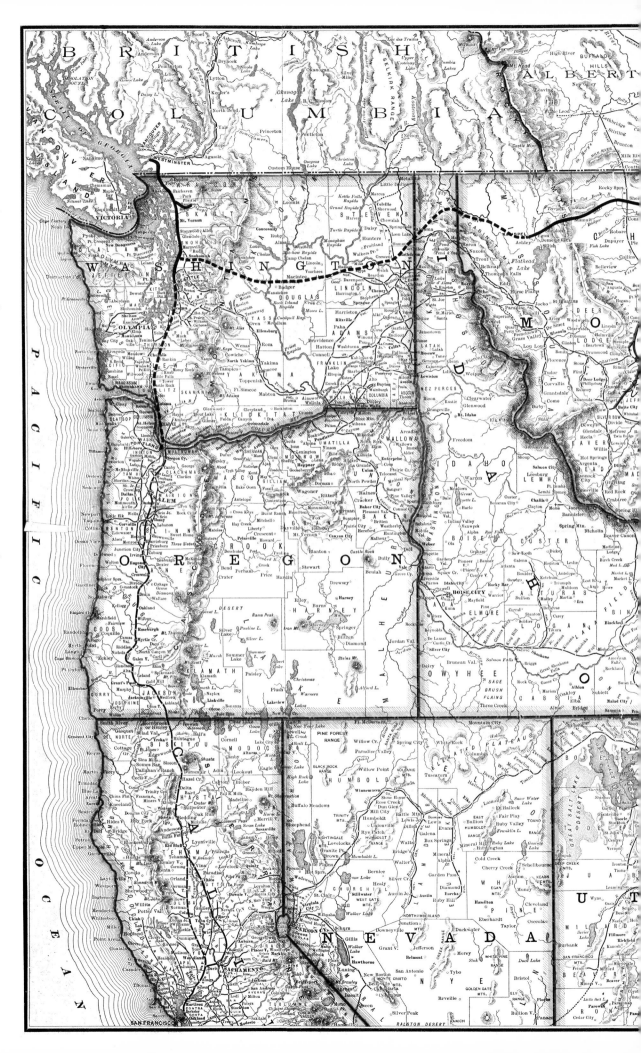

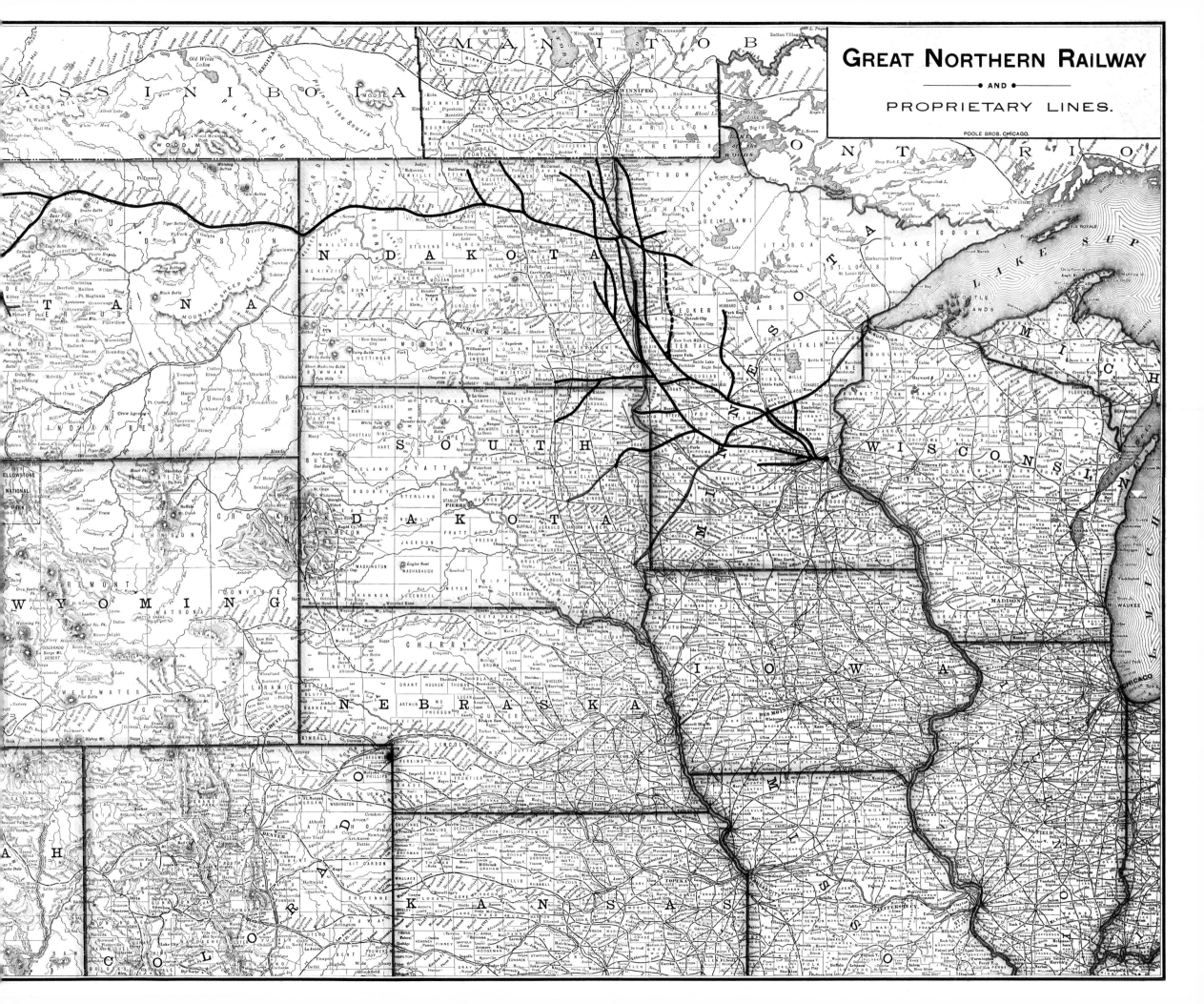

Illinois Central

1892

57. Rand McNally and Company. Map of Illinois Central R.R. Chicago, 1892. 92 × 62 cm (36 × 24 in).

"Part of the Illinois Central Railroad Depot at Chicago," 1859.

A railroad map of the central United States from the Great Lakes to the Gulf of Mexico, showing relief by hachures, rivers, cities and towns, roads, and the railroad network.

The Illinois Central was the first great railroad network projected west of the Allegheny Mountains and the first to receive lands granted by the passage of the "Illinois Central Land Grant Bill." The company pioneered the colonization and agricultural development of Illinois and the Midwest. Originally it transported coal from the Illinois and Kentucky coal mines but expanded to carry grains, livestock, fruits and vegetables, and manufactured goods. It was also a very popular passenger carrier.

The line was chartered on February 10, 1851, and opened its first fourteen-mile section from Chicago to Kensington in May 1852. It completed 706 miles of its main line from La Salle to Chicago by January 1855. It was opened to traffic along the entire network in 1856, becoming at the time the longest railroad in the World. With subsidiary lines, the system was extended outside the state in the latter part of the nineteenth century to many distant points, including Memphis, Tennessee, Vicksburg and Natchez, Mississippi, Baton Rouge, Louisiana, St. Louis, Missouri, and Albert Lea, Minnesota; and in the present century, among other places, to Birmingham, Alabama, Meridian, Mississippi, and Fort Myers, Florida.

The system became operational from Chicago, Peoria, and Springfield, Illinois; westward to Sioux Falls, South Dakota, and Omaha, Nebraska; southward to New Orleans, Louisiana, and Gulfport, Mississippi; southeastward to Tampa and Miami, Florida; eastward to Indianapolis, Indiana, and Louisville, Kentucky; and northward to Madison, Wisconsin.

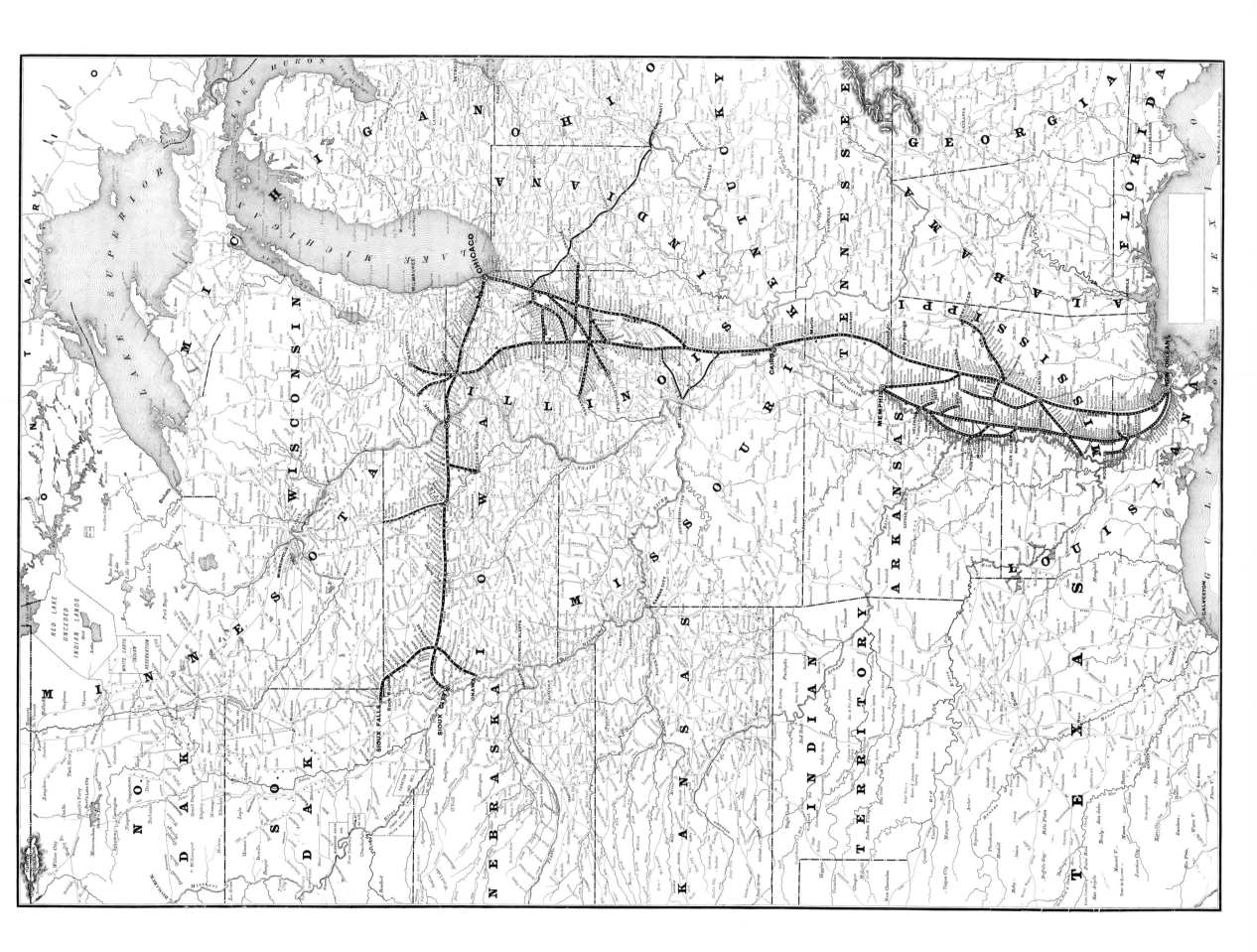

Lehigh Valley

1871

58. Sayre, Robert H. Map of the Lehigh Valley Rail Road, Penna. & N.Y. Canal & Railroad and connecting lines. 1871 Engr. by J. Schedler. Printed by Geo. Schlegel. New York, 1871. 29 × 49 cm (11½ × 19½ in).

The initiative for a railroad project in the Lehigh Valley was taken by the Philadelphia financier Edward R. Biddle, who was president of the Morris Canal. He obtained a charter, and on April 21, 1846, the Delaware, Lehigh, Schuylkill & Susquehanna Railroad Company was incorporated. The company was sold to Asa Packer, the real builder of the line, who changed its name to the Lehigh Valley Railroad Company on January 7, 1853. This line is one of the famous anthracite railroads of Pennsylvania and extends through the states of New Jersey, Pennsylvania, and New York, from the Atlantic seaboard to the Great Lakes. The main line runs from Jersey City, New Jersey, to Buffalo, New York, a distance of 442 miles, with an important branch line extending from Depew, New York, to Niagara Falls.

In 1865, under Packer's auspices, the Pennsylvania & New York Canal & Railroad Company was formed to take over the North Branch Canal and build a railroad on its bed over the entire 104 miles from Wilkes-Barre to the New York state line, and the Lehigh Valley subscribed to the capital stock of this company to aid it in completing its work as rapidly as possible. It would furnish, it was thought, an outlet for the Lehigh Valley to the North, and permit the company to find new markets for coal as its capacity for tonnage increased and the war-time demand came to an end. This line was opened all the way to Waverly, New York, on the Erie, in 1869.

This map shows relief in light brown color and rivers in light blue. It depicts Pennsylvania, most of New York, and part of New Jersey. The two main railroads appear as solid red lines and the Morris Canal, from New York City to the Delaware River, appears as a red dashed line. Connecting railroads are shown by black cross-hatched lines.

Engine on the Lehigh Valley Railroad, 1897.

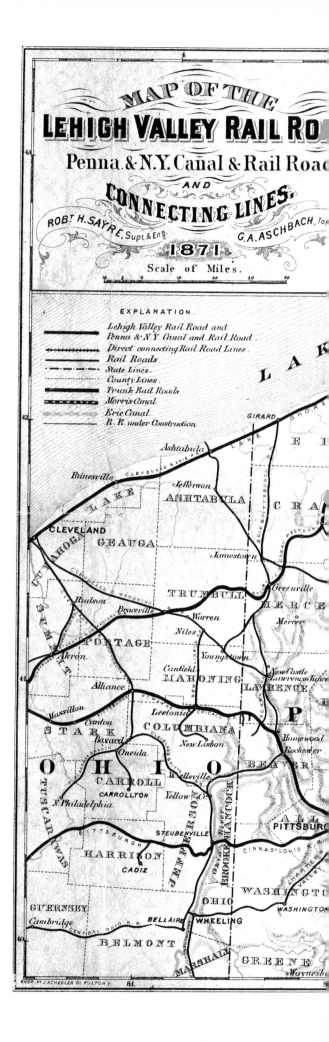

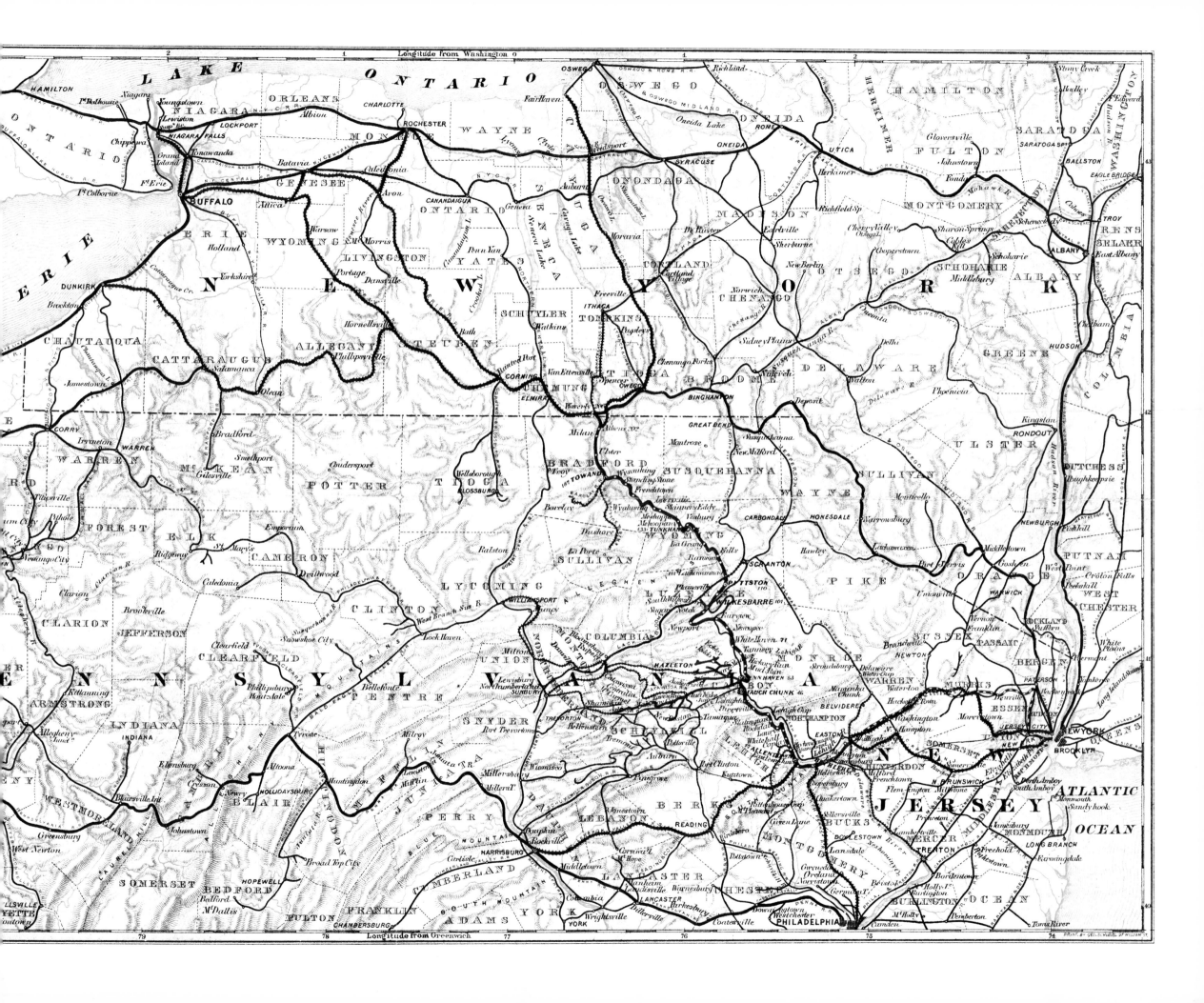

Pacific Railroad

1877

59. Williams, Henry T. New trans-continental map of the Pacific R.R. and routes of overland travel to Colorado, Nebraska, the Black Hills, Utah, Idaho, Nevada, Montana, California and the Pacific Coast. c1877. 58 × 93 cm (23 × 36½ in).

An attractive colored map of the western United States, printed by the Osborne photolithographic process, showing relief by hachures, drainage, cities and towns, stage routes, railroads completed and projected. Main lines in heavy black. Tourist and travel information, timetables, and steamship rates are printed on the verso of the map.

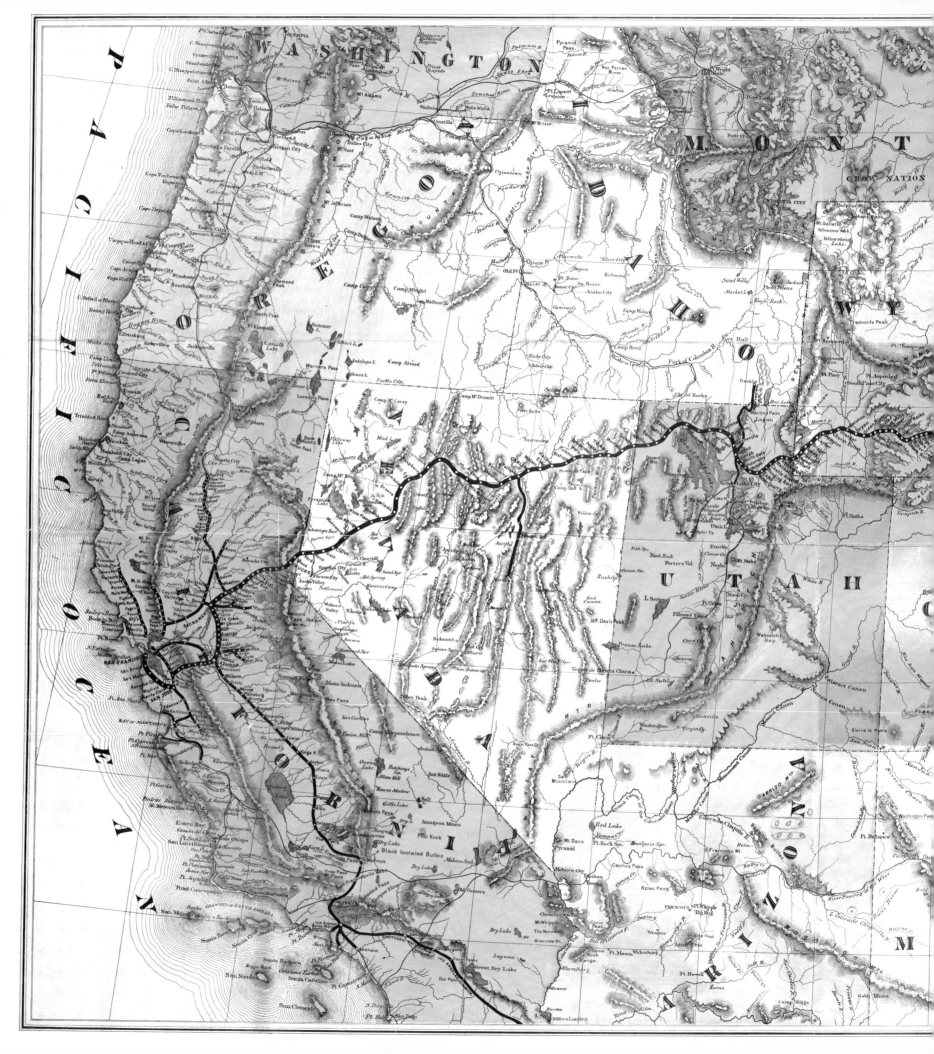

116

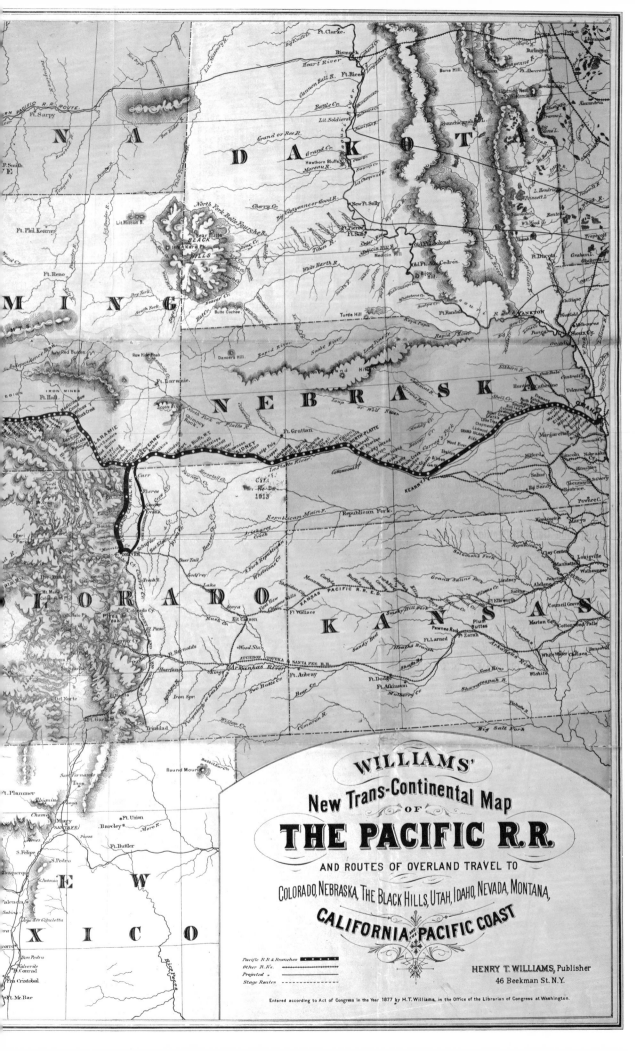

Devil's Gate Bridge, Medicine
Bow vicinity, Wyoming,
ca. 1868.

WILLIAMS'
New Trans-Continental Map
OF
THE PACIFIC R.R.
AND ROUTES OF OVERLAND TRAVEL TO
COLORADO, NEBRASKA, THE BLACK HILLS, UTAH, IDAHO, NEVADA, MONTANA,
CALIFORNIA AND PACIFIC COAST

Pacific R.R. & Branches
Other R.R's
Projected
Stage Routes

HENRY T. WILLIAMS, Publisher
46 Beekman St. N.Y.

Entered according to Act of Congress in the Year 1877 by H.T. Williams, in the Office of the Librarian of Congress at Washington.

St. Paul, Minneapolis, and Manitoba

1882

60. American Bank Note Company. The St. Paul, Minneapolis & Manitoba Railway. New York, 1882. 42 × 77 cm (17 × 30 in).

This timetable and advertising map was produced to promote settlement in the fertile wheat belt's Red River Valley and to show connections with the Canadian Pacific Railway for points in Manitoba and the Northwest Territory.

The verso of the map includes advertisements for sale of lands owned by the railroad company and for acquisition of public lands by the Homestead, Pre-emption, and Timber Culture Acts. It also promotes health and pleasure resorts for tourists.

The map indicates completed lines, lines under construction, and connections with other lines. It embraces parts of Wisconsin, Minnesota, North Dakota, and adjacent parts of Canada, and shows drainage, in blue, relief by hachures, townships and counties, cities and towns, railroad stations and junction points, forts, and Indian reservations. An inset shows through lines and connections to Chicago, Sioux City, and Winnipeg.

This company was organized in 1879 by James J. Hill, the famous railroad executive who became president of the line in 1882, the date of this map. The line was consolidated into the Great Northern System in 1890. It was known as the Red River Line and traversed the park region to the new Northwest.

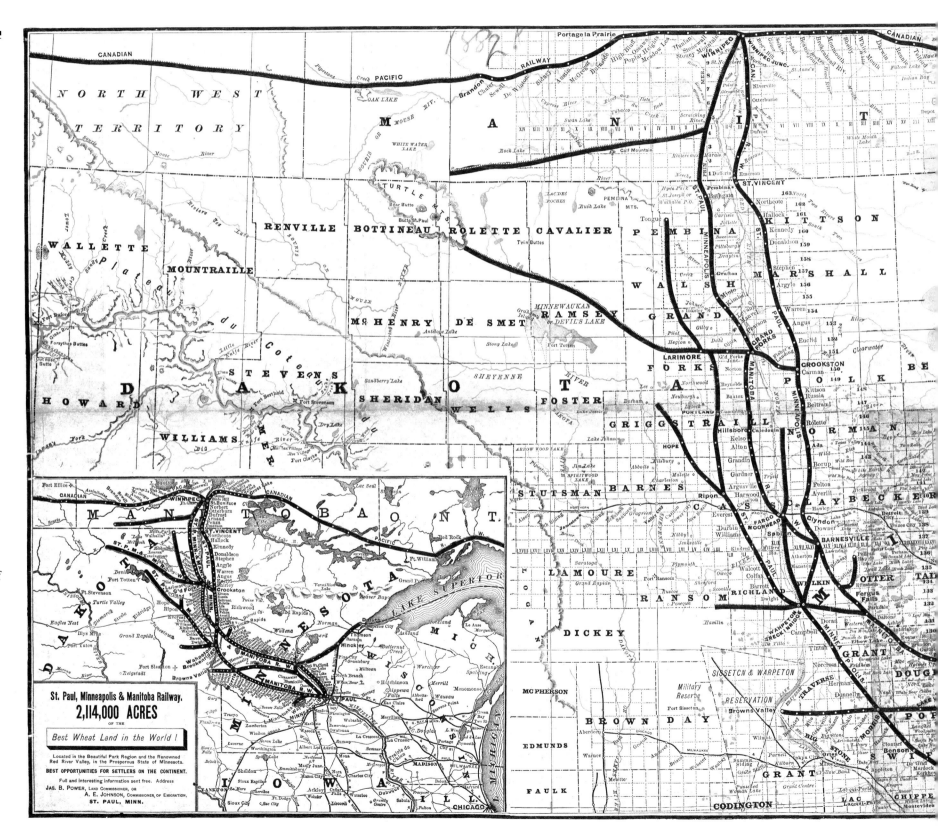

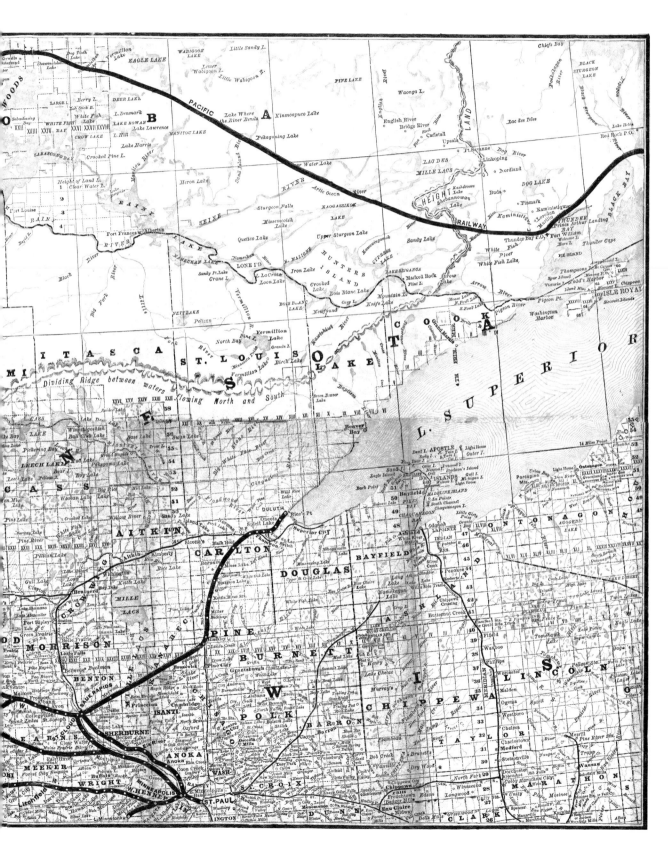

Dormitory cars for the construction crews of the St. Paul, Minneapolis, & Manitoba Railroad, sometime in the 1880s. Courtesy of Great Northern Railroad.

"Clear Spring Farm." From Frederick W. Beers's *County Atlas of Lebanon, Pennsylvania.*

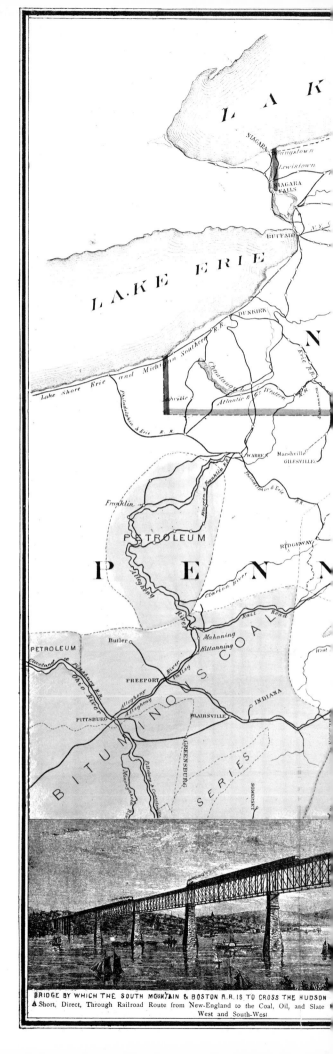

BRIDGE BY WHICH THE SOUTH MOUNTAIN & BOSTON R.R. IS TO CROSS THE HUDSON
A Short, Direct, Through Railroad Route from New-England to the Coal, Oil, and Slate West and South-West.

South Mountain and Boston

1875

61. Price, R. M., Jr. Map of the South Mountain & Boston Railroad & connections showing territory passed through, railroads & canals crossed or connected, together with mineral & geographical features of country passed through. New York, Ferd. Mayer, Genl Lith., 1875. 42 × 67 cm (16 × 26 in).

A hand-colored map of the northeastern states showing the mineral and mining areas of Pennsylvania. Shows major mountain ridges by hachures, drainage, major cities and towns, anthracite and bituminous coal regions, iron, zinc, slate and petroleum deposits, and the named railroads serving and connecting these regions with Boston, New York, and Philadelphia. Indicates connections to the narrow-gauge Lebanon and Pine Grove Rail Road serving the famous Cornwall ore banks of South Mountain, which are further identified on the map as "Immense Deposits of Iron."

The map appears in Frederick W. Beers, *County Atlas of Lebanon Pennsylvania* (Philadelphia: F. A. Davis, 1875), in which there is a historical sketch of the railroad and information describing the benefits of this line to Lebanon County. It also appears in the *New Illustrated Atlas of Westmoreland Co., Pennsylvania* (Reading, Pa.: A.M. Davis, 1876). The line began its construction near Jonestown to tap the rich and fertile agricultural and mining regions of Lebanon Valley.

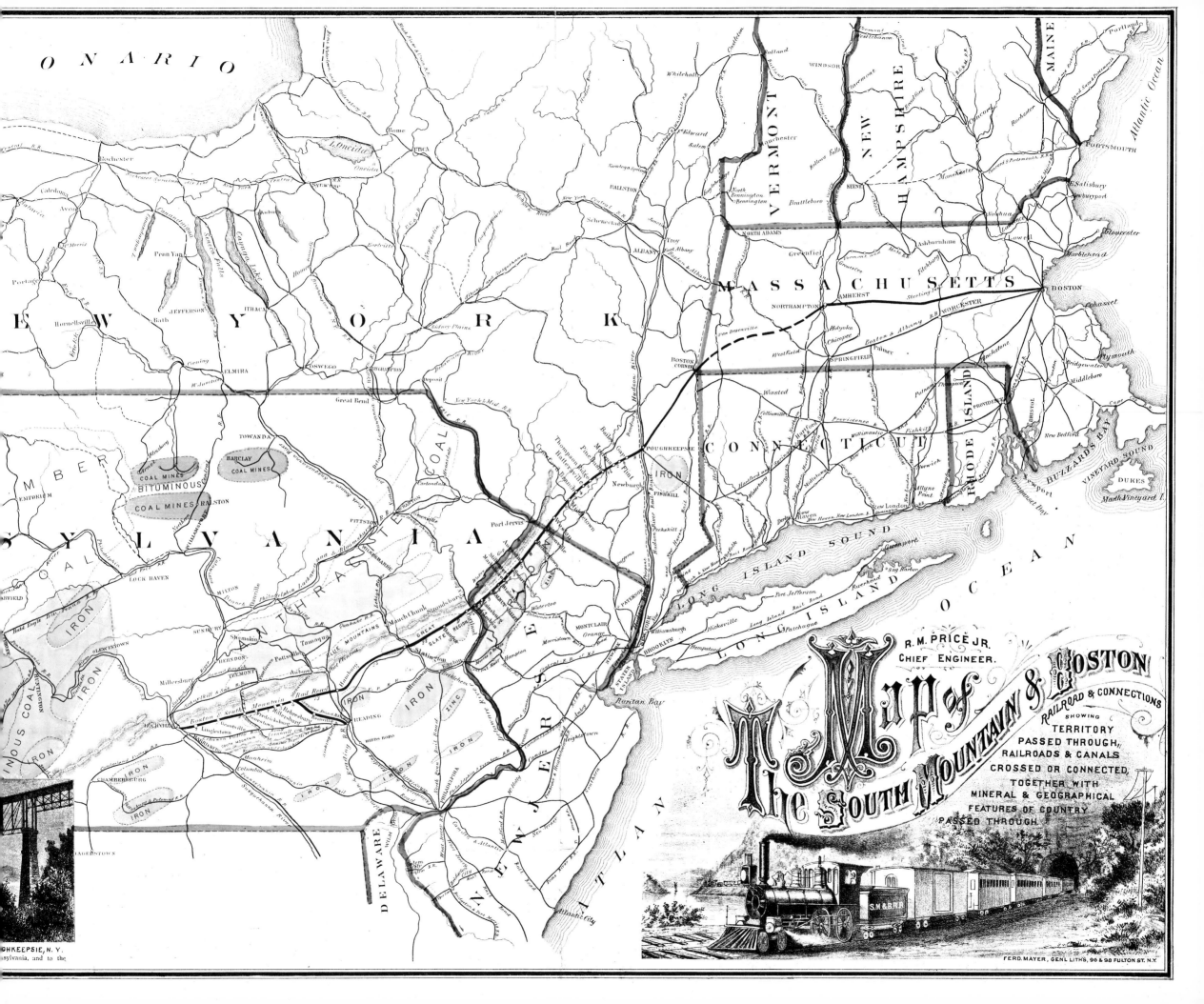

Map of The South Mountain & Boston

R. M. PRICE JR.
CHIEF ENGINEER.

Railroad & Connections

SHOWING
TERRITORY
PASSED THROUGH,
RAILROADS & CANALS
CROSSED OR CONNECTED,
TOGETHER WITH
MINERAL & GEOGRAPHICAL
FEATURES OF COUNTRY
PASSED THROUGH.

FERD. MAYER, GENL LITHS, 96 & 98 FULTON ST. N.Y.

Seaboard Air Line

1896

62. Rand McNally and Company. Map of the
Seaboard Air Line and its principal connections north,
south, east & west. 1896. Chicago, 1896. c1895. 27 × 35
cm (11 × 14 in).

The map shows relief by hachures,
drainage, cities and towns, and the railroad
network emphasizing the main line. Published
with Stanley G. Fowler's *Farms and Farm
Lands Along the Seaboard Air Line* (Portsmouth, Va.: General Passenger Department,
1896).

This uncolored map of the eastern
United States, accompanied by a promotional
booklet, was published to encourage settlement along the main line and its tributary
lines in Virginia, North and South Carolina,
and Georgia. Its aim was to attract workers in
the manufacturing, lumbering, quarrying, farming, and cattle raising occupations.

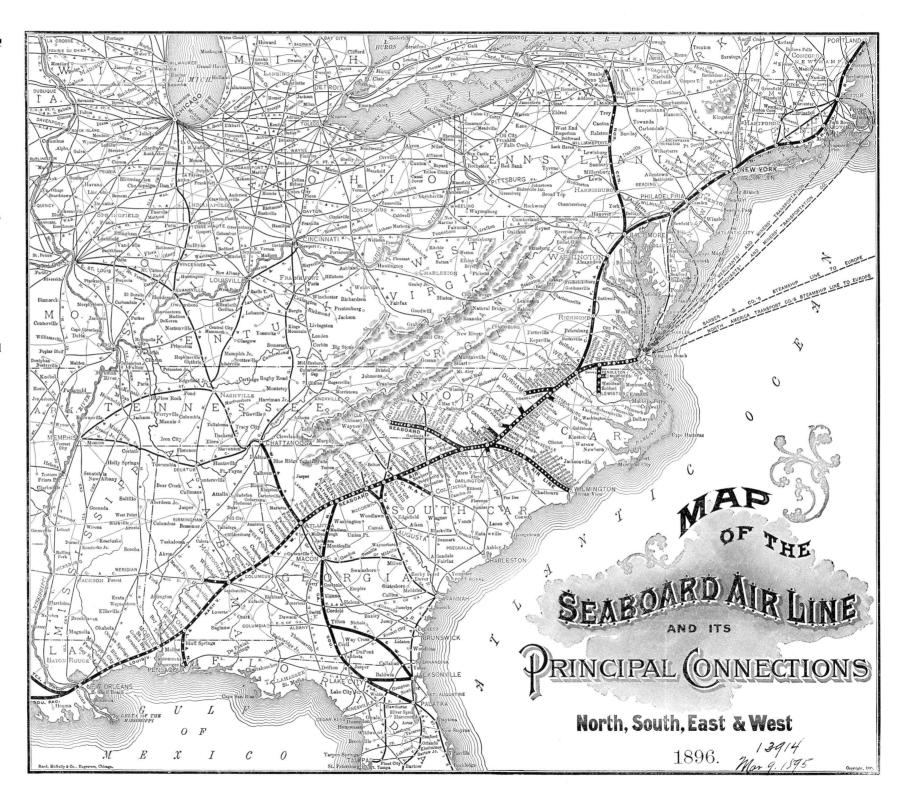

MAP OF THE SEABOARD AIR LINE AND ITS PRINCIPAL CONNECTIONS North, South, East & West 1896.

Texas and Pacific

1873

63. Colton (G. W. and C. B.) and Company. Map of the state of Texas showing the line and lands of the Texas and Pacific Railway reserved and donated by the State of Texas. 1873. New York, 1873. 47 × 60 cm (18½ × 23½ in).

Colored map which shows relief by hachures, drainage, cities and towns, counties, railroads, and the land grant. Includes an inset map of the Continental United States showing the Texas & Pacific Railway and its major connections.

The main map depicts the extent of the 14 million acres of land granted to the Texas and Pacific Railway in the state of Texas and indicates that another 15 million are available in Arizona, California, and New Mexico. The main lines are shown in red and connecting lines in blue. Includes a table of distances and the 1870 census of population by counties.

This line was formerly known as the Southern Pacific and was sometimes called the Memphis and El Paso Road. It began at Shreveport, Louisiana, in 1858, reached Marshall, Texas, in 1859, Longview in 1870, Dallas in August 1873, and Fort Worth in July 1876. In 1873 a section of the northern branch of this road was opened from Sherman to Brookston (shown as Brookville on this map). In March of 1875, the line reached Paris and Clarkville in July, and Texarkana in August.

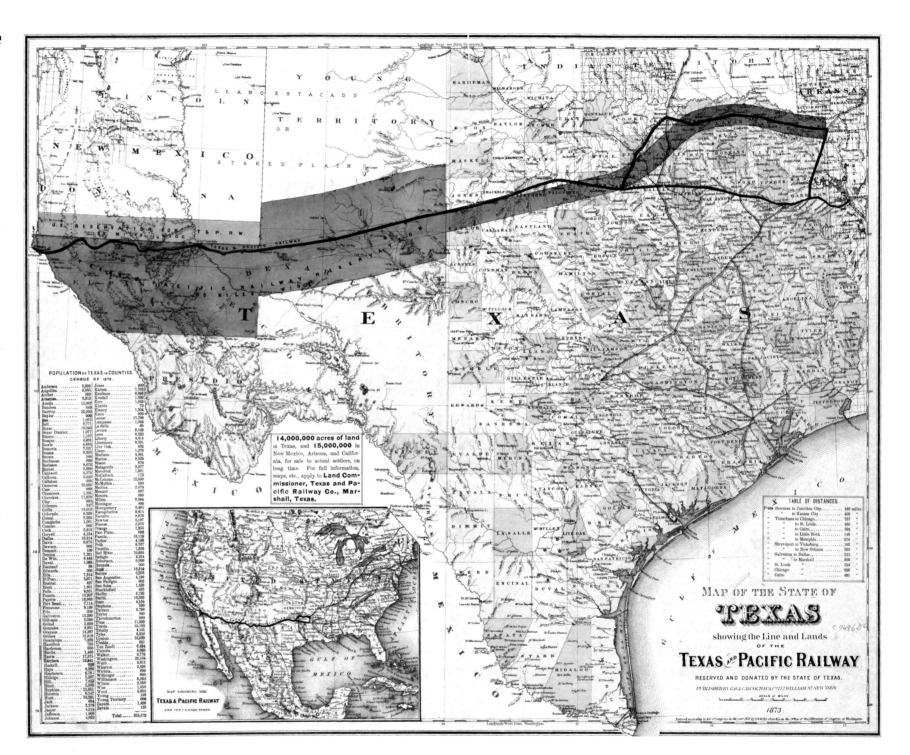

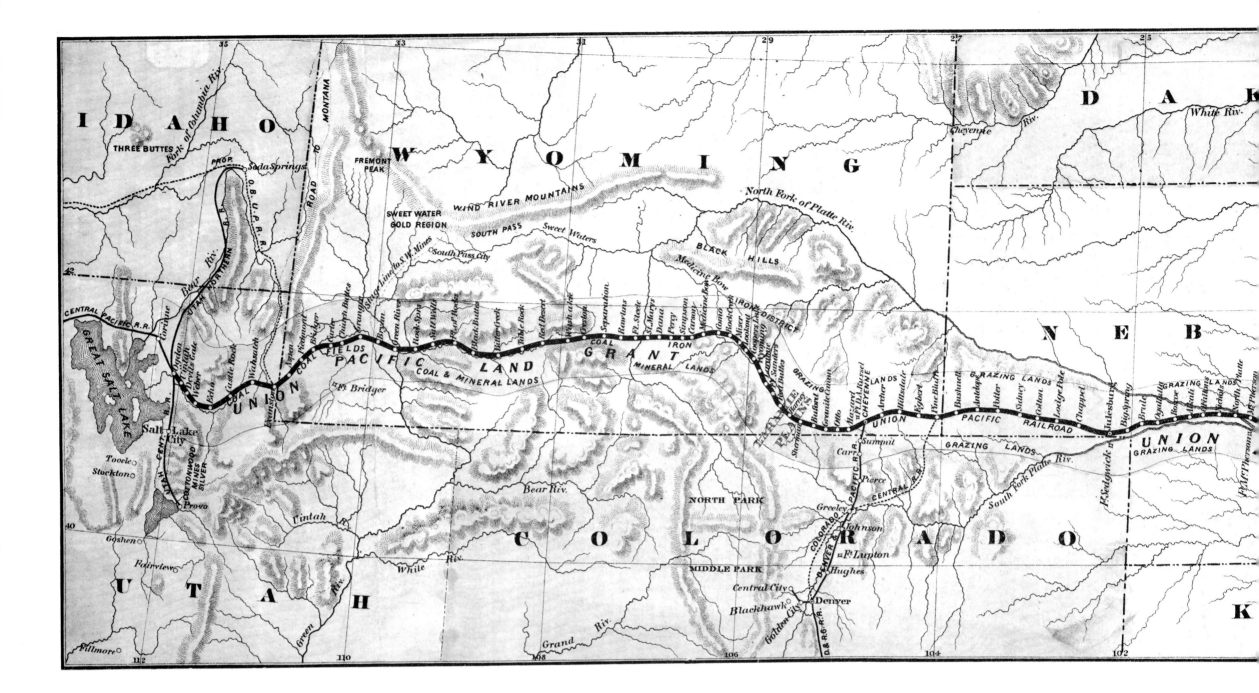

Union Pacific

1872

64. National Railway Publishing Company. Map of the land grant & connections of the Union Pacific Railroad, 1037 miles of road, 12,000,000 acres of land. 1872. Thos. L. Kimball, General Ticket Agent. O. F. Davis, Land Commissioner, Omaha. Philadelphia, 1872. 18 × 70 cm (7 × 27½ in).

A strip map stretching from Chicago to Great Salt Lake, Utah, showing railroad connections and the land grant of the Union Pacific between Omaha, Nebraska, and the lake. Indicates the path of the Union Pacific tracks and its stations, coal and mineral lands, and agricultural and grazing lands. Indicates stage line connections from Bryan, Wyoming, to the Sweetwater gold region in the Wind River Mountains, Wyoming.

On July 1, 1862, the Union Pacific Railroad Company was created by the Pacific Railroad Act. Ground was broken at Omaha in December 1863, and the first rail was laid in July 1865. Thereafter, despite the primitive construction methods available and numerous attacks by Indians, progress was rapid. On

May 10, 1869, Union Pacific construction forces met those of the Central Pacific at Promontory, Utah, to complete the country's first transcontinental railroad. The golden spike that symbolized completion of the line is owned by Stanford University and is on permanent exhibition there.

Although Council Bluffs, Iowa, was designated by President Abraham Lincoln on November 17, 1863, as the railroad's eastern terminus, train service between that city and Omaha was not available until the completion of the first railroad bridge across the Missouri River in 1872. Prior to that time freight and passengers were ferried across the river. The original bridge was replaced by a double-track bridge in 1887.

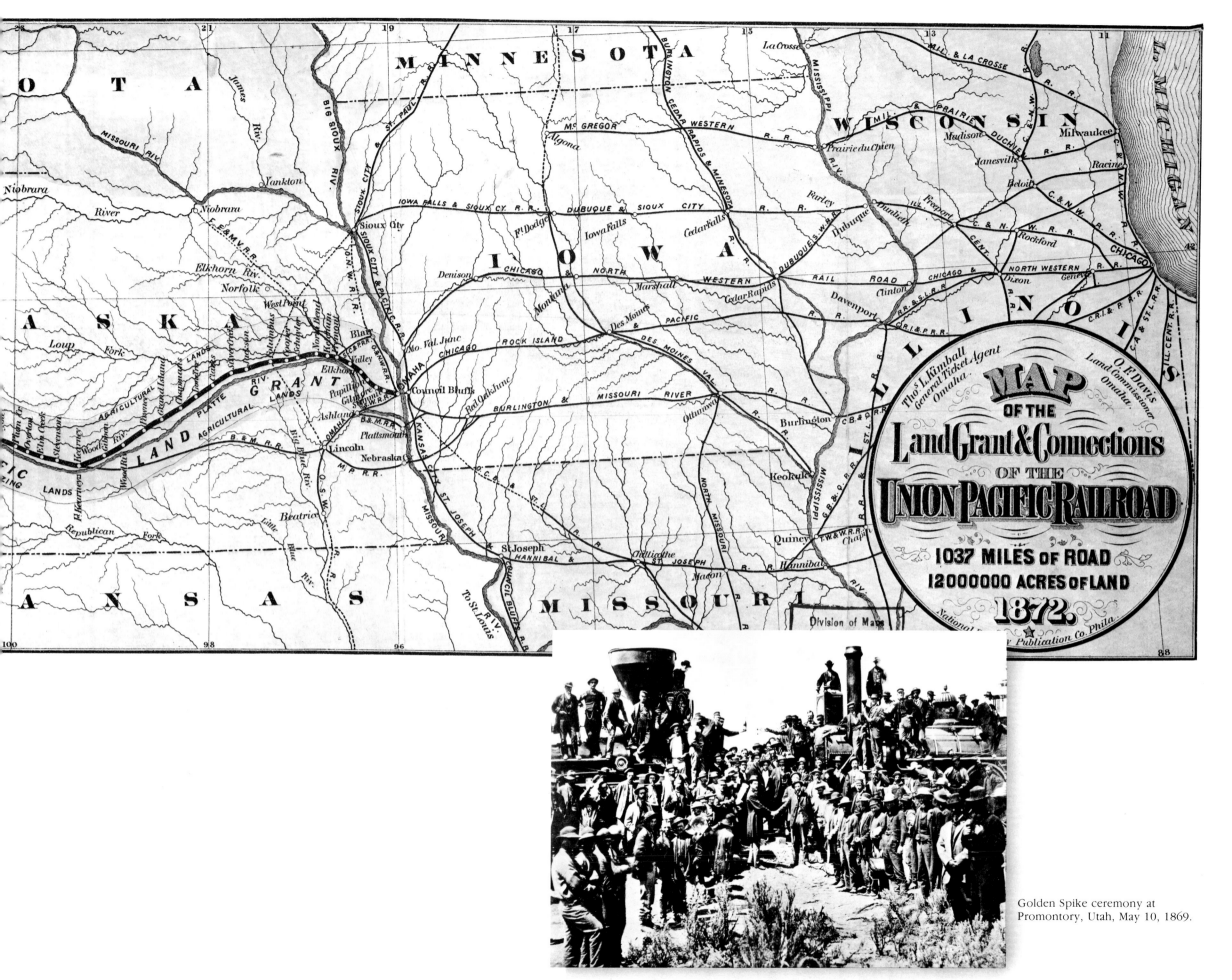

Golden Spike ceremony at
Promontory, Utah, May 10, 1869.

Union Pacific

1900

65. Rand McNally and Company. The Union Pacific system of railroad and steamship lines. 1900. Chicago, 1900. 48 × 66 cm (19 × 26 in).

Map of the western United States showing relief by hachures, drainage, cities and towns, and the railroad network coded by color to show the Union Pacific (red), Oregon Short Line (blue), Oregon Railroad and Navigation Company and its steamship lines (orange), Leavenworth, Kansas and Western Railway (black), and connections (thin black). Shows lines as reorganized by Edward H. Harriman after the business depression of 1893. It was incorporated again in 1897 and assumed operation February 1, 1898.

At the time of its meeting with the Central Pacific, the Union Pacific consisted of a single line extending from Omaha westward for 1,086 miles. The line began to grow quickly, however, absorbing smaller lines and building additional tracks. Early financing was obtained through the Credit Mobilier of America. In January 1880, a new federal corporation, the Union Pacific Railway Company, was formed by consolidating the Union Pacific Railway Company, the Kansas Pacific Railway Company, and the Denver Pacific Railway & Telegraph Company. The system had expanded to 7,691 miles of line by 1893. That year, as the result of severe competition, drought, crop failures, and the panic of 1893, the railroad was unable to meet its fixed charges and was placed in the hands of receivers. The properties of the Union Pacific Railway Company were sold at foreclosure in November 1897, and title to the railroad passed to the present Union Pacific Railroad Company, a Utah corporation.

Soon after the new company was organized, Edward R. Harriman, one of the participants in the reorganization, emerged as the dominant figure in its management. Under his direction the property underwent extensive rehabilitation which included the acquisition of modern locomotives and cars, the elimination of curves and grades, the replacement of wooden bridges by steel and masonry spans, and the installation of hundreds of miles of double track.

Union Pacific Railroad at Weber Canyon, Utah, in the 1870s.

"Building the Union Pacific Railroad in Nebraska." Wood engraving, 1867.

126

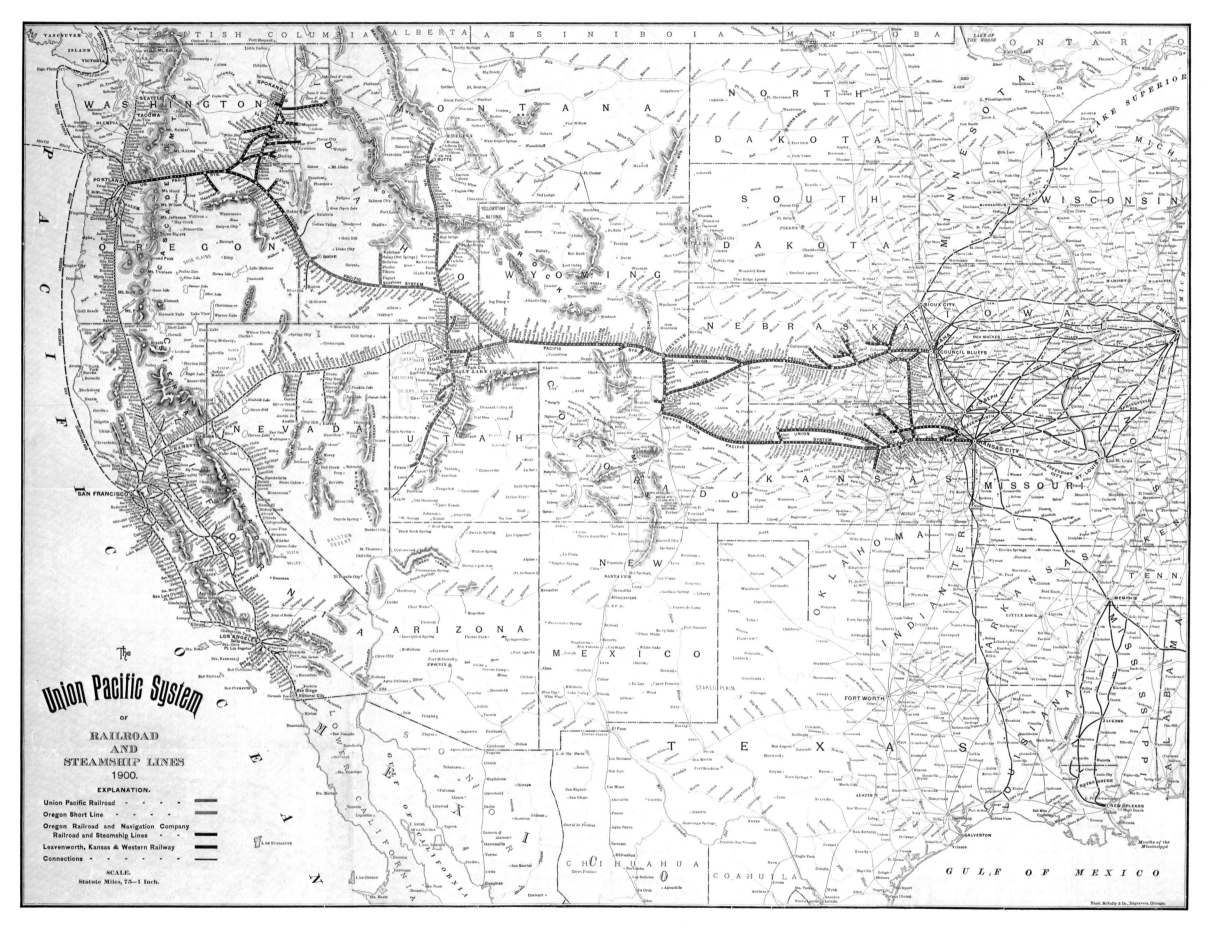

The

Union Pacific System

OF

RAILROAD
AND
STEAMSHIP LINES
1900.

EXPLANATION.

Union Pacific Railroad ....
Oregon Short Line ....
Oregon Railroad and Navigation Company
Railroad and Steamship Lines .
Leavenworth, Kansas & Western Railway
Connections ....

SCALE.
Statute Miles, 75-1 Inch.

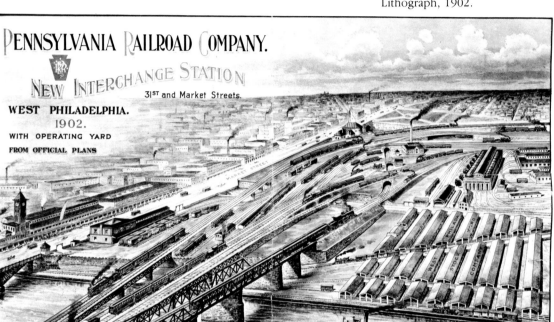

Pennsylvania Railroad Company.
New Interchange Station.
Lithograph, 1902.

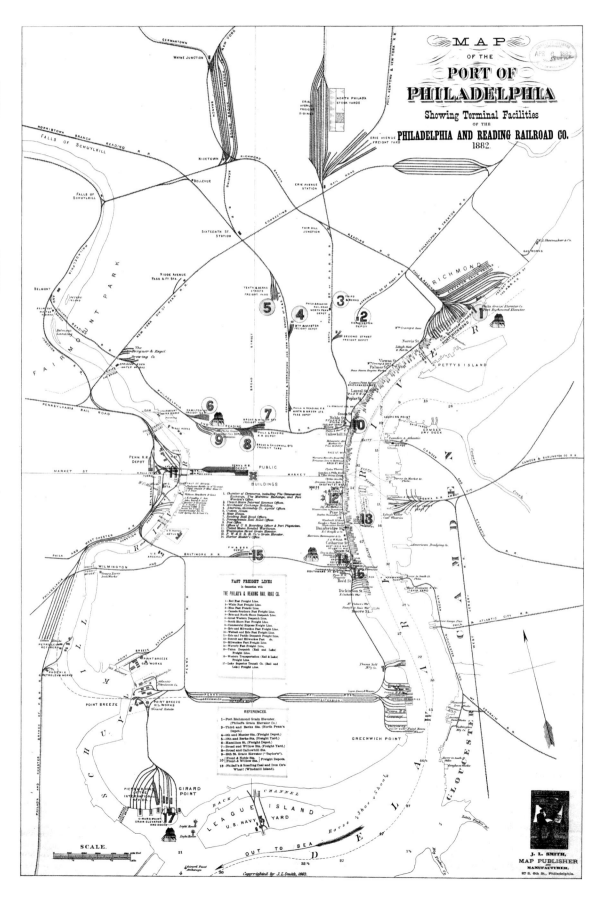

Philadelphia and Reading

1882

66. Smith, J. L. Map of part of Philadelphia showing terminal facilities of the Philadelphia and Reading Railroad Co. Philadelphia, 1882. 64 × 44 cm (25 × 17 in).

A skeleton map of Philadelphia and Camden, New Jersey, showing in detail the railroad, steamship, and ferry terminal facilities, depots and wharves, and the track alignment and connections within the cities. The company's properties are indicated in blue and are keyed by reference numbers. The map also shows gas works, oil refineries, iron works, grain elevators, U.S. Navy facilities, water works, and names of connecting railroads. The shipping channels and depths in the Delaware River are also identified.

The publishing company that produced this map, J. L. Smith, which began making maps in 1860, continues in business today under the proprietorship of Michel B. Patterson.

The line was incorporated on April 4, 1833, and later became the Reading Railway Systems, one of the principal anthracite carriers in the world.

Boston and Vicinity

1865

67.   Chase, J. G. Rail road map showing the street rail road routes in and leading from Boston, with the terminus of each road in suburban cities or towns. Boston: J. H. Bufford, Lith., 1865. 64 × 55 cm (25 × 21½ in).

An outline map of the city and vicinity showing drainage, town boundaries, and major streets. The steam railroads are indicated by dashed black and white lines, and the street railroads by solid red lines, with their names printed along the lines. Distances are given in quarter-mile circles from the city center.

The central city area delimited in red on this map appears in great detail in a companion map (not reproduced here) entitled *Rail Road Map of All Street and Steam Railroads in Boston and Vicinity, 1865.* This map is reduced from the city engineer's large-scale plan of 1864, on which detailed railroad information has been overprinted in red. It is not legible in reproduced form.

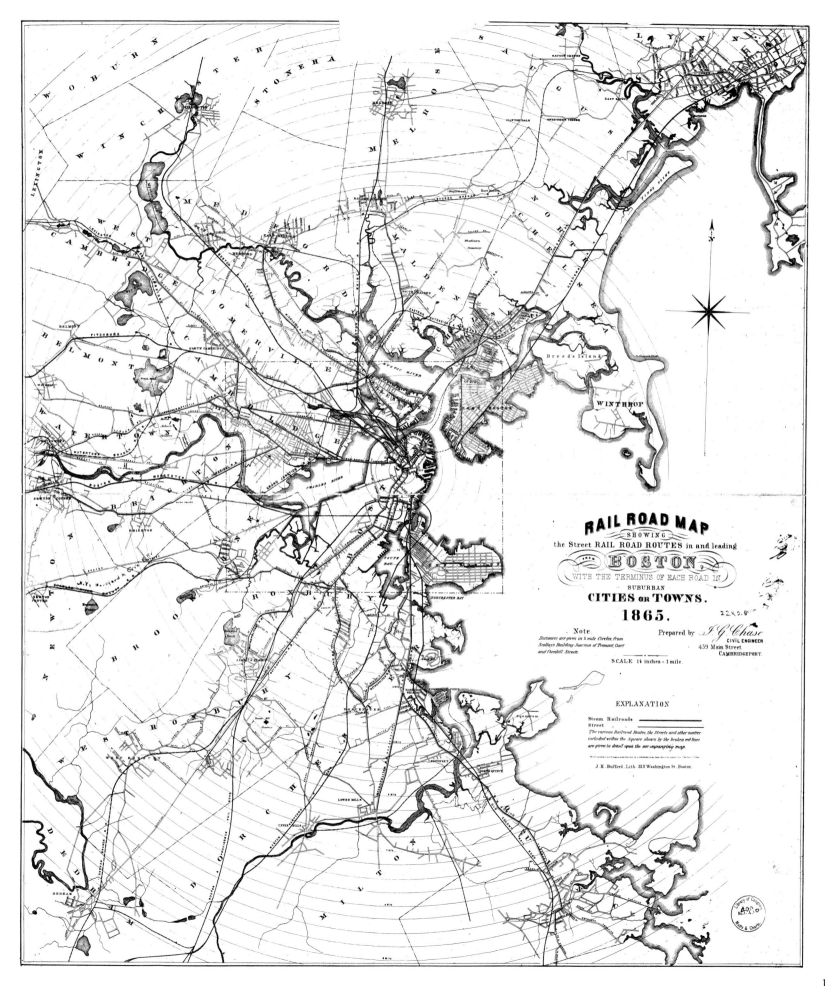

Boston and Maine

1905

68. Walker, George H. Plan of Boston & Maine R. R. export terminals, Boston. Boston, 1905. 70 × 100 cm (27 × 29 in).

A spectacular colored lithographic bird's-eye-view map of Boston's shipyards, identifying individual buildings and facilities. It shows a busy and prosperous harbor and railroad terminal. The view is toward the west, from across the East Boston docks. Colored flags of eleven world shipping lines using the harbor and port facilities decorate the top of the map. The Boston and Maine terminals are prominently displayed and labeled. A useful table provides the warehouse floor space area, grain elevator capacity, and acreage of terminal facilities.

This is a unique adaptation of the popular cartographic form used to depict North American cities and towns during the nineteenth and early twentieth centuries. Panoramic, bird's-eye-view, or perspective maps are representations of cities, portrayed as if viewed from above at an oblique angle. Although not generally drawn to scale, they show street patterns, individual buildings, and major landscape features in perspective.

Preparation of panoramic maps involved a great amount of painstakingly detailed labor. For each project a frame or projection was developed, showing in perspective the pattern of streets. The artist then walked the streets, sketching buildings, trees, and other features to present a complete and accurate landscape as though seen from the air.

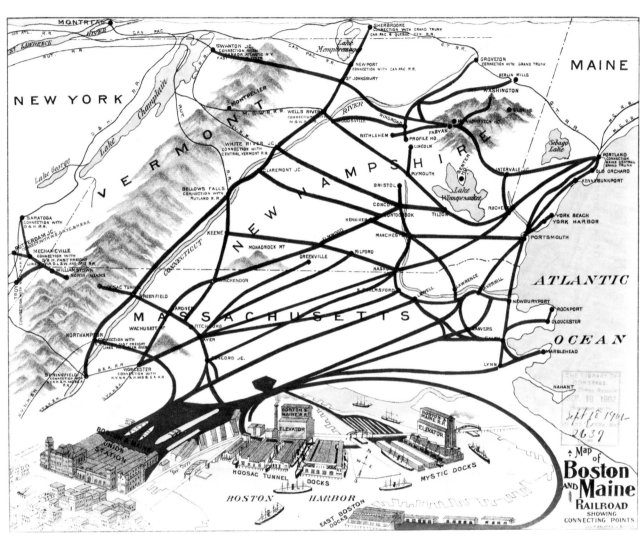

"Map of Boston & Maine Railroad." Illustration for back of railroad stationery, entered for copyright 1902.

Preparation and sale of nineteenth-century panoramas were motivated by civic pride and the desire of the city fathers to encourage commercial growth. Many views were prepared for and endorsed by chambers of commerce and other civic organizations and were used as advertisements of a city's commercial and residential potential.

Advances in lithography, photolithography, photoengraving and chromolithography, which made possible inexpensive and multiple copies, coupled with a prosperous populace willing to purchase prints, made panoramic maps popular wall hangings during America's Victorian Age.

130

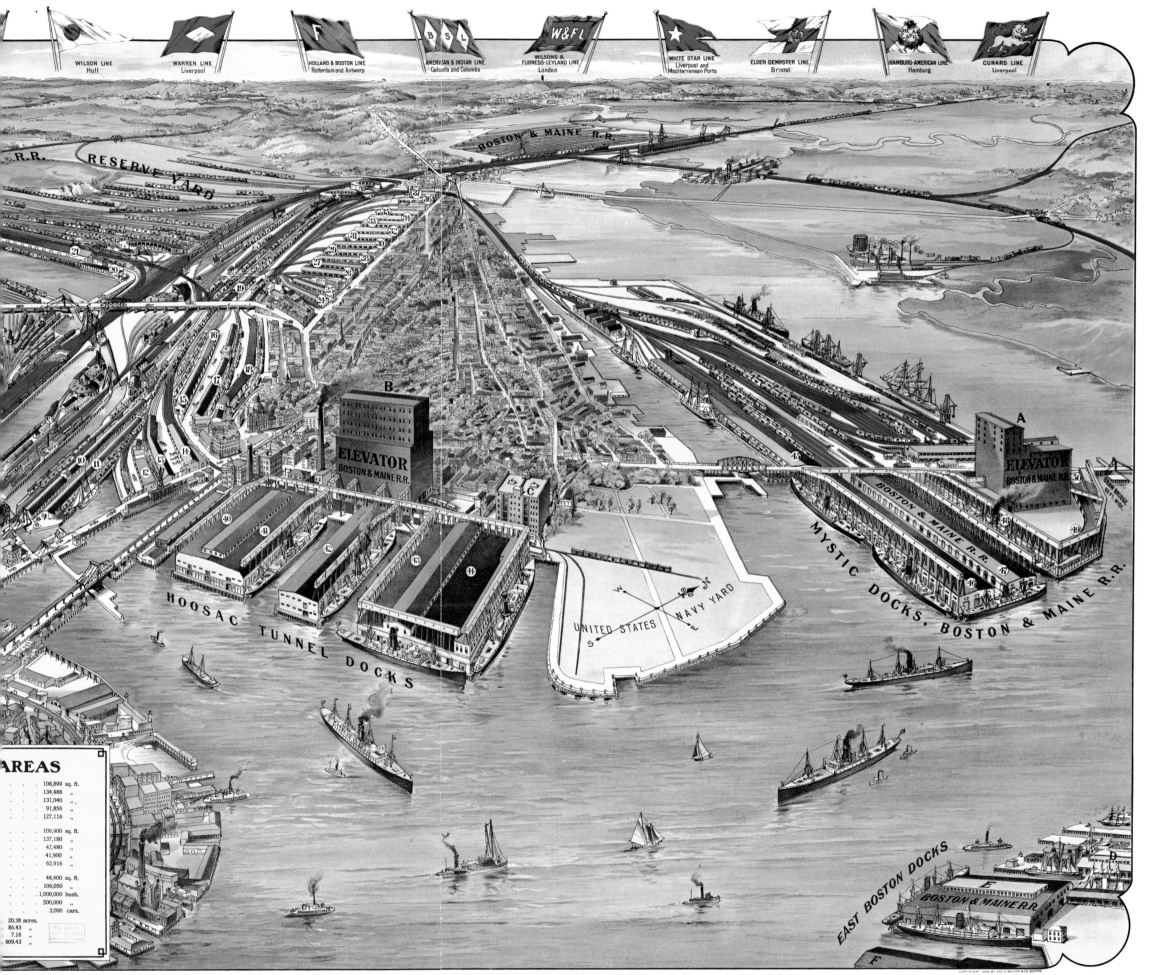

WILSON LINE
Hull

WARREN LINE
Liverpool

HOLLAND & BOSTON LINE
Rotterdam and Antwerp

AMERICAN & INDIAN LINE
Calcutta and Colombo

WILSONS &
FURNESS-LEYLAND LINE
London

WHITE STAR LINE
Liverpool and
Mediterranean Ports

ELDER DEMPSTER LINE
Bristol

HAMBURG-AMERICAN LINE
Hamburg

CUNARD LINE
Liverpool

BOSTON & MAINE R.R.

RESERVE YARD

ELEVATOR
BOSTON & MAINE R.R.

ELEVATOR
BOSTON & MAINE R.R.

MYSTIC DOCKS, BOSTON & MAINE R.R.

BOSTON & MAINE R.R.

HOOSAC TUNNEL DOCKS

UNITED STATES NAVY YARD

EAST BOSTON DOCKS

BOSTON & MAINE R.R.

AREAS

108,899 sq. ft.
134,486 "
131,040 "
91,856 "
127,116 "

109,900 sq. ft.
137,180 "
42,480 "
41,900 "
62,916 "

48,400 sq. ft.
106,050 "
1,000,000 bush.
500,000 "
3,000 cars.

20.38 acres.
86.43 "
7.16 "
609.43 "

PLAN OF BOSTON & MAINE R.R. EXPORT TERMINALS, BOSTON.

Boston Terminal Facilities

1906

69. Walker, George H. Map showing the terminal facilities of Boston. Boston, 1906. 66 × 90 cm (26 × 35 in).

Street map of Boston and vicinity over-printed in colors to show lines and facilities of the Boston & Maine (red), Boston & Albany (blue), New York, New Haven and Hartford, and the Union Freight (green). Various symbols indicate terminal companies and businesses. Important buildings, hotels, schools, parks, play grounds, and yacht clubs are indicated. At the bottom center of the map the "American League Baseball Grounds" are identified. A table lists railroad connections to wharves and steamship lines.

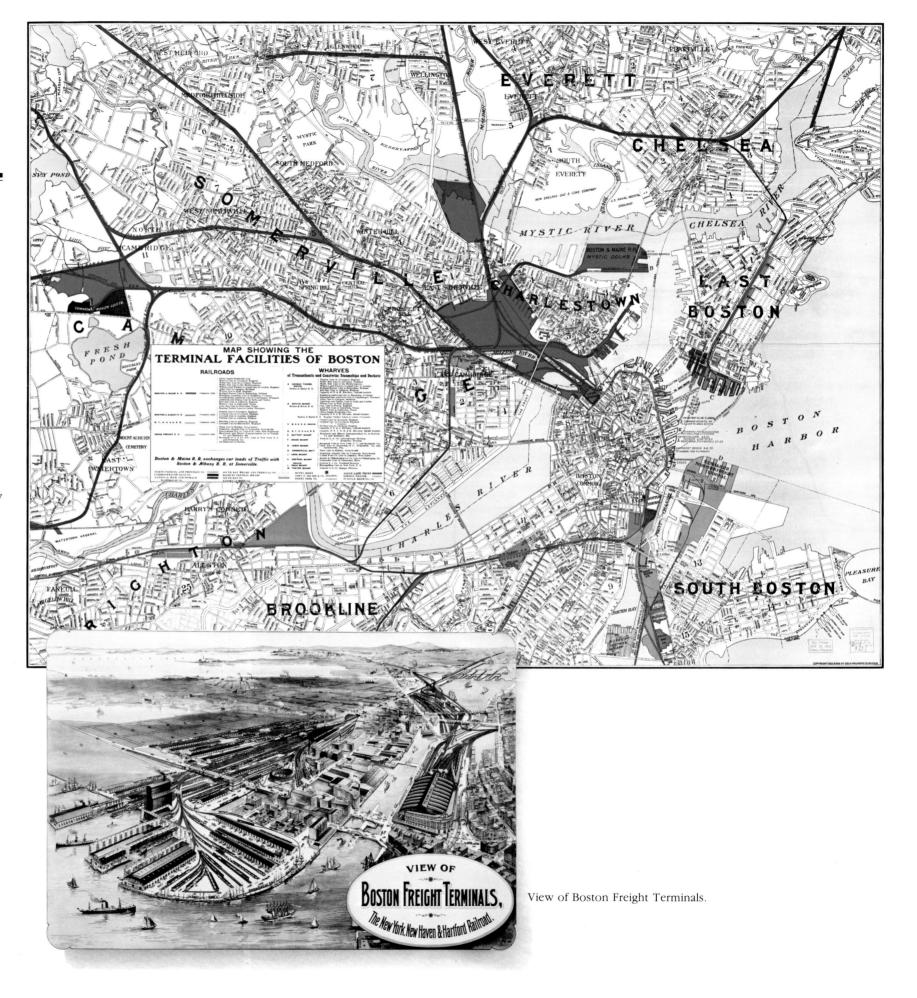

View of Boston Freight Terminals.

132

Chicago and Calumet

1887

70.   Snyder (L. M.) & Company. Map showing location of the Chicago and Calumet Terminal Railway around Chicago, Illinois. Chicago, 1887. 62 × 53 cm (24½ × 20½ in).

Map of Chicago and vicinity accentuating in red the tracks of the Calumet line and its terminals. Rivers, lakes, parks, and boulevards are emphasized. The major railroad network is overprinted in blue, and roads, streets, and tollgates are shown. Distances are measured from the courthouse in one-mile concentric circles. Shows township and range lines, cities, towns, and railroad stations, and names counties.

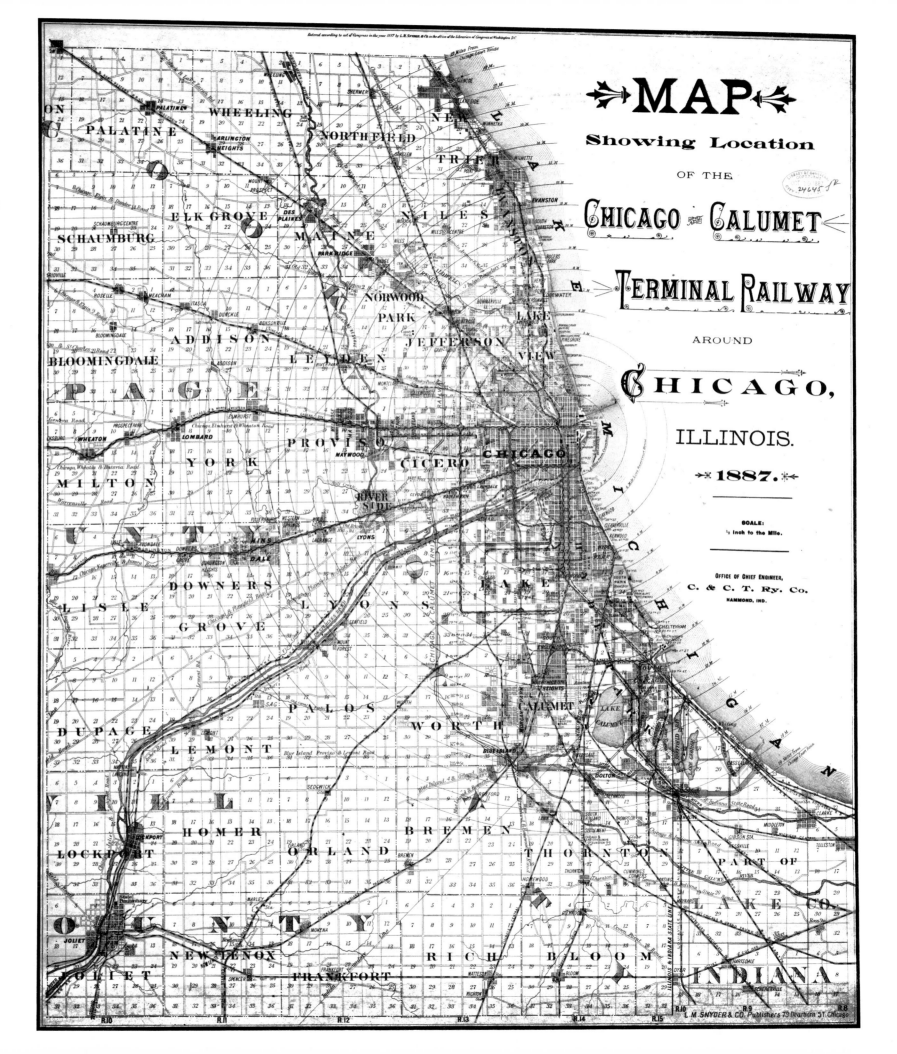

Chicago and North-Western

1902

71. Walker, George H. Terminals of the Chicago and North-Western Railway at Chicago. Boston, 1902. 66 × 102 cm (26 × 40 in).

A striking, colored, lithographic panorama of central Chicago, looking toward the northwest as if from a point above Grant Park. The map shows the rail lines in red and emphasizes the company's properties. The offices and passenger and freight stations are keyed by number to a tabulation in an inset map of the city, which is located in the lower left of the main map. Appearing on the panorama are names of major streets and parks, prominent buildings, steam and elevated railroads, and shipping and manufacturing facilities.

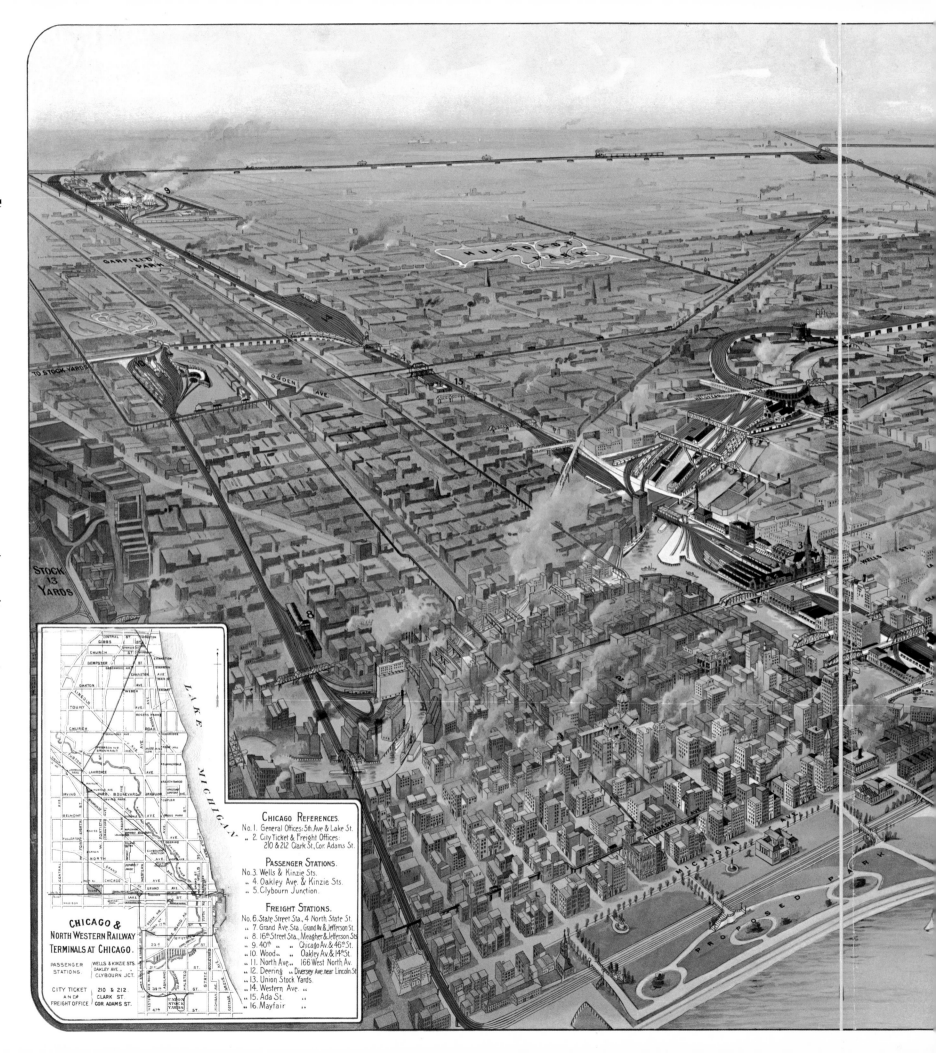

CHICAGO &
NORTH WESTERN RAILWAY
TERMINALS AT CHICAGO.

| PASSENGER STATIONS. | WELLS & KINZIE STS. OAKLEY AVE. CLYBOURN JCT. |
| CITY TICKET AND Cº FREIGHT OFFICE | 210 & 212 CLARK ST. COR ADAMS ST. |

CHICAGO REFERENCES.
No.1. General Offices: 5th Ave & Lake St.
" 2. City Ticket & Freight Offices:
210 & 212 Clark St, Cor. Adams St.

PASSENGER STATIONS.
No.3. Wells & Kinzie Sts.
" 4. Oakley Ave. & Kinzie Sts.
" 5. Clybourn Junction.

FREIGHT STATIONS.
No.6. State Street Sta., 4 North State St.
" 7. Grand Ave. Sta., Grand Av. & Jefferson St.
" 8. 16th Street Sta., Meagher & Jefferson Sts.
" 9. 40th " .. Chicago Ave. & 46th St.
" 10. Wood " .. Oakley Av. & 14th St.
" 11. North Ave. .. 166 West North Av.
" 12. Deering " Diversey Ave. near Lincoln St.
" 13. Union Stock Yards.
" 14. Western Ave. "
" 15. Ada St. "
" 16. Mayfair "

134

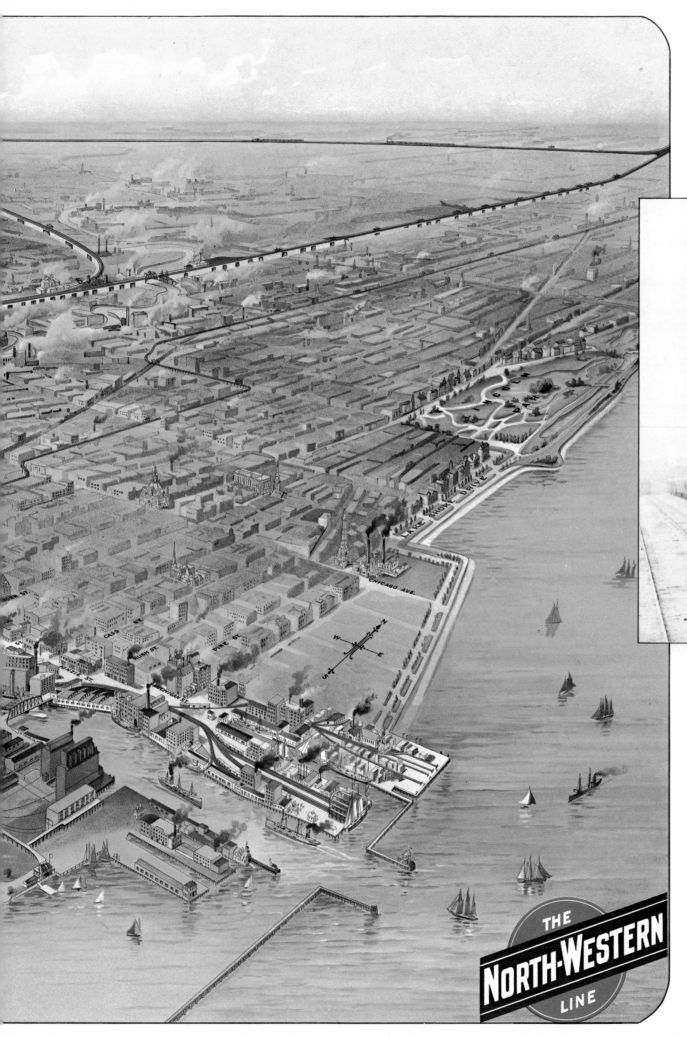

THE **North-Western** LINE

Passenger Station of the Chicago &
North-Western Railway, Council
Bluffs, Iowa, ca. 1899.

Port Arthur Route

1896

72. Hornbeck, F. A. Uncle Sam and his search light. Looking over the "Port Arthur Route" [Panoramic map of the Kansas City, Pittsburg & Gulf Railroad]. St. Louis: Woodward & Tiernan, 1896. 54 × 78 cm (21 × 31 in).

A colorful promotional map advertising the area between Kansas City and the Gulf of Mexico for business, farming, and settlement. Port Arthur, established in 1895, was named for the first president of this line, Arthur Edward Stilwell, the prominent real estate and insurance executive, and railroad promoter. Stilwell was the grandson of Hamlin Stilwell, the enterprising New York businessman who, early in the nineteenth century, helped build the Erie Canal and the New York Central Railroad and was one of the founders of Western Union telegraph.

The terminus of the "Port Arthur Route," which in 1900 became the Kansas City Southern Railway, ensured the prosperity and growth of this industrial and shipping center.

The tracks of this line were built with the aid of funds from George M. Pullman, of sleeping car fame, parallel to the borders between Kansas and Missouri, Arkansas and Oklahoma, and Texas and Louisiana, making it the shortest distance to the gulf. Later in the twentieth century it was known as the "Route of the *Flying Crow*."

The statements "Uncle Sam and his search light" and the "Schombrurgk line" refer to the U.S. Congress's 1895 recommendation for a commission to arbitrate the Venezuela-British Guiana boundary dispute. This crisis arose in 1885 from the way Sir Robert H. Schombrurgk's placement of the border line between the two countries gave to British Guiana land originally claimed by Venezuela. An American commission was appointed, and the line finally drawn in 1899 made an award generally considered favorable to Great Britain.

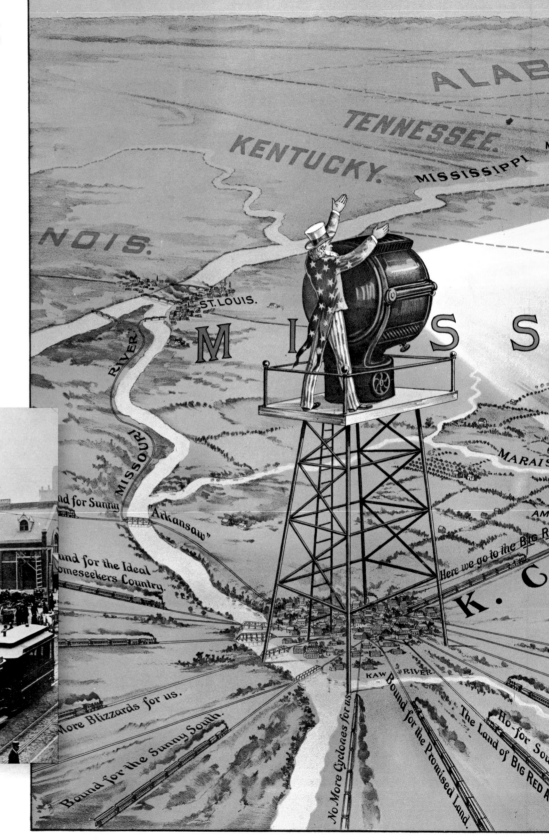

"The Great Market, Kansas City, Missouri." Photograph by B. W. Kilburn, 1890.

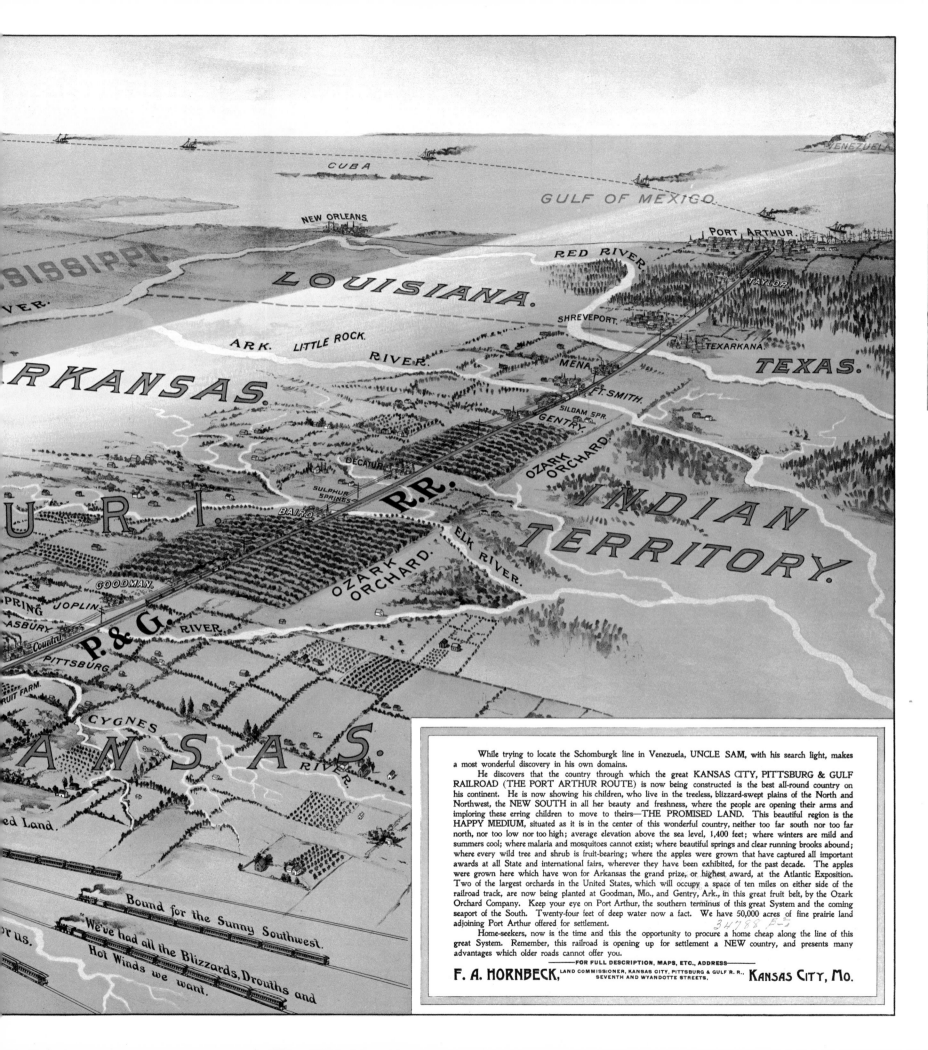

Tank cars, Port Arthur vicinity, Texas, 1901.

Southwestern United States

1887

73. Pierce, Herbert L. Wichita, Kansas 1887.
Chicago, Poole Bros., 1887. 44 × 60 cm (17 × 23½ in).

A colorful map of the southwestern
United States showing railroads completed
and under construction, converging on the
city of Wichita from ten large distant cities
around the country. The map advertises the
advantages of settling in Wichita and
Sedgwick County, Kansas. Railroads are
named along their lines, and stage coach
routes are shown pictorially. Such statistics as
real estate transactions, population of western
cities, miles of railroad lines built in Kansas,
buildings erected in the city, and amount of
corn produced are labeled on the map. An inset map of the city shows steam and electric
railroad lines and horse-drawn streetcar lines.
Stockyards and railroad depots are keyed by
number to a tabulated list. Schools and col-
leges are also indicated. The "Train of Thirty-
one Cars of Corn Donated by Sedgwick
County to the Ohio Flood Sufferers in 1886"
is pictured at the bottom of the map.

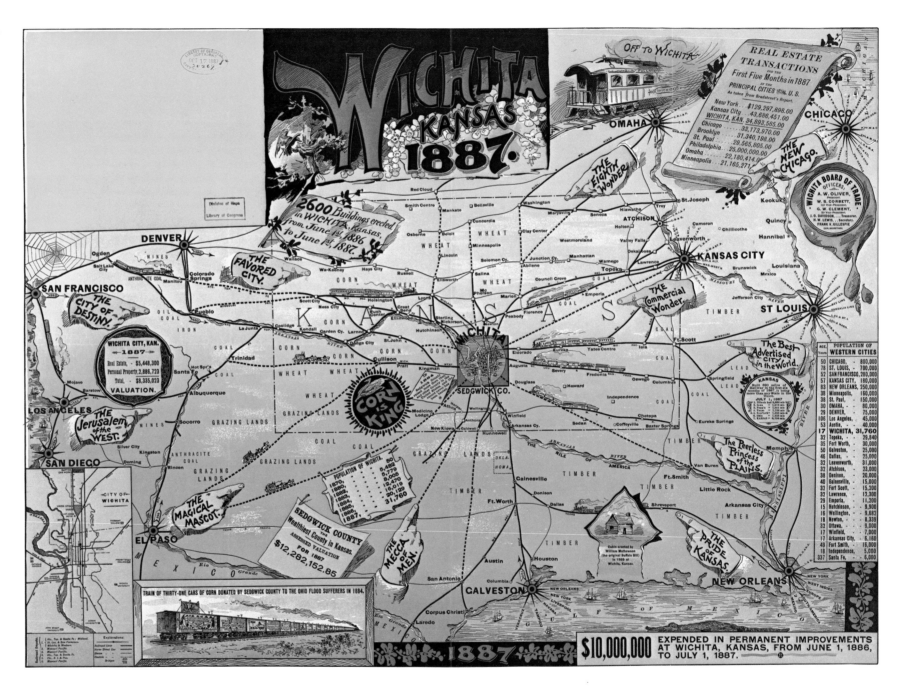

138

McClure & Co.

1886

74. Devlin, James S. Plan of that part of the Connellsville coal and coke regions between Connellsville and Mt. Pleasant showing the railroad lines coke ovens &c. James S. Devlin, Civil and Mining Engineer. Pittsburgh, Armor Lithographic Co. Lim'd., 1886. 50 × 65 cm (20 × 25½ in).

"McClure & Co. Manufacturers of Connellsville Coke. Blast Furnace a Specialty."

Colored map and view of the McClure & Company coal mines mostly in Bullskin and Upper Tyrone Townships, Fayette County, Pennsylvania. The map shows tributary rail lines terminating at the company's coal mines. This area was once a center of the world's greatest coke producing regions. The view shows how the McClure Company extracted, manufactured, and shipped coal and coke in the 1880s.

Coke furnaces in Pennsylvania.

Canada

Canada Southern Railway.
Executed by the American
Oleograph Co., Chicago.

Intercolonial

1864

75. Fleming, Sandford. General map to accompany report on the intercolonial Railway: — Exploratory survey of 1864. Made under the instruction from the Canadian government. Montreal, Burland, Lafricain & Co., 1864. 81 × 143 cm (32 × 56 in).
From his *Report on the Intercolonial Railway Exploratory Survey* (Quebec, G. E. Desbarats, 1865).

Portion of survey map showing Nova Scotia, New Brunswick, Prince Edward Island, and part of Maine. It indicates drainage, counties, townships, cities and towns, railroad stations, and existing railroads (overprinted in red). Lines surveyed in 1864, projected lines, and airline distances are shown, mostly in New Brunswick, in the five-hundred-mile span of territory required to link Truro and Halifax with the Grand Trunk Railway at Riviere-du-Loup.

This survey was entrusted by the Canadian government to the young and distinguished civil engineer Sandford Fleming. Before this survey, in 1862, Fleming presented to the government the first detailed and carefully worked-out plan for building a railroad to the Pacific. He was appointed engineer-in-chief of this government-owned enterprise to link the Maritime Provinces with central Canada. He later was made chief engineer on the Canadian Pacific Railway, and is well-known for devising a system of standard time.

The following explanatory notice accompanies the map:

This map is copied, by permission, chiefly from Wilkinson's Map of New Brunswick, published under the authority of the Legislature of that Province, by "Wyld," of London.

In the unsurveyed Districts, it is not (as might have been expected) strictly correct, but the general accuracy of the whole, or at least of that portion North of the Bay of Fundy, may, it is believed, be relied on.

The Nova Scotia portion of the Map does not possess the same degree of accuracy.

The position of the Line surveyed last summer, northerly from Amherst to the Shediac Railway, is, in part, incorrect. It should intersect the existing Railway about six miles easterly from Moncton, instead of about one mile as shown. The sheets were printed before this inaccuracy was discovered.

There are other inaccuracies, but they are not of great moment, as the main object of the Map is to render the descriptions of the various routes, referred to in the accompanying Report, more intelligible.

Engine used on a coal mine railroad near Stellarton, Nova Scotia, September 17, 1894.

GENERAL MAP
To accompany Report on the
INTERCOLONIAL RAILWAY-EXPLORATORY SURVEY,
of 1864.
Made under instruction from the
CANADIAN GOVERNMENT.
By

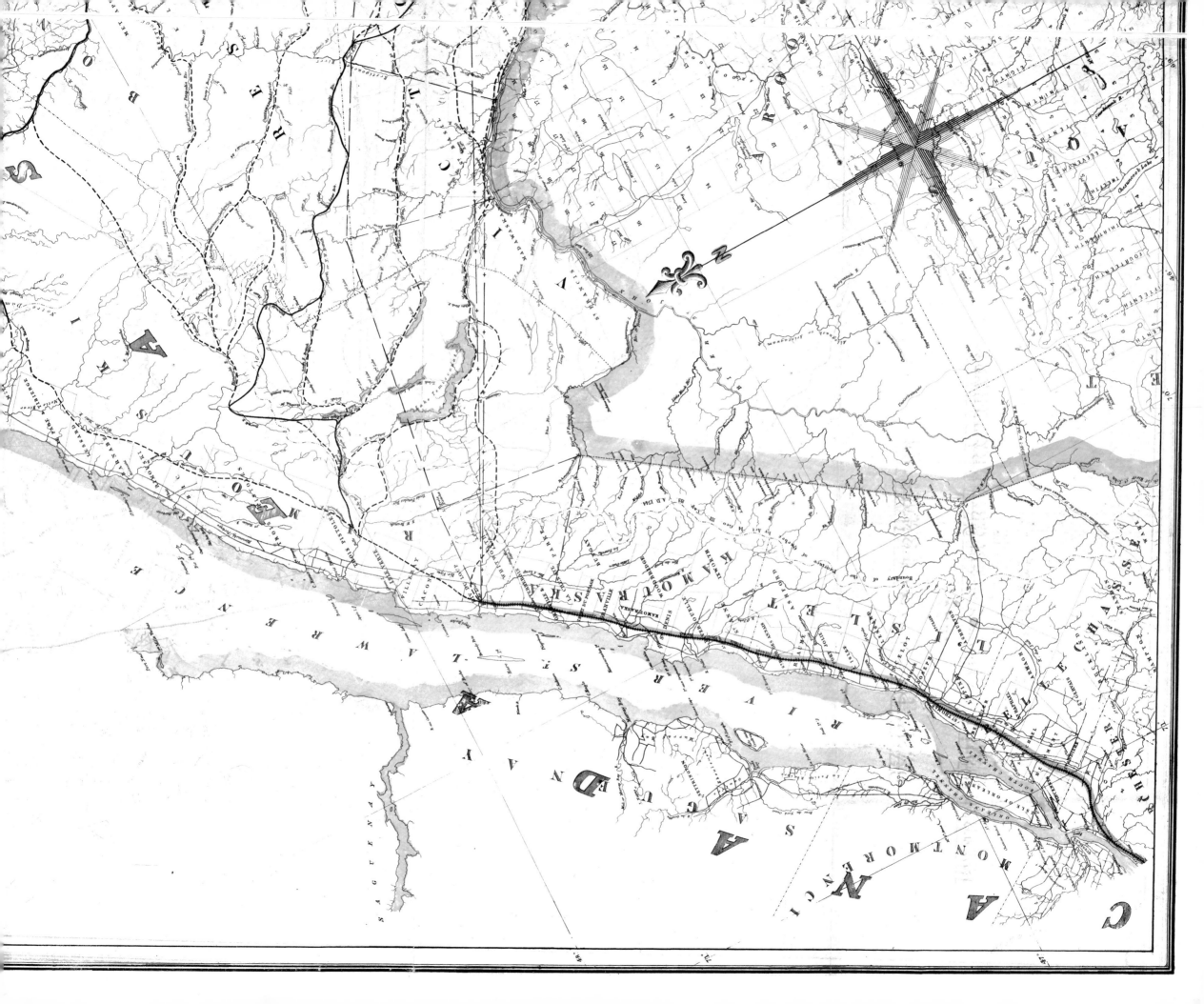

Lake Louise, Canada, ca. 1916.

Canadian Pacific

1874

76. Fleming, Sandford. Map from the Pacific Ocean across the Rocky Mountain zone to accompany report on exploratory survey. Canadian Pacific Railway. January 1874. Sheet no. 8. Ottawa, 1874. 62 × 78 cm (24 × 30½ in).

From Sir Sandford Fleming's *Report of Progress on the Explorations and Surveys up to January, 1874* (Ottawa: Printed by MacLean, Roger & Co., "Times" Office, 1874.).

A colored lithographic print, one of sixteen maps, charts, and profiles appended to the report, covering the area of British Columbia and part of western Alberta from Edmonton to Vancouver Island. Shows explored and unexplored railroad survey routes. Fleming's own route may be traced on the map from a point south of Ft. Edmonton to the route marked in a solid red line and labeled "Line common to Routes No's 1 to 6," then through Yellow Head Pass to Kamloops, then southwest along "route No. 2" to the Fraser River and west to New Westminster. This map represents one of the many survey maps resulting from Fleming's transcontinental expedition, organized in 1872, to follow the proposed route for the new railroad.

The expedition set out across the Great Lakes by steamer to the area where advance parties were already inching their way in a land untouched by the white man. The expedition included Fleming's son, and the remarkable Presbyterian minister George Monro Grant, who was to become one of the most distinguished educators and literary figures of his time. Also on the journey were John Macoun, the famous Canadian botanist, and Charles Horetzky, formerly of the Hudson's Bay Company, as the official photographer. At Ft. Edmonton the party split up, Fleming and Grant went south through Yellow Head Pass, and Horetzky and Macoun went north, by way of the Peace River, and then headed for Fort St. James and the Pacific coast (Route No. 7 on the map).

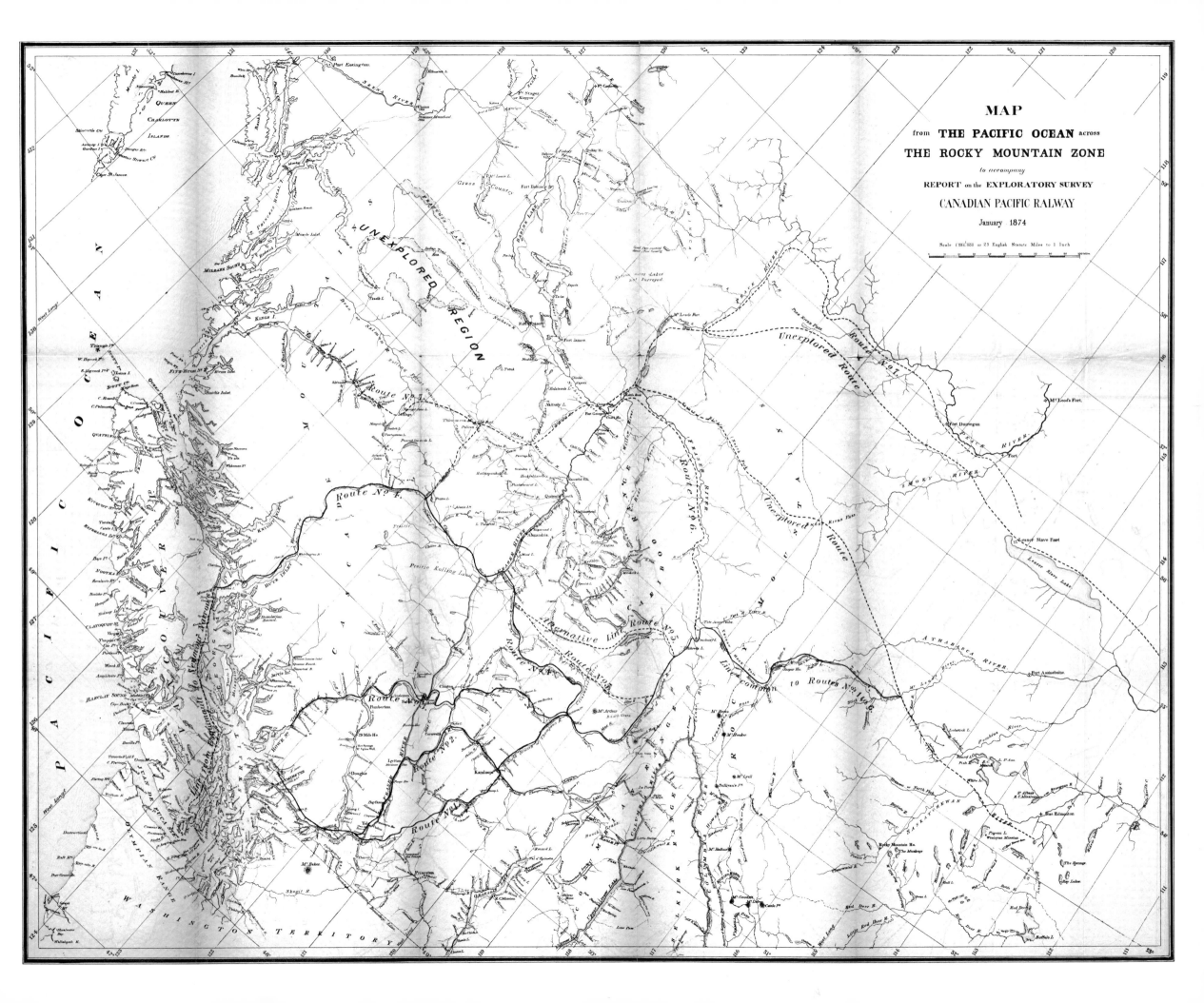

MAP

from **THE PACIFIC OCEAN** across

THE ROCKY MOUNTAIN ZONE

to accompany

REPORT on the EXPLORATORY SURVEY

CANADIAN PACIFIC RAILWAY

January 1874

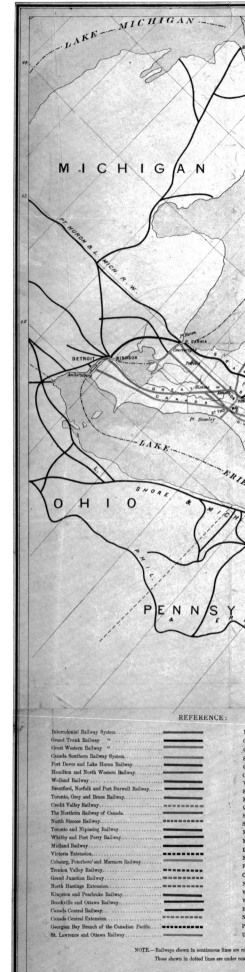

"Great Tubular Bridge, Grand
Trunk Railway, Montreal,
Canada." From *Frank Leslie's
Illustrated Newspaper*,
December 20, 1856.

Canada

1876

77. Macdonald, Alan. Map shewing the railway
systems in the eastern provinces of Canada. Prepared by
the authority of the Hon. the Minister of Public Works
under the direction of William Kupford engineer in
charge. Montreal: Burland Desbarats Lith. Company,
1876. 64 × 96 cm (25 × 38 in).

Outline map of Canada overprinted in
colors to show the railroad network with
connections in the eastern United States. The
map covers the area from Nova Scotia to On-
tario and part of Michigan. Large cities are
shown and counties are delimited. Fifty-two
railroads are keyed by color and name.
Railroads indicated by continuous lines have
been completed, and those shown by dotted
lines are under construction.

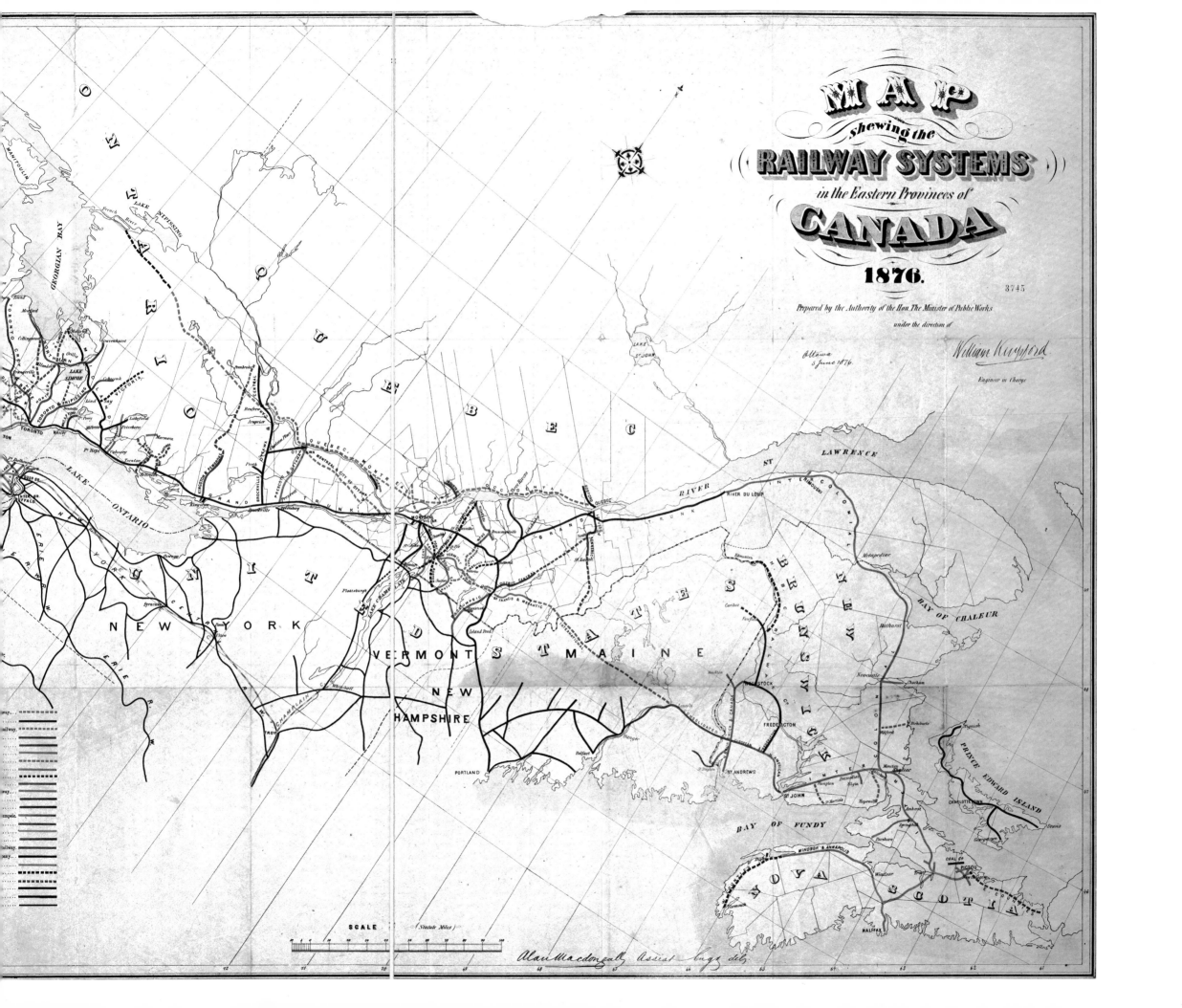

MAP

shewing the

RAILWAY SYSTEMS

in the Eastern Provinces of

CANADA

1876.

3745

Prepared by the Authority of the Hon. The Minister of Public Works

under the direction of

Ottawa
5 June 1876

William Kingsford

Engineer in Charge

SCALE (Statute Miles)

Alan Macdonald, Assist. Engr. del.

Canada

1907

78. White, James. Railway map of the Dominion of
Canada. Ottawa: Department of the Interior, 1907. 53 ×
89 cm (21 × 35 in).

A general railroad map of Canada showing drainage, provincial boundaries, major
cities and towns, and the railroad network
and its connections with United States lines,
overprinted in colors to distinguish the
ownership of lines. A legend in the lower left
corner of the map names various lines in the
system.

Distances in miles between Canadian cities
and European ports are also given. Includes
expenditure tabulations and total mileage for
lines completed and under construction.

Advertisement for the Grand
Trunk Railway, 1857.

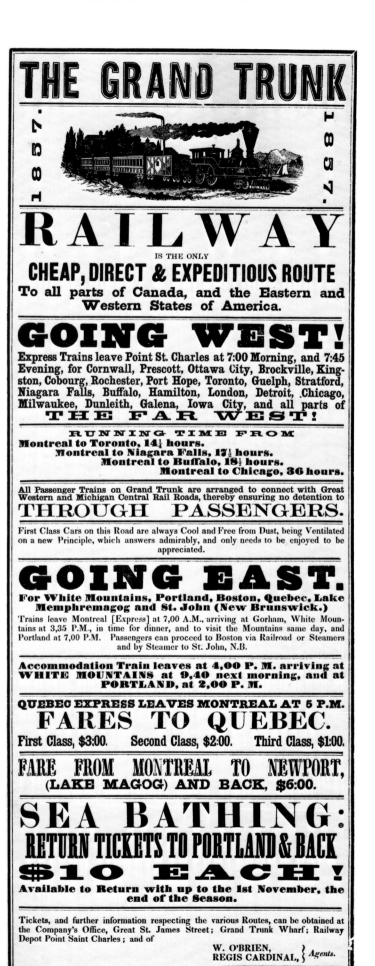

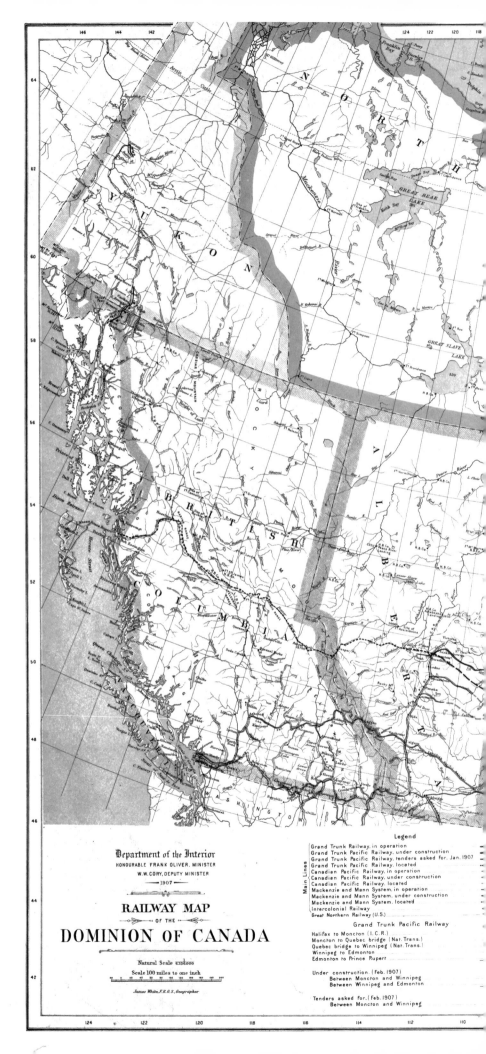

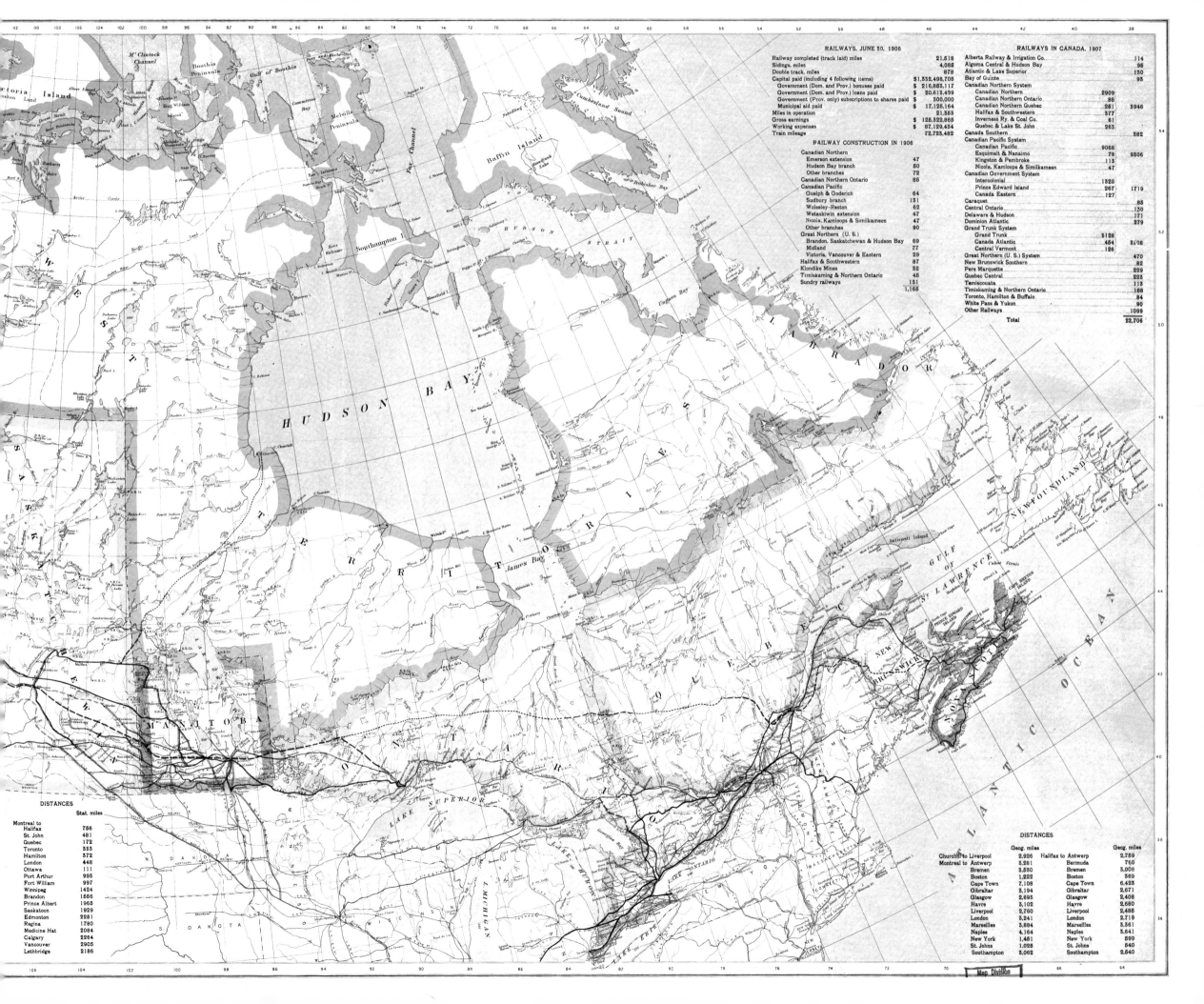

Newfoundland Railway

1890

79. Blackman, Albert L. Map of Newfoundland showing the Newfoundland Railway and proposed extension. Reduced from the Admiralty Chart, with latest official surveys. London: G. W. Bacon & Co., [1890]. 75 × 64 cm (30 × 25 in).

This map, using British Admiralty hydrographic charts as a base, includes drainage, relief by hachures, bathymetry, existing and proposed ocean telegraphic cables, roads and trails. A heavy line emphasizes the completed railroad from St. John's to Mings Bight, in the north central part of the island; dashed lines indicate branches and extensions to be completed. The map shows potential agricultural and grazing lands, forest and timber areas, and extensive copper mining districts. An inset "Map Showing the Comparative Latitudes of Newfoundland and Western Europe" appears in the upper right of the map.

This 3.5-foot narrow-gauge railroad was begun in 1881 but was not completed until 1898. To cross the 300 miles between St. John's and Port-aux-Basques, in the southwest corner of the island, it required building 550 miles of tracks with sharper curves and steeper grades than any railroad had in the Rocky Mountains. The line averages a bridge every 4 miles. Under normal conditions a trip across the island took thirty hours.

REID-NEWFOUNDLAND COMPANY

Rail	635
North Sydney to Port-au-Basques, Steamer	102
Port-au-Basques, Placentia Steamer	371
Placentia Bay Steamer	294
Trinity Bay Steamer	152
Bonavista Bay Steamer	142
Notre Dame Bay Steamer	362
St. John's and Labrador (Summer Service)	1021
Bay of Islands and Battle Harbor Service	379
Total Miles Operated	**3464**

USEFUL INFORMATION.

Ticket Offices—Passengers are requested to procure tickets at ticket offices and in ample time to enable the proper checking of baggage. When tickets are procured on train the Conductor will collect ten (10) cents additional to regular fare.

Tickets, Direction Honored—Tickets of all classes are good for passage only in the direction printed.

Round Trip Tickets—Round trip through tickets can be obtained at reduced fares; they are good only for time specified and are not transferable nor good for stop-over at any intermediate station, unless specially stamped "Good to stop off."

Children—Children not exceeding five years of age, accompanied by their parents or friends will be carried free. Children over five and under twelve will be carried at half fare.

Stop-Over will be allowed in exchange on such tickets as entitle holders to stop-over and when so stamped.

Lost Tickets—Proper care should be taken so as to guard against the loss of a ticket, as Railways are not responsible for lost tickets; also, care should be taken of baggage checks, making a memorandum of check numbers for use in case of loss.

Personal Baggage—Consisting of wearing apparel only, and not exceeding 150 lbs. weight, will be checked free on each whole fare ticket, and 75 lbs. free on each half fare ticket. Baggage in excess of free allowance will be charged for, and passengers paying excess charges will receive an excess baggage ticket which must be delivered to Agent with baggage check when baggage is claimed. Storage will be charged on each piece of baggage, either checked or not checked, remaining at stations over twenty-four hours.

Baggage for Flag Stations—Must be claimed at baggage car door immediately on arrival, otherwise it will be carried to next station where agent is on duty and held for further orders.

Caution—It is unlawful to carry dangerous articles, such as gunpowder, matches, etc., in baggage.

Customs—When baggage is examined at Canadian and Newfoundland points, passengers are required to attend to this personally, otherwise baggage will be held by the Customs.

Time of Trains—It is not guaranteed that the starting time or the arriving time of trains shall be as published herein, neither will this Railway be liable for loss or damage arising from delays or detentions, nor will this railway assume any responsibility beyond its own line.

Reference Marks—
*—Flag Station—Trains stop only when signalled or when there are passengers to set down, and under the conditions named herein.
†—Indicates that trains do not stop.

Disputes—Conductors and Agents are governed by rules which they are not authorized to change, therefore, in the event of any disagreement about tickets required, privileges allowed, etc., passengers should pay Conductor's or Agent's claim, obtain receipt and refer the matter to the General Passenger Agent for his decision.

Seat Space—A passenger is entitled only to seat space in car sufficient for one person, baggage and parcels that cannot be placed under car seat or in the passenger's portion of the parcel rack must not be taken into the car. Baggage which cannot be stowed away as above mentioned should be delivered at the baggage room. If found in the car it will be removed.

Obstruction of the Car Aisles Will Not Be Permitted.

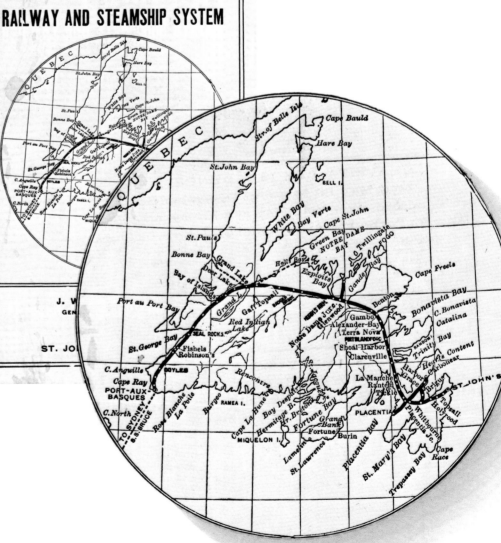

SEASON OF 1908

REID NEWFOUNDLAND COMPANY

RAILWAY AND STEAMSHIP SYSTEM

Brochure for the Reid-Newfoundland Company Railway and Steamship System, 1908.

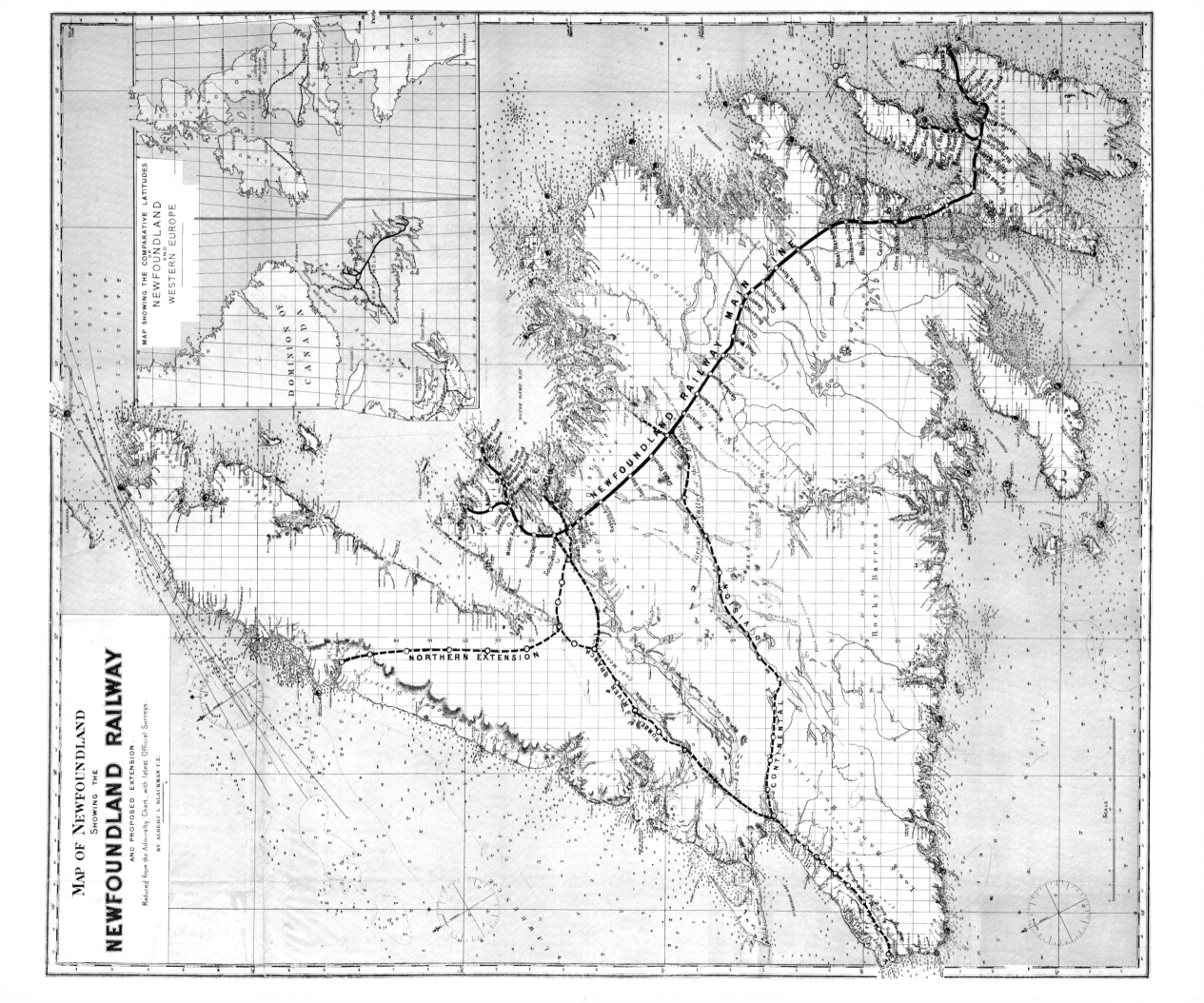

MAP OF NEWFOUNDLAND
SHOWING THE
NEWFOUNDLAND RAILWAY
AND PROPOSED EXTENSION.
Reduced from the Admiralty Chart, with latest Official Surveys.
BY ALBERT L. BLACKMAN C.E.

MAP SHOWING THE COMPARATIVE LATITUDES
OF
NEWFOUNDLAND
AND
WESTERN EUROPE

NORTHERN EXTENSION

NEWFOUNDLAND RAILWAY MAIN LINE

CONTINENTAL DIVISION

HUMBER RIVER BRANCH

DOMINION OF CANADA

Manitoba

1888

80. Brownlee, J. H. Brownlee's railway & guide map of Manitoba published by authority of Provincial government. Winnipeg, March 1888. Montreal: Canada Bank Note Co. Ltd., 1888. 40 × 64 cm (16 × 25 in).

Typical example of a detailed uncolored tourist and settler's map showing drainage, relief by hachures, township and range lines, municipal and county boundaries, cities, towns, railroad stations, schools, post offices, grain elevators and warehouses, and the Hudson's Bay Company's posts. Railroads in operation are shown by solid black lines; those under construction or projected are indicated by dashed lines.

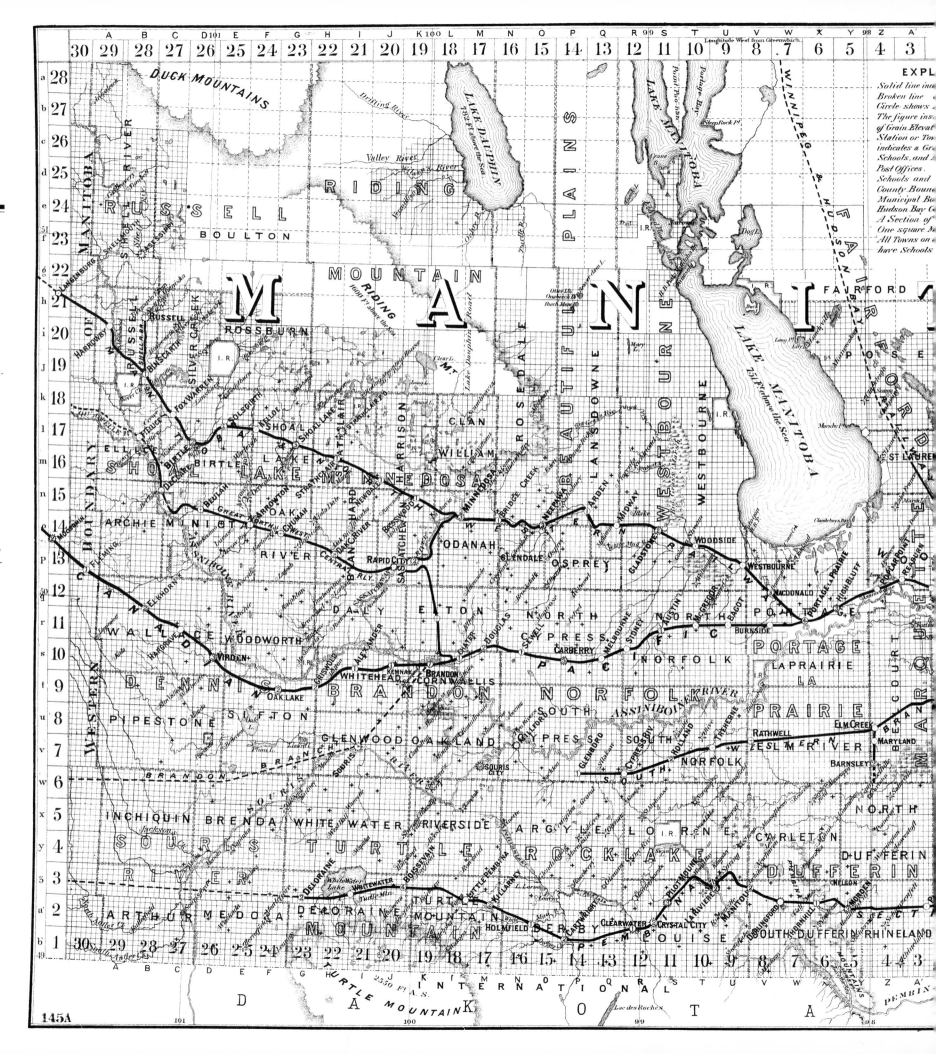

Threshing scene in western
Canada, ca. 1922.

Canadian Pacific

1897

81. Poole Brothers. Map of Canadian Pacific Railway Kootenay District, British Columbia. Chicago, 1897. 45 × 30 cm (18 × 12 in) on sheet measuring 45 × 71 cm (18 × 28 in).

This colored guide map covers the mining regions of southeast British Columbia and shows lakes and major rivers in blue and relief by brown shading. County and township lines, cities and towns, railroad stations, mining camps, and wagon roads are indicated. The Canadian Pacific is shown by a heavy solid line, and its lake steamer connections are indicated by dashed lines. Below the lakes, the construction of Canadian Pacific branch lines is indicated by dashed lines.

During the 1890s mining brought the first permanent population to this area of British Columbia. Mining was also responsible for the introduction of transportation facilities and associated forestry and water power developments. Prospectors, mainly from the United States, began mining gold and other minerals, and numerous mining towns soon arose.

In 1920 a large Canadian National Park was created in this scenic area, which contains high peaks, deep canyons, and mineral hot springs.

Packing silver ore across a glacier, British Columbia. Photograph by H. H. Ives, ca. 1926.

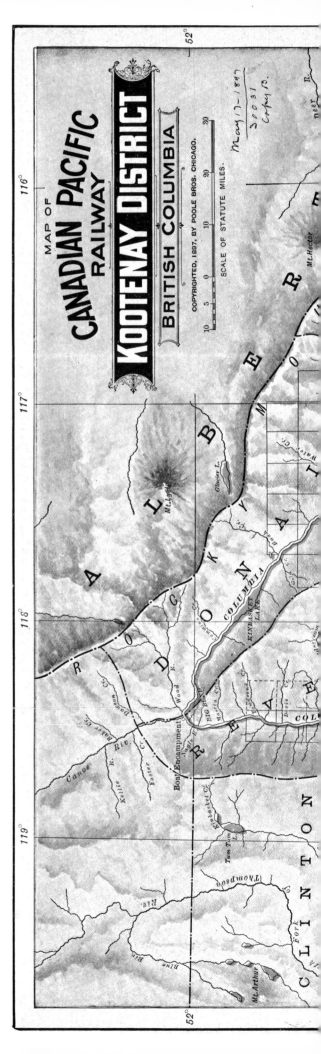

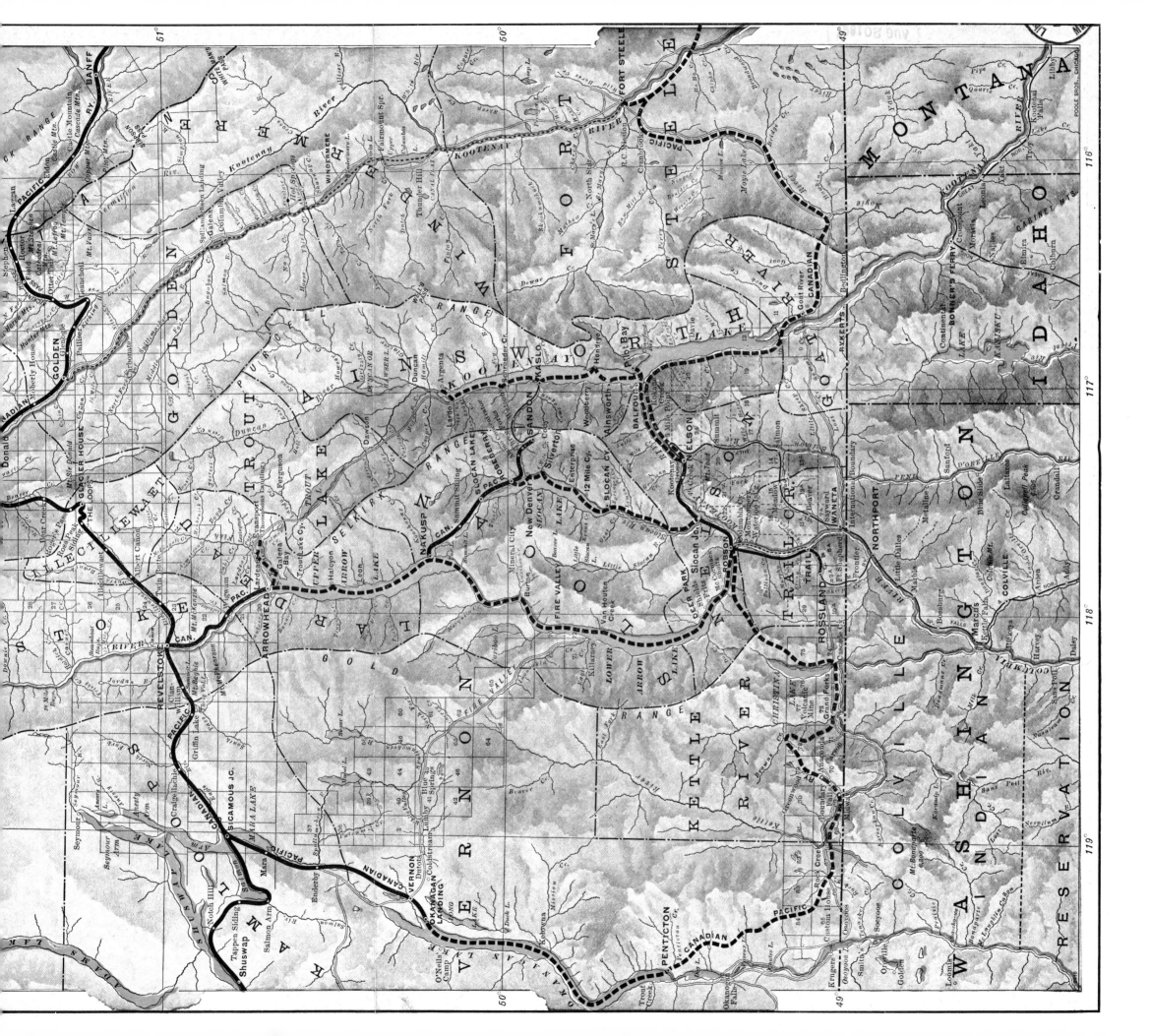

155

Yukon Gold Fields

1898

82. Poole Brothers. Map of Canadian Pacific Railway and connections showing routes to the Yukon gold fields. Alaska, Klondike and the northwestern mining territories of Canada. Chicago, 1898. 44 × 68 cm (17½ × 27 in).

General map covering Alaska and northwestern Canada from Saskatchewan west. Shows major drainage, relief by shading, forts, cities and towns, and railroad stations. The Canadian Pacific Railway is indicated in solid black and its unfinished routes are shown in black dashed lines. Indicates connections to trails and wagon roads, which are shown by parallel red lines, and inland water routes indicated by thin red dashed lines. A water route is shown from Green Lake in Saskatchewan, near Prince Albert, through the Great Slave Lake and the MacKenzie and Yukon Rivers, to the Bering Sea. This water route is interrupted only by a short portage in the far north at Ft. McPherson. A shaded area in the Alaska panhandle is labeled "Disputed Territory."

This copy of the map is signed in ink by Marcus Baker, the nineteenth-century U.S. government geographer, cartographer, and explorer of Alaska, who was one of the founders of the National Geographic Society, a director of the U.S. Geological Survey, and the first executive secretary of the U.S. Board on Geographic Names, which was established in 1890.

"Women Prospectors on their way to Klondyke." Photograph by B. W. Kilburn, 1898.

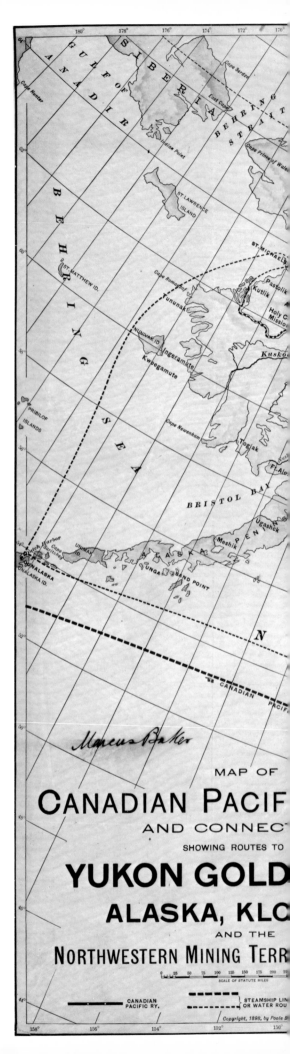

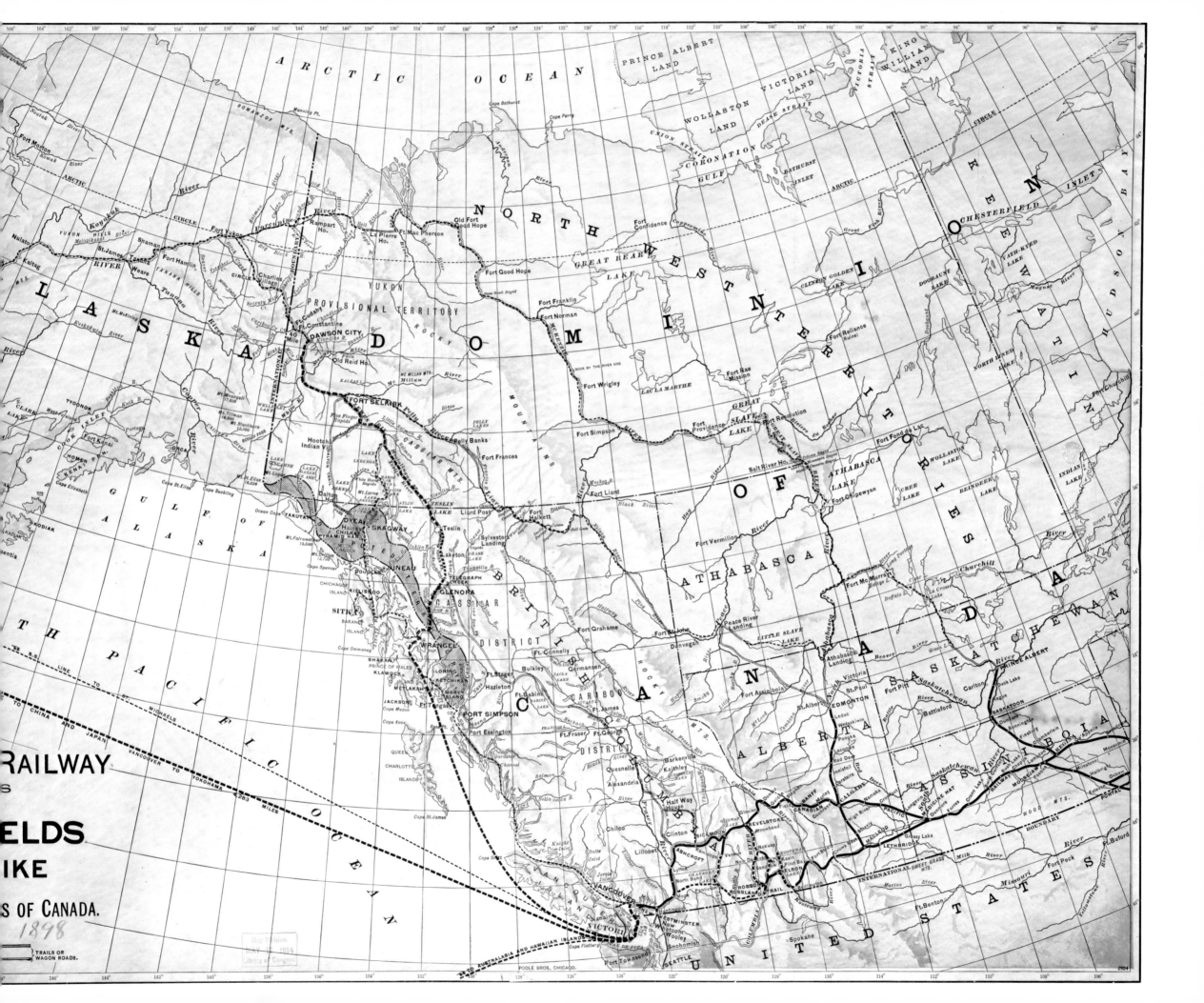

Railroad Lines

Canadian Pacific

1912

83. **Poole Brothers.** Around the world by Canadian Pacific route. Chicago, 1892. 79 × 45 cm (31 × 17½ in).

A colored tourist map advertising the advantages of traveling across the North American continent via the Canadian Pacific Railway Company and its steamer connections. The verso of the map gives geographic information on exotic and interesting places to visit by globe-circling excursions that use the company's new transpacific steamships and Atlantic Ocean connections. Drawn on a polar projection, the map covers all of North America, emphasizing the main line and U.S. connections and indicating shipping lines and ports of call around the Eurasian continent. It is described as follows by the railroad company:

It is not the intention to turn the old world upside down, but it was necessary to publish the map in the manner it has been to properly show the course as well as the advantages of the Canadian Pacific Route around the world. And also the route to and from the far East. We are so accustomed to view the picture of the world on Mercator's projection that we are apt to forget that the world is round . . . .

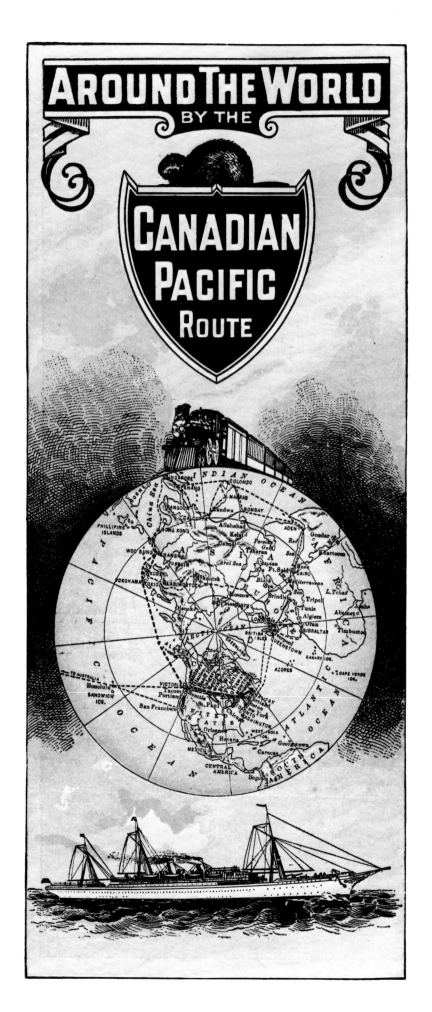

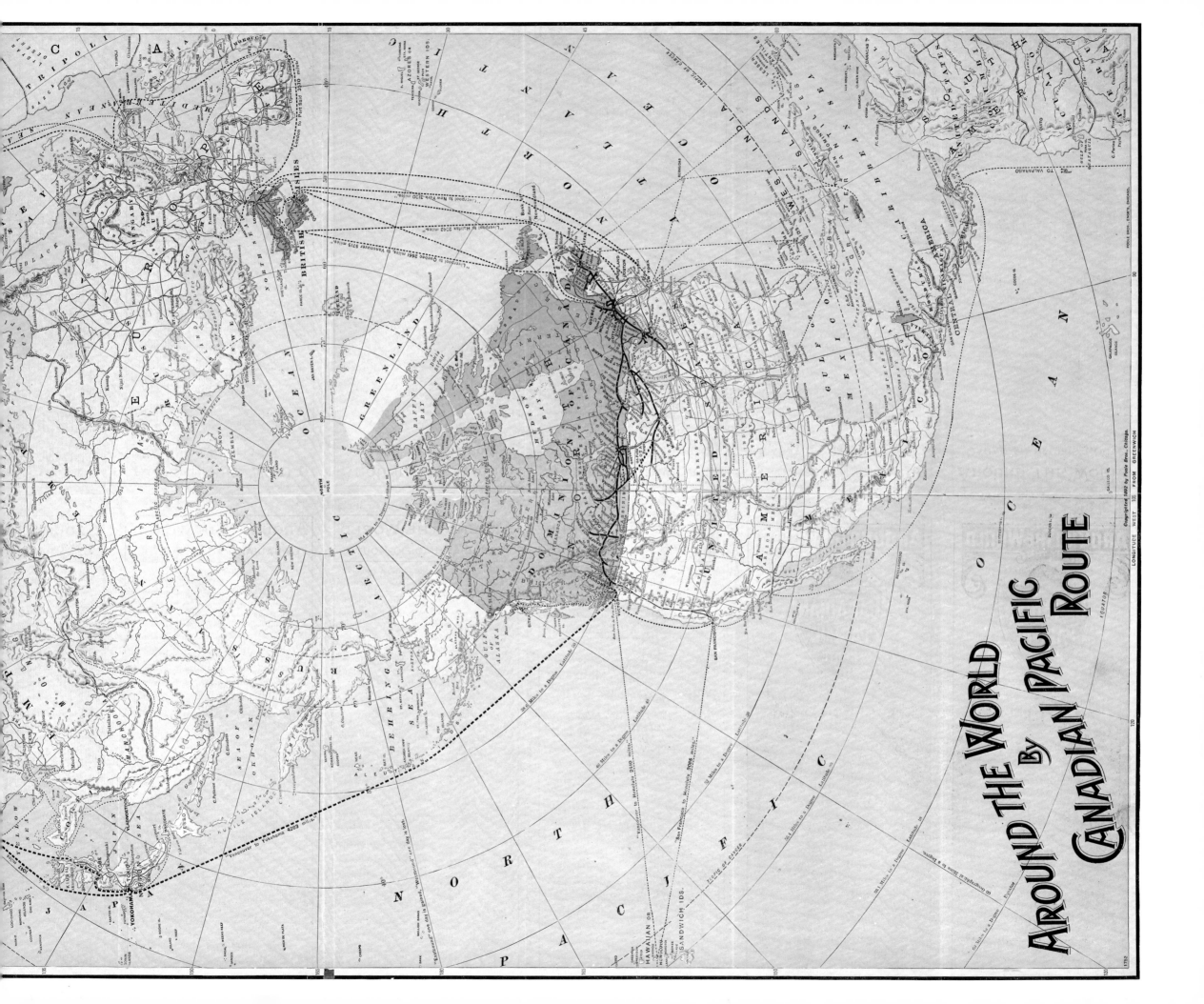

Around the World by Pacific Canadian Route

Grand Trunk

1896

84. Rand, Avery Supply Company. Map of the Grand Trunk and Great Western Railways of Canada and their connections. Boston, 1896. 33 × 69 cm (13 × 27 in).

A tourist and traveler's timetable map of Canada and the United States portraying the major rail network in Canada and showing connections with lines in the United States. Names of railroads appear along the lines. Indicates major drainage, relief by hachures, cities and towns, railroad stations, and junction points. The verso of the map contains detailed timetable and tourist information and includes tables of organization and a list of officers.

The decorative cover title on the verso reads: "Grand Trunk Railway of Canada the International Route Between East and West; Great Western Division of the Grand Trunk Ry. of Canada, the Great International Route Between East and West."

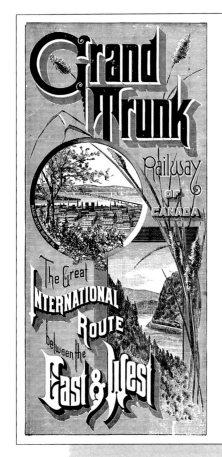

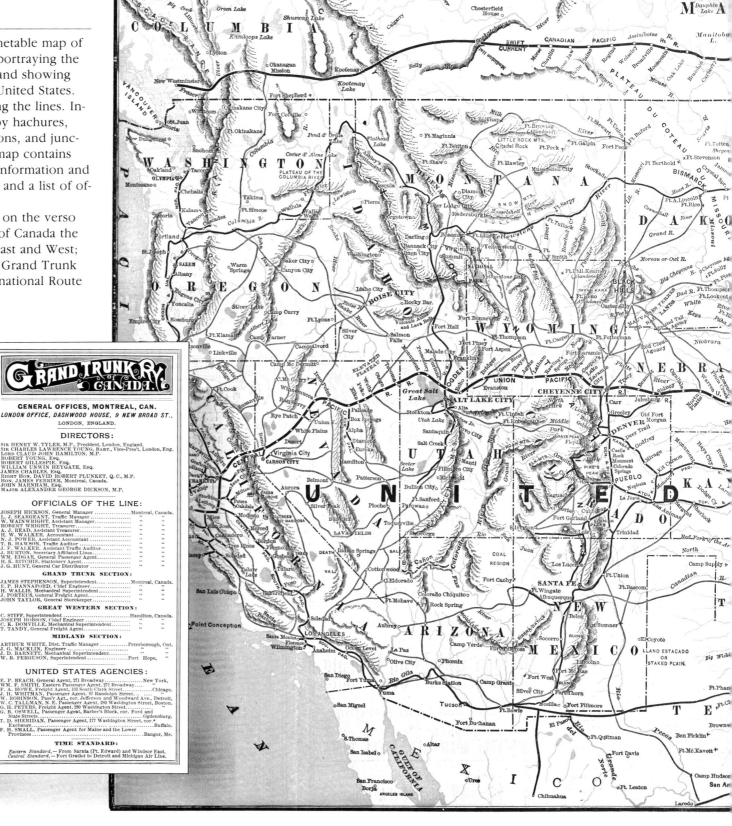

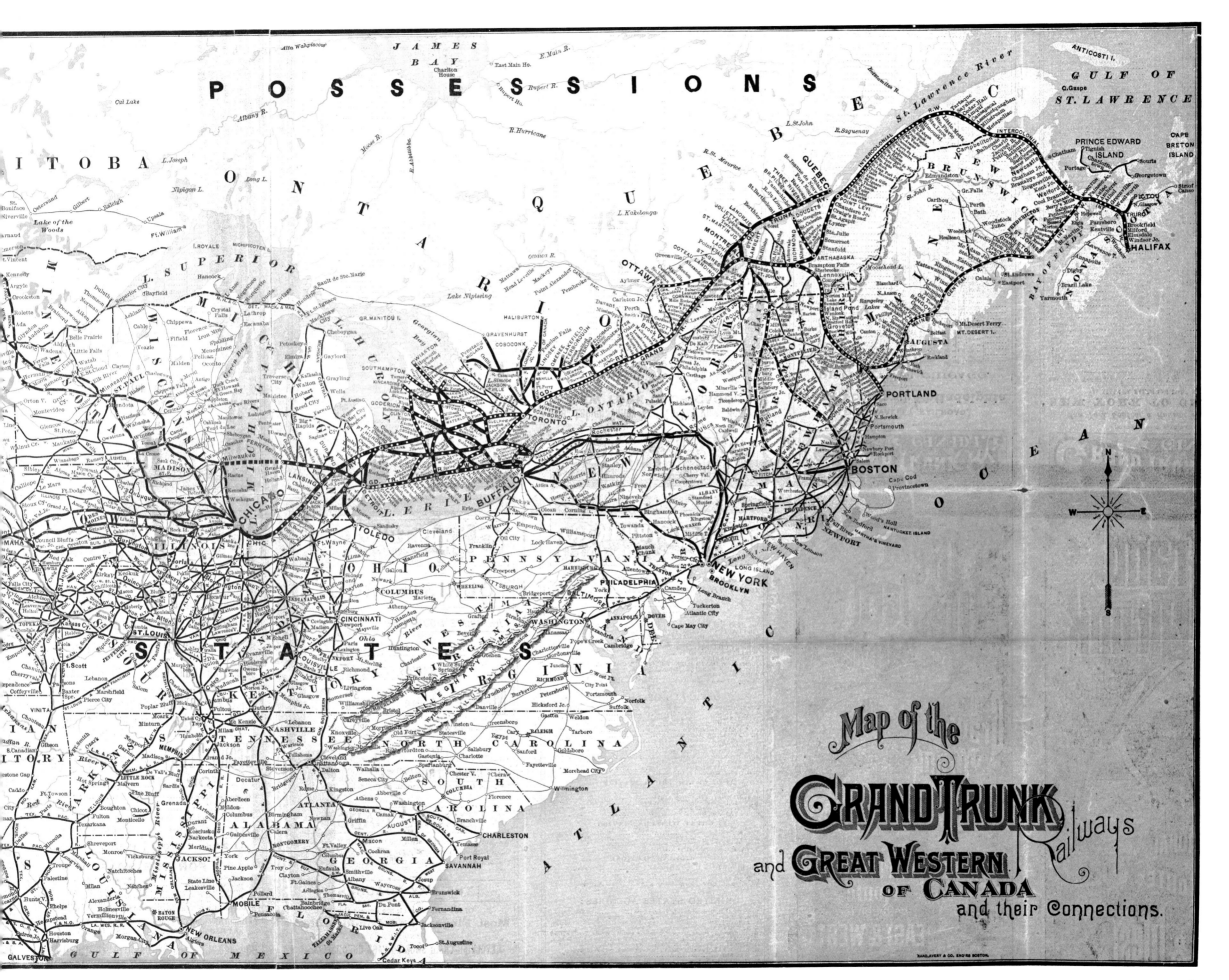

Map of the **Grand Trunk** and **Great Western** of **Canada** *Railways* and their Connections.

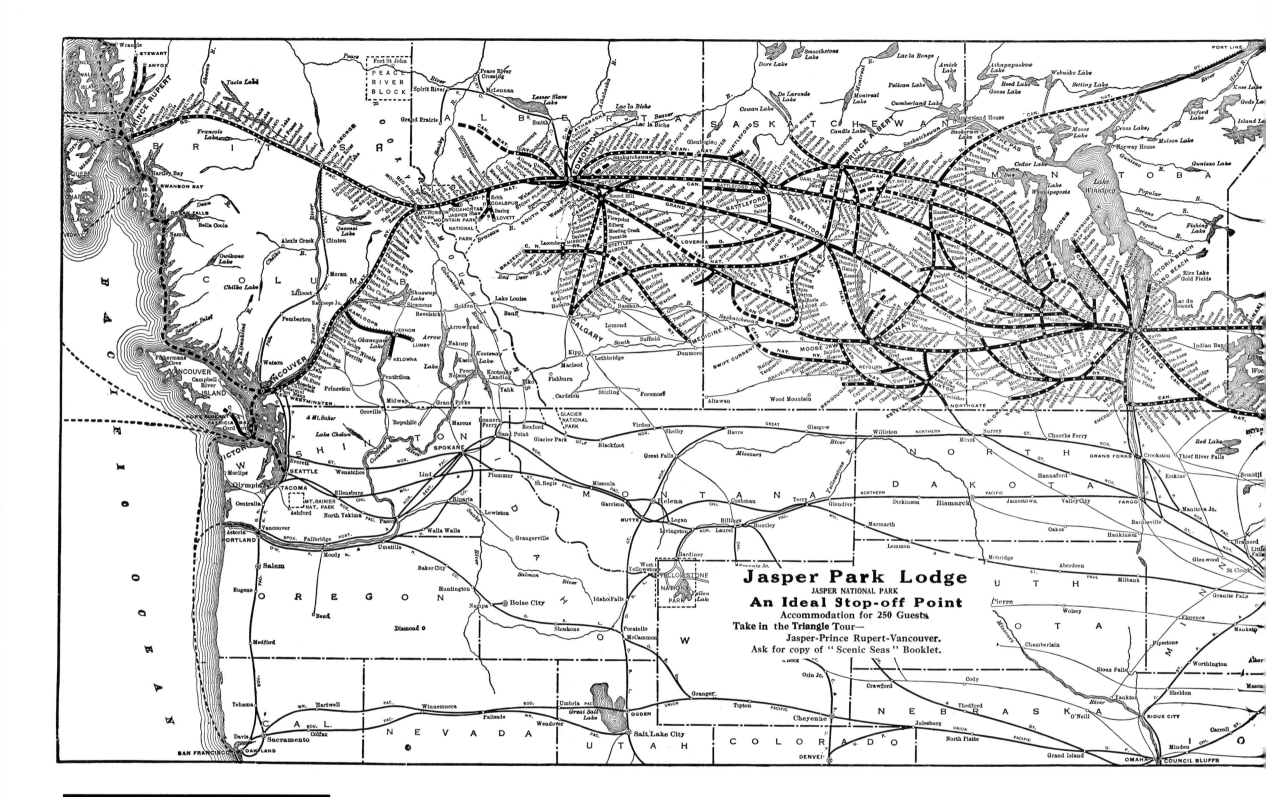

Jasper Park Lodge
JASPER NATIONAL PARK
An Ideal Stop-off Point
Accommodation for 250 Guests
Take in the Triangle Tour—
Jasper-Prince Rupert-Vancouver.
Ask for copy of "Scenic Seas" Booklet.

Canadian National

1921

This uncolored map is inserted into a 1923 detailed illustrated timetable folder. It advertises worldwide railroad and steamship connections between both oceans, the Great Lakes, and the northern United States.

85. **Poole Brothers.** Canadian National Railways. Grand Trunk Railway System. Chicago, 1921. 24 × 79 cm (9½ × 31 in).

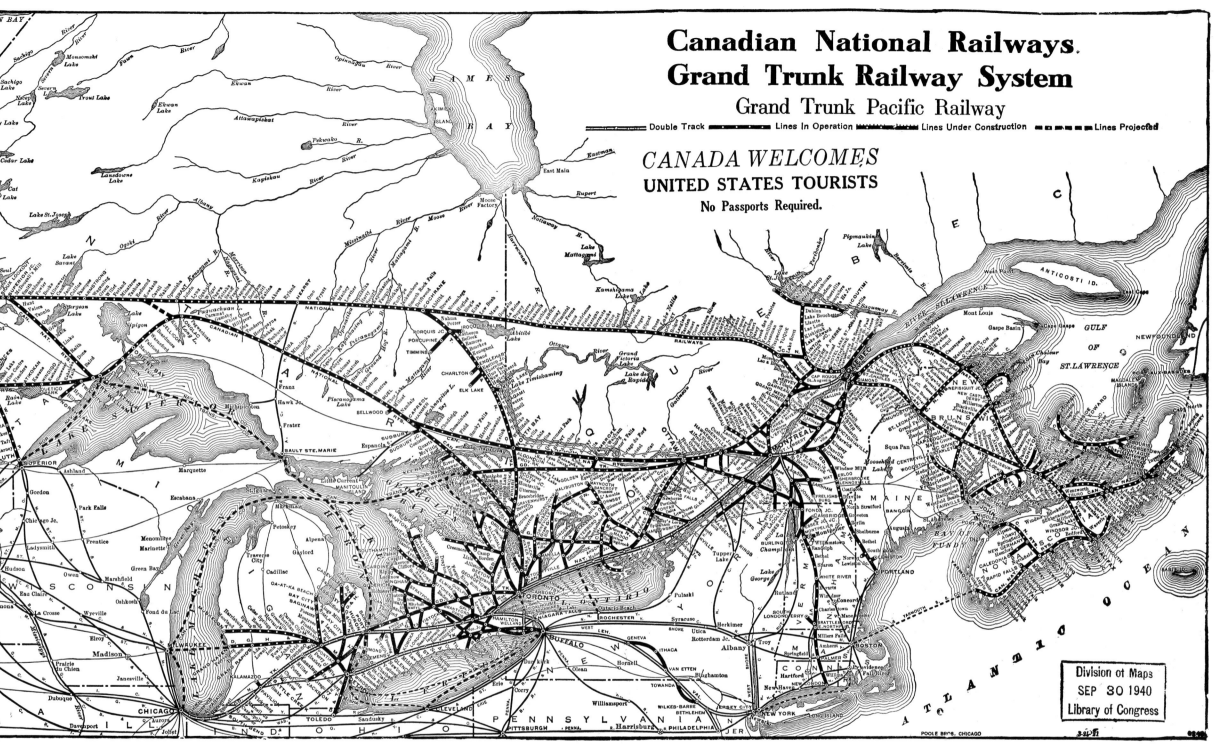

Canadian National Railways.
Grand Trunk Railway System
Grand Trunk Pacific Railway

Double Track — Lines In Operation — Lines Under Construction — Lines Projected

CANADA WELCOMES
UNITED STATES TOURISTS
No Passports Required.

POOLE BROS. CHICAGO

Maligne Lake, Jasper National Park, Alberta, Canada. Photograph by L. K. Mulford, 1945.

Mexico

Constructing the Mexican National
Railroad near Toluca.

Surveys

Tehuantepec Railroad

1851

86. Barnard, John G. Map of the Isthmus of Tehuantepec embracing all the surveys of the engineering & hydrographic parties and showing the proposed route of the Tehuantepec Rail Road. Surveyed under the direction of Maj. J. G. Barnard U.S. Engrs. Chief Engineer. Drawn by Chas. C. Smith. Lith. of Sarony & Major, New York. [New Orleans: Tehuantepec Railroad Company] 1851. Map 103 × 68 cm (41 × 26½ in).

The opening of a line of communication across the Isthmus of Tehuantepec was proposed in the time of Cortez, and a survey of a route for a canal was made in the eighteenth century. As early as November 4, 1824, the Mexican government took steps to attract proposals, and on March 1, 1842, a concession was granted to Jose Garay for a railroad line. This was amended in 1846.

Garay's concession was sold in 1848 to the English firm of Manning and Mackintosh, who, unable to finance the project, assigned it to Peter A. Hargous of New York in 1849. The Tehuantepec railroad company was then incorporated in Louisiana, and a survey was made in 1850 under the direction of Gen. John G. Barnard. An elaborate report of this survey was published in 1852. Before construction work could begin, the Mexican government, fearful of American influence, declared the concession void in 1851. The result of this action was to divert the attention of promoters to a rival line, and a railroad was constructed across the Isthmus of Panama during 1850-55, thus making it more difficult to obtain capital for the Tehuantepec project. After many concessions the line was finally built and formally open to traffic in January 1, 1907.

"El Cafetal de Temasopa, Mexico."
Detroit Photographic Co., ca.
1885.

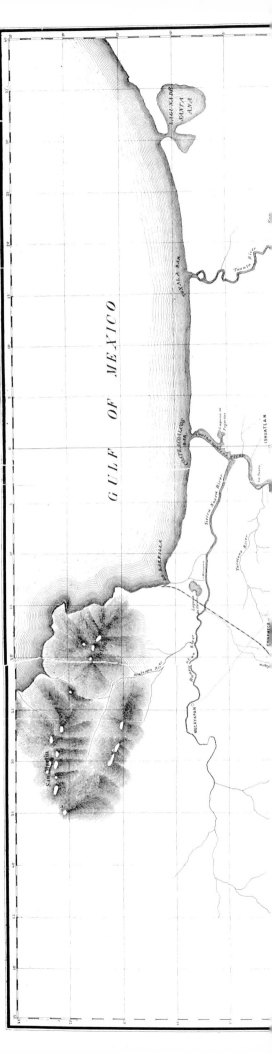

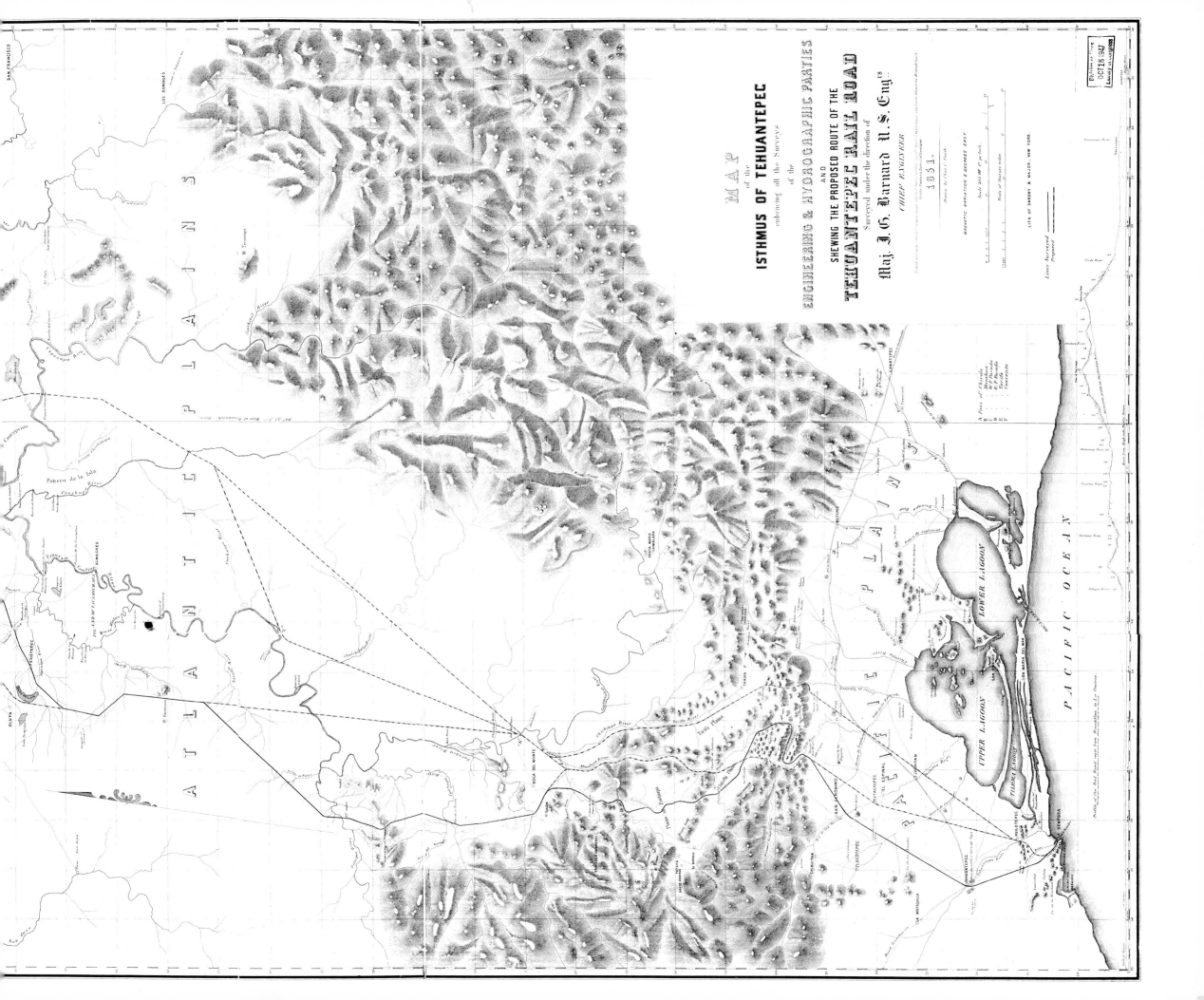

MAP
of the
ISTHMUS OF TEHUANTEPEC
embracing all the Surveys
of the
ENGINEERING & HYDROGRAPHIC PARTIES
AND
SHEWING THE PROPOSED ROUTE OF THE
TEHUANTEPEC RAIL ROAD
Surveyed under the direction of
Maj. J. G. Barnard U. S. Eng.rs
CHIEF ENGINEER

1851.

Drawn by Chas.l Smith.

MAGNETIC VARIATION 9 DEGREES EAST.

Scale 105.68 T.p inch.

Scale of Statute miles

LITH. OF SARONY & MAJOR, NEW YORK.

Lines Surveyed ————
Proposed ————

A Plan of Chivela
B   Morales
C   W.t Phivela
D   E.t Phivela
E   Tarifa
F   Cuanato

ATLANTIC OCEAN

PACIFIC OCEAN

SAN FRANCISCO

LOS DOMINGOS

PLAINS

ATLANTIC PLAINS

PACIFIC PLAINS

UPPER LAGOON
LOWER LAGOON
TILEMA LAGOON

SANTA MARIA CHIMALAPA

Mexican National

1881

87. Von Motz, Albert. Map of the northern part of the Mexican National Railway shewing the lines of the vicinity of the Rio Grande del Norte, granted by the Mexican Government to the Mexican National Constrn. Co. (Palmer and Sullivan concession) E. Miller, Chief Engr. Northn. Divn. 1881. Compiled from the latest authorities and drawn by Albert von Motz, C. E., Laredo, Texas, Sept. 1881. 64 × 66 cm (25 × 26 in).

Pen-and-ink manuscript map showing relief by hachures; railroads in operation, under construction, and proposed; roads; rivers and streams; and cities and towns in northeastern Mexico and southern Texas. This is the final manuscript version, which was used for printing reduced lithographic prints of this map.

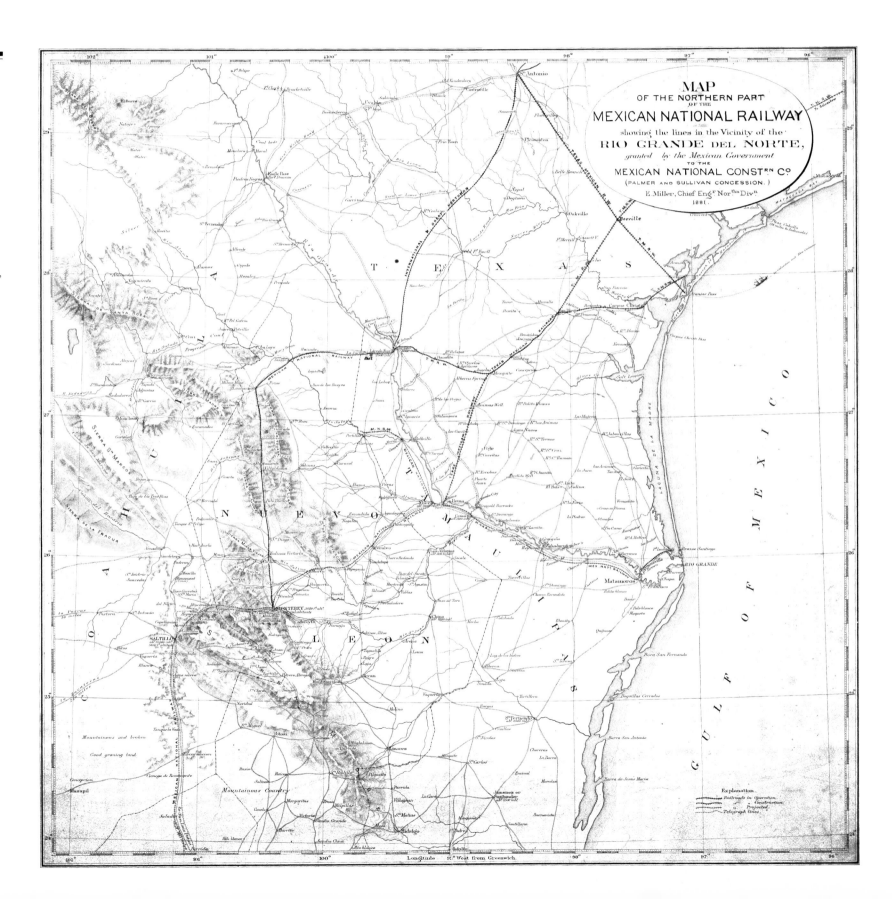

Mexican Railroads

1888

88. Gaetschy, Gaspar. Mapa de los ferrocarriles Mexicanos propiedad de El Monitor Mexicano. Mexico, D.F., Lith. Em. Moreau, 1888. 59 × 80 cm (23 × 32 in).

Cover Title: Mapa e itinerarios de los ferrocarriles Mexicanos. Propiedad exclusiva de ''El Monitor Mexicano.''

A colorful railroad timetable and advertising map of Mexico showing Mexican railroads, in heavy black lines, and connections to United States railroads in lighter lines. The map indicates province boundaries, major cities, and railroad stations. Railroads under construction are indicated by heavy dashed lines. Bordering the map are individual advertisements for such products and services as pool table distributors, life insurance companies, flower shops, restaurants, and the Jockey Club. The verso of the map has timetables reproduced from the 1888 edition of the *Monitor Mexicano*.

Mexican Central

1890

89. American Bank Note Company. Mexico. Mapa de las lineas del Ferrocarril Central y conecciones. New York, 1890. 53 × 62 cm (21 × 24½ in).

A colorful cover to the map contains an English title which reads: "The Mexican Central Railway. The Highway to Mexico the Egypt of the New World." The verso of the map includes ticket information, advertisements for side excursions, pullman cars, and itineraries for Kansas City, St. Louis, and New Orleans. The map provides thumbnail descriptions of the twenty important cities of Mexico.

This lightly colored map of North America emphasizes the main line of the Mexican Central Railway in red. Connecting lines in black are shown north of the Rio Grande. Drainage, relief by brown hachures, state boundaries, major cities, towns, and railroad stations are clearly shown. The four continental time zones and a special zone for Mexico city are shown by miniature clock faces. "Perfil del Ferrocarril Central de Mexico a Paso del Norte" appears in the lower left corner of the map. This map is accompanied by a leaflet in English entitled *Round Trip Excursions to Mexico via the Mexican Railway. El Paso Route.*

WINTER
EXCURSION TRIPS
TO A TRULY SUMMER LAND.

MEXICO

The · Most · Charming · Winter · Resort

IN THE WORLD.

A Genial and Balmy Climate,

The Fruits, Flowers and Tropical Foliage of California and Florida Combined,

And an Antiquity which rivals Egypt and Palestine.

THE TOURIST'S PARADISE

THE GRAND OLD

CITY OF MEXICO,

For the Season of 1889 and 1890,

WITH VASTLY IMPROVED HOTEL ACCOMMODATION

And a rapidly increasing English-speaking Population,

Presents to the thousands who annually escape from the frost and snow of the Northern, Western and Eastern States,

· A Winter Home ·

In an incomparable climate, surrounded by picturesque scenery, and in a locality more interesting than any part of Europe.

Height above sea level, 7350 feet.

Mean temperature during twelve months, 68 degrees Fahrenheit.

3

· · THE ONLY LINE · ·
RUNNING

PULLMAN DRAWING-ROOM SLEEPING CARS

From the Rio Grande to the City of Mexico,

PASSING EN ROUTE ALL THE PRINCIPAL CITIES OF THE REPUBLIC, AND THE

Only Standard Gauge Road

Extending from the United States to the City of Mexico.

⟶ SOLID DAILY TRAINS ⟵

From El Paso to City of Mexico without transfer.

In addition to this map folder, the Mexican Central R'y Co. issues a book describing the principal places of interest in Mexico; a leaflet folder descriptive of the principal cities on the line of the Mexican Central R'y; and a time-table folder showing the time from various sections of the United States to Mexico, via El Paso and Eagle Pass.

The above and other information may be obtained upon application to any of the agents named below.

G. W. KEELER, Gen'l Eastern Agent, 261 Broadway, New York.
M. H. KING, Gen'l Western Agent, 236 S. Clark St., Chicago, Ill.
C. E. MINER, Gen'l Trav. Agent, Laclede Hotel, St. Louis, Mo.
R. W. GILLESPIE, Trav. Pass'r Ag't, 34 St. Charles St., N. O., La.
W. P. FOSTER, Trav. Pass'r Ag't, 116 N. 4th St., St. Louis, Mo.

4

Mexican Central
⟶ RAILWAY ⟵
· CONDENSED TIME TABLE ·
BETWEEN
EL PASO AND EAGLE PASS
AND
═ CITY OF MEXICO ═

EXPRESS No. 52	KILO-METRES		CITY OF MEXICO TIME.		MILES.	EXPRESS No. 51
6 20 p.m.	....	Lv.	....El Paso....	Ar.	....	7 15 a.m.
6 35 p.m.	0	Ar.	*Juarez City..	Ar.	0	7 10 a.m.
7 00 a.m.	361 4	Lv.	..*Chihuahua..	Lv.	224 0	7 35 p.m.
7 25 a.m.	....	Lv.	..*Chihuahua..	Ar.	....	7 00 p.m.
11 10 a.m.	524 2	Lv.	..Santa Rosalia..	Lv.	324 9	3 05 p.m.
12 55 p.m.	597 0	Ar.	....Jimenez....	Lv.	370 2	1 30 p.m.
1 20 p.m.	....	Lv.	....Jimenez....	Ar.	....	1 05 p.m.
3 55 p.m.	670 5	Lv.	....Escalon....	Lv.	415 9	11 20 a.m.
6 25 p.m.	829 1	Lv.	....Lerdo....	Lv.	514 4	8 00 a.m.
6 32 p.m.	834 3	Ar.	*Torreon Junction..	Lv.	517 6	7 50 a.m.
		Lv.	....Eagle Pass....	Ar.		7 10 a.m.
9 00 p.m.		Lv.	..Piedras Negras..	Ar.		5 00 a.m.
1 00 a.m.		Lv.	....Sabinas....	Ar.		1 00 a.m.
6 15 a.m.		Lv.	....Monclova....	Ar.		7 30 p.m.
11 30 a.m.		Lv.	....Jaral....	Ar.		1 55 p.m.
		Ar.	*Torreon Junction..	Lv.		7 30 a.m.
6 55 p.m.	834 3	Lv.	*Torreon Junction..	Ar.	517 6	7 25 a.m.
8 45 p.m.	901 6	Ar.	..*Jimulco....	{ Lv. Lv. }	561 3	5 45 a.m. 5 55 a.m.
6 33 a.m.	1206 8	Lv.	....Fresnillo....	Lv.	749 1	8 12 p.m.
7 30 a.m.	1234 8	Lv.	..*Calera....	{ Ar. Lv. }	766 5	7 10 p.m. 6 40 p.m.
7 55 a.m.	1264 4	Lv.	..Zacatecas....	Lv.	784 9	5 36 p.m.
8 55 a.m.	1385 2	Lv.	*Aguascalientes..	Ar.	859 9	1 35 p.m.
1 05 p.m.		Lv.		Ar.		1 05 p.m.
1 45 p.m.	0	Lv.	Aguascalientes..	Ar.	0	12 25 p.m.
7 00 p.m.	224 7	Ar.	San Luis Potosi..	Lv.	141 0	7 15 a.m.
4 15 p.m.	1495 4	Lv.	....Lagos....	Lv.	928 4	10 10 a.m.
5 56 p.m.	1554 5	Lv.	....Leon....	Lv.	965 1	8 42 a.m.
6 45 p.m.	1587 7	Ar.	..*Silao....	{ Lv. Ar. }	985 8	7 55 a.m. 7 25 a.m.
7 10 p.m.		Lv.		Ar.		
*7 00 p.m.	0	Lv.	....Silao....	Ar.	14 0	7 10 a.m.
7 45 p.m.	.18	Lv.	..Marfil....	Lv.	2 9	*6 25 a.m.
By Str'tR'y	.23	Ar.	..Guanajuato....	Lv.		By Str'tR'y
7 55 p.m.	1617 5	Lv.	...Irapuato....	Ar.	1004 3	6 54 a.m.
8 45 a.m.	0	Lv.	...Irapuato....	Ar.	155 2	5 15 p.m.
4 45 p.m.	259 1	Ar.	..Guadalajara..	Lv.	0	9 15 a.m.
9 27 a.m.	1678 8	Lv.	....Celaya....	Lv.	1042 4	5 10 a.m.
10 35 p.m.	1724 8	Lv.	..Queretaro....	Lv.	1070 9	4 05 a.m.
12 10 a.m.		Lv.		Lv.		2 30 a.m.
12 20 a.m.	1779 7	Lv.	*San Juan del Rio..	{ Lv. Lv. }	1105 1	2 20 a.m.
4 37 a.m.	1890 3	Lv.	....Tula....	Lv.	1173 8	10 22 p.m.
7 15 a.m.	1910 3	Ar.	....Mexico....	Lv.	1225 5	8 30 p.m.

* Trains stop for Meals.   All trains run daily.

BAGGAGE REGULATIONS.

One hundred and fifty pounds of baggage will be checked free on each whole through ticket issued from or to points in the United States and seventy five pounds on each half through ticket.   On local tickets between points in Mexico, thirty three pounds of baggage will be carried free for each passenger.   Baggage will be re-checked at El Paso and Eagle Pass.

5

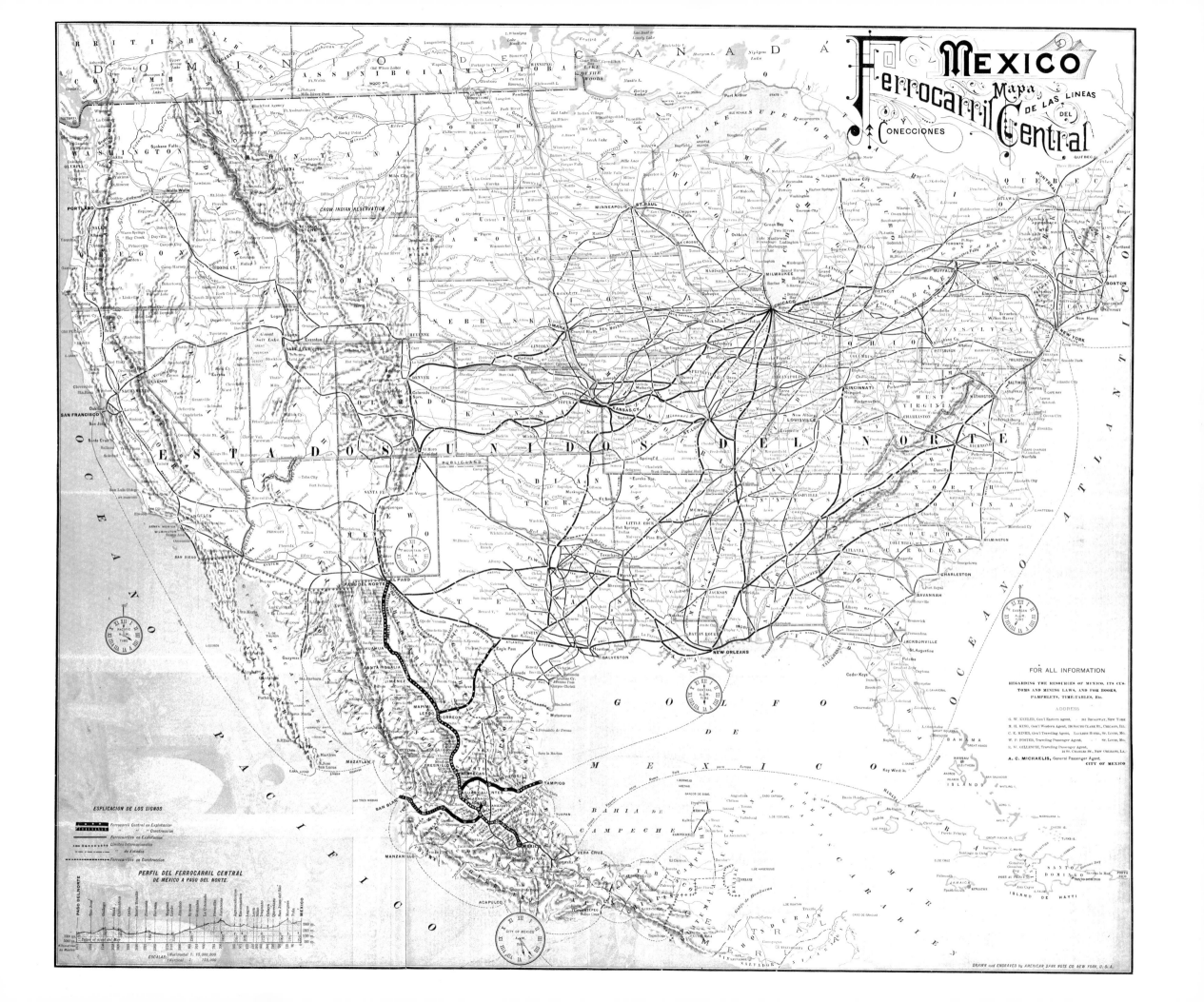

MEXICO
Ferrocarril Central
Mapa DE LAS LINEAS
y CONECCIONES DEL

FOR ALL INFORMATION

REGARDING THE RESOURCES OF MEXICO, ITS CUSTOMS AND MINING LAWS, AND FOR BOOKS, PAMPHLETS, TIME-TABLES, Etc.

ADDRESS

G. W. KEELER, Gen'l Eastern Agent, . . . 311 BROADWAY, NEW YORK

M. H. KING, Gen'l Western Agent, 196 SOUTH CLARK ST., CHICAGO, ILL.

C. E. MINER, Gen'l Traveling Agent, . LACLEDE HOTEL, ST. LOUIS, MO.

W. P. FOSTER, Traveling Passenger Agent, . . . ST. LOUIS, MO.

R. W. GILLENTIE, Traveling Passenger Agent, 24 ST. CHARLES ST., NEW ORLEANS, LA.

A. C. MICHAELIS, General Passenger Agent,
CITY OF MEXICO

ESPLICACION DE LOS SIGNOS

Ferrocarril Central en Explotacion
"   "   en Construccion
Ferrocarriles en Explotacion
Limites Internacionales
"   de Estados
Ferrocarriles en Construccion

PERFIL DEL FERROCARRIL CENTRAL
DE MEXICO A PASO DEL NORTE

ESCALAS: { Horizontal 1 : 15,000,000
Vertical 1 : 150,000

DRAWN and ENGRAVED by AMERICAN BANK NOTE CO. NEW YORK, U.S.A.

Mexican National

1882

90. Stanford, Edward. Map of the Mexican National Railway showing also its relative position to the railway system of the United States, both as to the eastern & western halves of the continent. London: Stanford's Geographical Establishment, 1882. 45 × 57 cm (18 × 22½ in).

General map of the United States and Mexico overprinted in colors to show the international boundary and the Mexican National Railway and its connections. The map shows major drainage, relief by hachures, and major cities and towns. Important shipping centers in the United States are indicated by red circles and squares. Coal and iron deposits are shown in Mexico. Includes a table of distances.

The name Topolobampo is annotated in ink to the left side of the map by John William Draper (1811-1882), the great American scientist, philosopher, and historian, in whose collection this map was originally preserved. Topolobampo was the famous utopian colony and harbor on the Gulf of California, established by the railroad promoter Albert Kimsey Owen, who also built the Texas-Topolobampo Railroad.

In September 1880, Mexican President Porfirio Diaz granted a concession to the William J. Palmer and James Sullivan interests operating under the name of the "Mexican National Construction company" (*Compañia constructora Nacional Mexicana*).

General Palmer, the head of this enterprise and the builder of the Denver and Rio Grande railroad, was an advocate of narrowgauge railroads, particularly as a means of reaching mines in a rugged country.

The route covered by the Mexican National concession was from Mexico through Toluca, Acambaro, Celaya, San Luis Potosi, Saltillo, and Monterey to Laredo, and from Mexico through Acambaro, Morelia, Zamora, Guadalajara, and Colima to the port of Manzanillo. By subsequent purchases of state concessions, the route was extended from Monterey to Matamoros, from San Luis Potosi to Lagos and Zacatecas, from Zacatecas to Guadalupe Hidalgo, and from Mexico to El Salto.

Construction was carried on simultaneously at different points, and as sections were completed they were taken over by the operating company, the Mexican National Railway *(Ferrocarril Nacional Mexicano),* incorporated in Colorado, with General Palmer as president. The line from Laredo was opened to Monterey in 1882 and extended to Saltillo in 1883. From Mexico the line was open to Toluca in 1880, and through Acambro and Celaya to San Miguel de Allende in 1883. Work between Saltillo and San Miguel was not begun until 1886, and the main line from Mexico to Laredo was not completed until September 28, 1888. The line from Monterey to Matamoros was finished in 1905.

On the Pacific line, work was also carried on from both ends. The section from Acambaro was carried through Morelia to Patzcuaro in 1886, and stopped at Uruapan. From Manzanillo the line was built as far as Colima by 1889, after which the project was abandoned.

In 1887 the Mexican National Railway Company was reorganized as the Mexican National Railroad Company, and control passed to the English holders of the bonds of the original company. It was the new company that completed the main line. It also acquired the Mexican International (1901) and the Interoceanic (1903). The entire system was merged into the National Railways of Mexico in 1909.

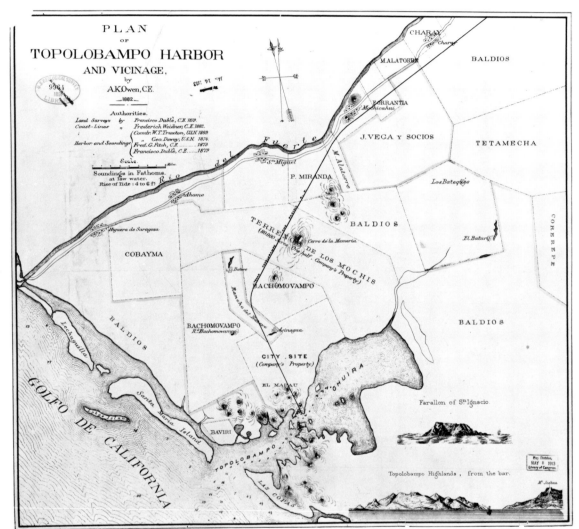

Map showing Topolobampo harbor.

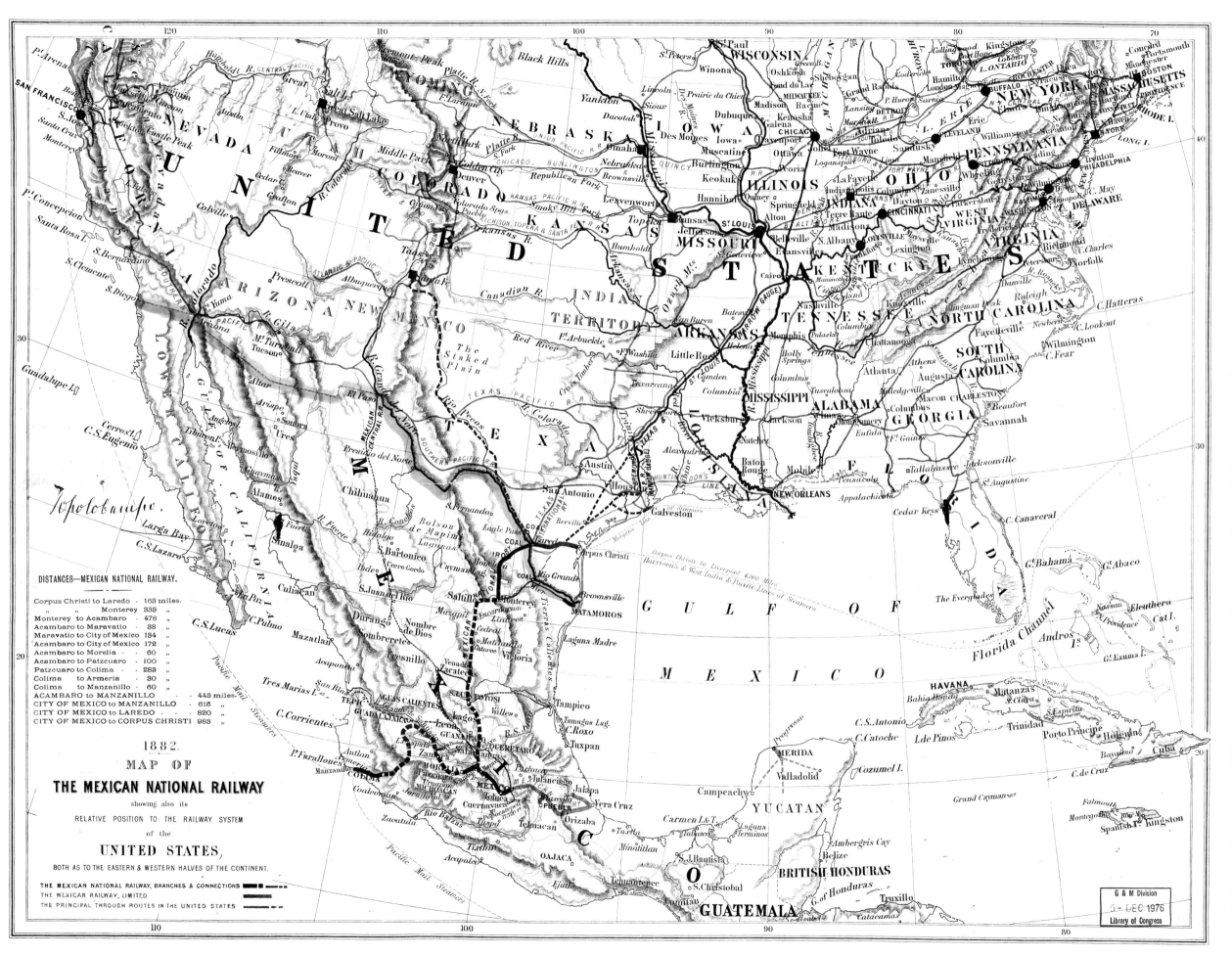

DISTANCES—MEXICAN NATIONAL RAILWAY.

Corpus Christi to Laredo - 163 miles.
"   Monterey   333 "
Monterey to Acambaro - 478 "
Acambaro to Maravatio - 38 "
Maravatio to City of Mexico 184 "
Acambaro to City of Mexico 172 "
Acambaro to Morelia - 60 "
Acambaro to Patzcuaro - 100 "
Patzcuaro to Colima - 288 "
Colima   to Armeria - 30 "
Colima   to Manzanillo - 60 "
ACAMBARO TO MANZANILLO - 443 miles.
CITY OF MEXICO TO MANZANILLO - 615 "
CITY OF MEXICO TO LAREDO - 820 "
CITY OF MEXICO TO CORPUS CHRISTI 983 "

1882.
MAP OF
THE MEXICAN NATIONAL RAILWAY
showing also its
RELATIVE POSITION TO THE RAILWAY SYSTEM
of the
UNITED STATES,
BOTH AS TO THE EASTERN & WESTERN HALVES OF THE CONTINENT.

THE MEXICAN NATIONAL RAILWAY, BRANCHES & CONNECTIONS
THE MEXICAN RAILWAY, LIMITED
THE PRINCIPAL THROUGH ROUTES IN THE UNITED STATES

173

Mexican Central

1896

91. Poole Brothers. Map of the Mexican Central Railway and Connections. May, 1896. Chicago, 1896. 54 × 63 cm (21 × 25 in).

A colored railroad map of Mexico emphasizing the routes of the Central Railway in heavy black lines. The unfinished work from Guadalajara to Ameca and Etzatlan is shown by dashed lines. Connections with the United States network are shown in lighter black lines. Eleven other lines in Mexico are distinguished by color and keyed to a list of railroads. Profiles for the main line and to Tampico and Guadalajara appear in the lower left of the map. Steamer connections to Tampico are shown by black dashed lines.

The year 1880 marks the beginning of railroad construction in Mexico by Americans. That year saw a change in the attitude of the Mexican government toward Americans as concessionnaires, as well as the organization of the Mexican Central Railway Company *(Ferrocarril Central de Mexico)* under the laws of Massachusetts.

On April 3, 1880, the Mexican government transferred to Robert R. Symon, agent of the company, the forfeited concession for a railroad from Mexico to Leon, originally granted to the Mexican Company, Ltd. *(Camacho-Mendizabal)* interests in 1874. With the idea of bringing into harmony the various contracts that had been entered into between the national and state governments and of facilitating the construction of through

"The Acqueduct at Queretaro, Mexico." W. H. Jackson & Co., ca. 1885.

lines, the Mexican congress on June 1, 1880, authorized the president to modify these contracts. By this means unification of gauge was made possible.

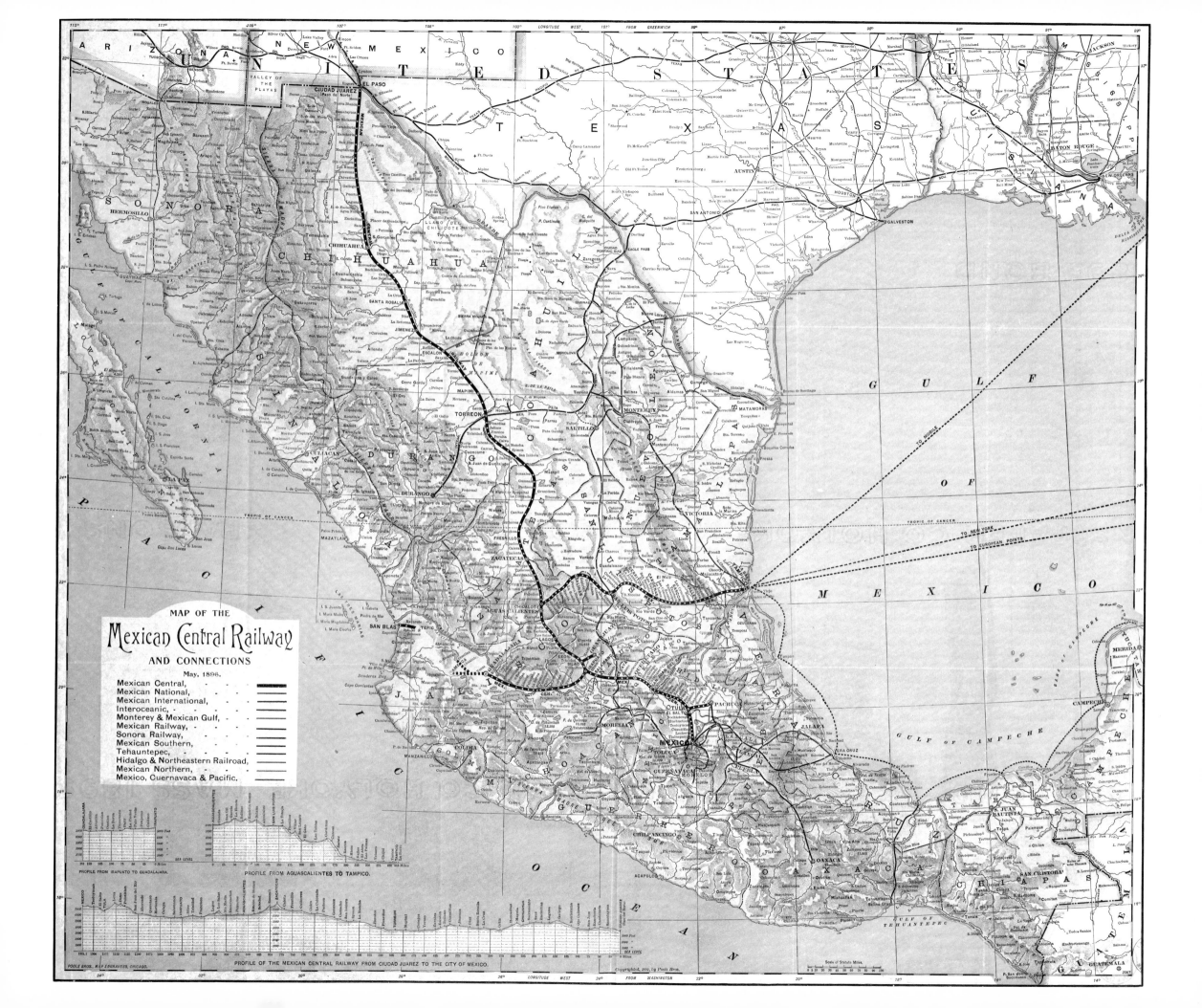

MAP OF THE

Mexican Central Railway

AND CONNECTIONS

May, 1896.

Mexican Central,
Mexican National,
Mexican International,
Interoceanic,
Monterey & Mexican Gulf,
Mexican Railway,
Sonora Railway,
Mexican Southern,
Tehauntepec,
Hidalgo & Northeastern Railroad,
Mexican Northern,
Mexico, Cuernavaca & Pacific.

PROFILE FROM IRAPUATO TO GUADALAJARA.

PROFILE FROM AGUASCALIENTES TO TAMPICO.

PROFILE OF THE MEXICAN CENTRAL RAILWAY FROM CIUDAD JUAREZ TO THE CITY OF MEXICO.

POOLE BROS. MAP ENGRAVERS, CHICAGO.

Copyrighted, 1892, by Poole Bros.

Scale of Statute Miles

Mexican International Railroad

1888

92. **Sagredo, G. Y. D.** Ferrocarril Internacional Mexicano y sus conecciones. 1888. New York, American Bank Note Co., 1888. 56 × 54 cm (22 × 21 in).

A colorful cover title in English reads: "Mexican International Railroad." The cover illustrates in color the international bridge over the Rio Grande between Piedras Negras, Mexico, and Eagle Pass, Texas. The detailed topographical map of Estado de Coahuila, Mexico, indicates the main line in red and connections in black. Railroads under construction are shown by dashed lines. The map portrays drainage, relief by contour form lines in green, cities, towns, ranches, and railroad stations.

Profiles for the main line, in feet and meters, appear at the bottom of the map. Timetable information and descriptive notes about cities and towns are printed on the verso of the map. Included on the verso is an outline map of North America showing the "Mexican International Railroad and Connections."

In 1881, General John B. Frisbie, representing Collis P. Huntington and the Southern Pacific interests, acquired from the Mexican government in the name of the International Construction Company, a concession for a railroad from Piedras Negras to Durango and from Durango through Zacatecas and Guanajuato to Mexico, with a branch through Nieves (Zacatecas) to a point on the Pacific coast between Mazatlan and Zihuatanejos (Guerrero), and another branch through San Luis Potosi to a point on the Gulf coast between Matamoros and Veracruz. The concession, when approved, was transferred to Huntington, acting for the construction company which was organized in Connecticut in March 1881.

In 1882, the company was reorganized and chartered as the International Railroad Company (*Ferrocarril Internacional Mexicano*). Construction work begun after the completion of the line of the Galveston, Houston, and San Antonio to Eagle Pass in 1883. In January 1884, the track was laid as far as Monclova. The line reached Torreon in 1888, thus connecting with the Mexican Central. On October 1, 1892, the line was opened to Durango. From Durango construction continued parallel to the western Sierra Madre as far as Tepehuanas, which was reached in 1902. This line provided an outlet for the extensive coal deposits of Coahuila, and it contributed to the success of Mexico's iron smelting industry.

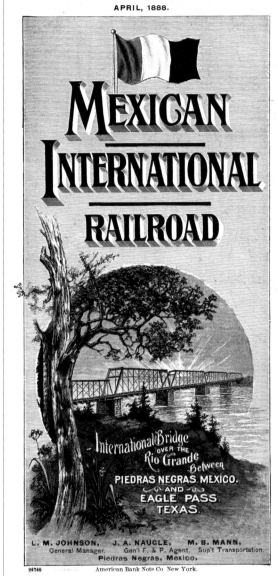

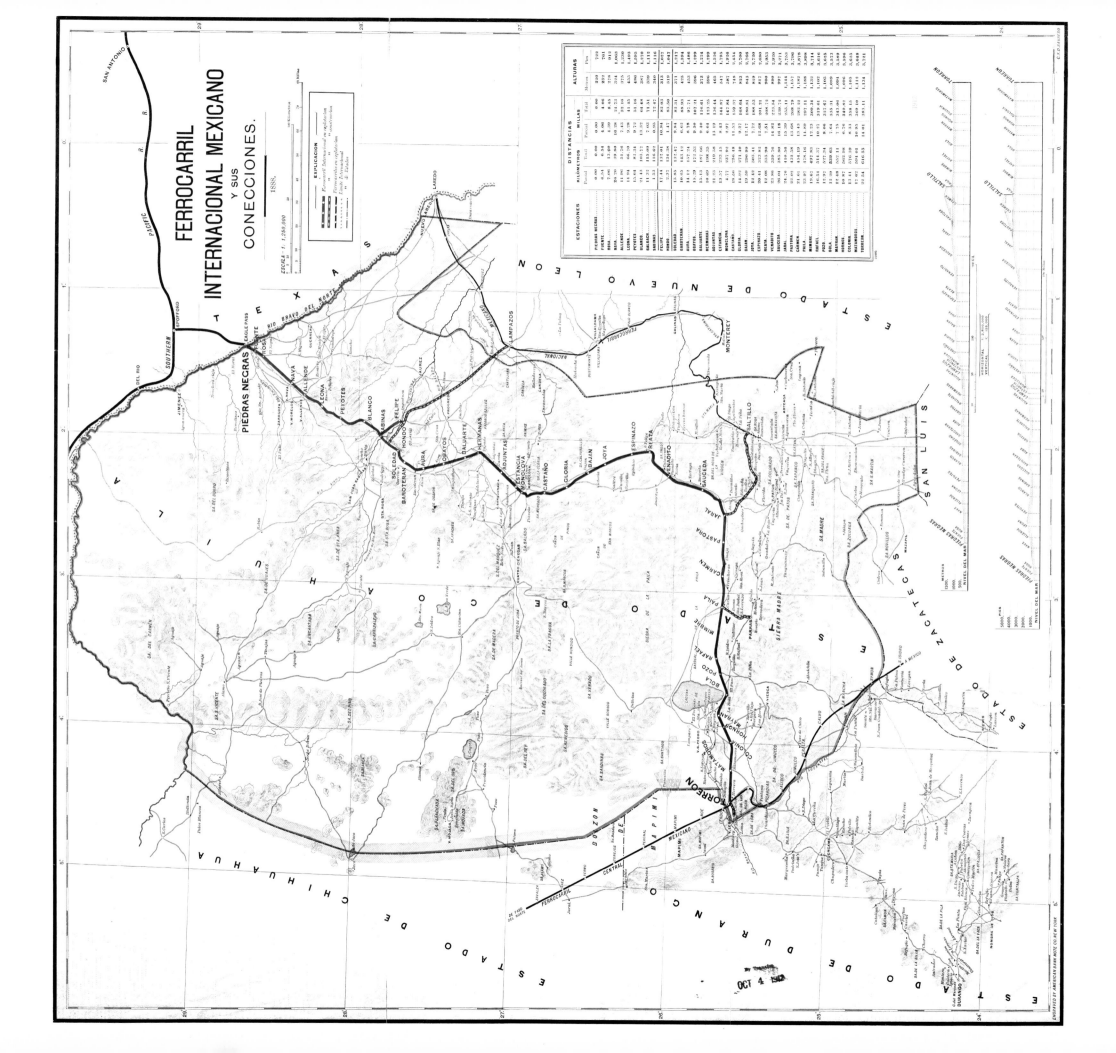

FERROCARRIL
INTERNACIONAL MEXICANO
Y SUS
CONECCIONES.
1888.

ESCALA 1: 1,250,000

EXPLICACION

Ferrocarril Internacional en explotacion
"   "   en construccion
Ferrocarriles en explotacion
Linea Internacional
Lim. de Estados

Photocopies of the illustrative material used in this book can be ordered from the Library of Congress, Photoduplication Service, Washington, D.C. 20540. Prices should be requested from the Photoduplication Service. When ordering, include the title of this book, **Railroad Maps of North America,** the page number, a brief description of each illustration ordered, and the negative number or division designation listed below.

iv. Passenger train on Markham Trestle: LC-USZ62-7498

vi. The World's Railroad Scene: LC-USZ62-1348

viii. Combination Atlas Map: LC-USZ62-38428
Railroad Station, Sharon, Massachusetts: LC-C801-307

ix. John Stevens's railway: LC-USZ62-58037
George Stephenson's engine: LC-USZ62-1390

x. Types of American Locomotives, no. 1: LC-USZ62-1402

xi. Types of American Locomotives, no. 2: LC-USZ62-1403

xii. New Railroad Bridge: LC-USZ62-37849

xiii. Mexican Central: LC-USZ62-60694

xiv. Mining for gold: LC-USZ62-8197
Northern Pacific Railroad car: LC-USZ62-12238

xv. "Camp Victory," Central Pacific Railroad construction: LC-USZ62-35633
Central Pacific, Kern County: LC-USZ62-51649

xvi. Deadwood Central Railroad Engineer Corp: LC-USZ6-7

xvii. The Great Palace Reclining-Chair Route: LC-USZ62-1371

xviii. Departure of emigrants: LC-USZ62-1372

xix. Map Drawing Room: G & M
Map Engraving Department: G & M
Cylinder Press Room: G & M

xx. In the Waiting Room: LC-USZ62-1372

xxi. Ensenore Glenn House: G & M

2. Railroad surveying crew: LC-USZ62-83479

15. First iron bridge: LC-USZ62-46243

19. Mid-nineteenth-century New Haven: LC-USZ62-17517

20. Federal troops clearing damage: LC-B8184-1319

22. Manassas Junction: LC-USZ62-83480

30. Lost Camp Spur Cut: LC-USZ62-51737

34. Through to the Pacific: LC-USZ62-25

36. View of Erie Canal: LC-USZ62-32565

38. Across the Continent: LC-USZ62-1

40. James J. Hill's first engine: LC-USZ62-51392

44. First commericial map of Georgia Railroad: G & M

50. Dining saloon: LC-USZ62-14133

52. Suspension bridge, Niagara Falls: LC-USZ62-34968

54. Railroad bridge: LC-USZ62-1385

56. Depot at Harrisburg: LC-USZ62-57214

58. The Dictator: LC-B8184-10212

60. Herman Haupt directs repair work: LC-B8184-622
Major General McCallum: LC-USZ62-83481

64. The Fast Mail: LC-USZ62-1368

66. The Cool Route: LC-USZ62-14192

68. Passengers boarding California Limited: LC-USZ62-33526

72. Flagler's first train: LC-USZ62-59404

74. First trip on Mohawk and Hudson: LC-USZ62-1344
First trip of the West Point: LC-USZ62-2509

80. Cascade Bridge: LC-USZ62-38597

84. Harper's Ferry: LC-USZ62-28104

86. Landing of American troops: LC-USZ62-8724

100. Alaska, Klondike gold rush: LC-USZ62-36836

102. Bird's-eye-view of Atchison: G & M

104. Bridge over the Ohio: LC-USZ62-28128

106. Saratoga Springs: LC-USZ62-60115

112. Illinois Central Depot: LC-USZ62-65013

114. Engine on the Lehigh Valley Railroad: **LC-USZ62-83490**

117. Devil's Gate Bridge: LC-USZ62-56274

119. Dormitory cars: LC-USZ62-59795

120. Clear Spring Farm: G & M

125. Golden Spike ceremony: LC-USZ62-5443

126. Weber Canyon: LC-USZ62-16883
Building the Union Pacific: LC-USZ62-43322

128. Pennsylvania Railroad Company: LC-USZ62-1363

130. Map of Boston and Maine Railroad: G & M

132. Boston Freight Terminals: LC-USZ62-66965

135. Passenger Station: LC-USZ62-70607

136. The Great Market: LC-USZ62-3180

137. Tank cars: LC-USZ62-83482

139. Coke furnaces: LC-USZ62-35547

140. Canada Southern Railway: LC-USZ62-20922

142. Engine used on coal mine: LC-USZ62-83489

144. Lake Louise: LC-USZ62-83484

146. Great Tubular Bridge: LC-USZ62-67317

148. Advertisement: LC-USZ62-43924

150. Reid Newfoundland company brochure: G & M

153. Threshing in western Canada: LC-USZ62-83485

154. Packing silver ore: LC-USZ62-83486

156. Women prospectors: LC-USZ62-2129

163. Maligne Lake: LC-USZ62-83487

164. Mexican National Railroad: LC-USZ62-83488

166. El Cafetal de Temasopa: LC-USZ62-47774

172. Topolobampo: G & M

174. Acqueduct at Queretaro: LC-USZ62-34872

Index

☆U.S. GOVERNMENT PRINTING OFFICE: 1985—476-193